D1280195

PORTRAIT OF
ENGLISH
LITERATURE

PORTRAIT OF ENGLISH LITERATURE

Ifor Evans

SIDGWICK & JACKSON
LONDON

Originally published as *A Short History of English Literature*
by Penguin Books Ltd, Harmondsworth, Middlesex, England.
First published 1940. Subsequent editions, 1963, 1970, 1976.
This first illustrated hardback edition published in Great Britain
by Sidgwick and Jackson Ltd, 1979.

ISBN 0 283 98557 7

Designed by Ray Hyden
Picture research by Faith Perkins
On previous page: Sculpture of
George Stephens by John Flaxman

Printed in Great Britain by
A. Wheaton & Co., Ltd., Exeter
for Sidgwick and Jackson Limited
1 Tavistock Chambers
Bloomsbury Way
London WC1A 2SG

CONTENTS

ACKNOWLEDGEMENTS

Photographs and illustrations were supplied by or are reproduced by kind permission of the following. The pictures on pp. 172 and 216 are reproduced by gracious permission of Her Majesty the Queen; on p. 73 by courtesy of the Master and Fellows of Campion Hall, Oxford; on pp. 30 and 110 by permission of the Trustees of the Chatsworth Settlement; on pp. viii (MS R. 17. 1, fol. 283 b) and 4 (MS R. 17. 1, fol. 263) by courtesy of the Master and Fellows of Trinity College, Cambridge; on p. 236 by courtesy of Trinity College, Dublin; Bodleian Library, Oxford 5 l & r (Filmstrip: Caedmon Genesis), 13 r (MS. Douce 104, fol. 39), 13 l (MS. Rawl Q.B.6. fol. 254 u), 51 (Filmstrip: Landmarks in English Literature), 129 r; British Film Institute Library 197; BBC Copyright Photographs 109, 239 (Photo: David Edwards); The British Library 91; British Museum 3, 10; Camera Press 193, 241 insert; Dorset County Museum 177; Mary Evans Picture Library 54, 168, 224; Fotomas Index 14, 32, 63 l & r, 105 l & r, 140, 155 l, 162; John Freeman (photographer) 119, 202, 205, 207, 211; Ray Gardner 18 l, 84; Illustrated London News 183; Imperial War Museum 71, 235; A. F. Kersting (photographer) 28, 155 r; Gemma Levine (photographer) 244; London Diocesan Committee (Photo: Jason Shenai) iii; The Mander and Mitchenson Theatre Collection 87, 90, 96, 98, 101, 115, 116, 122, 124, 126, 129 l, 131, 134, 135, 137, 138; The Mansell Collection 8, 11, 17, 22, 26 b, 29, 34, 40, 47, 49 l, 79, 106, 144 l & r, 146, 148, 150, 156, 158, 166, 174, 178, 204, 208, 214, 215, 219, 222, 227; National Maritime Museum, Greenwich 103 l; National Portrait Gallery, London 61, 66, 175; Oslo University Library 6 r; Particam of Amsterdam (Photo: Nigel Luckhurst) 243; Pierpont Morgan Library, New York 6 l (M. 917 fol. 109); Radio Times Hulton Picture Library 56, 78, 181, 189, 241; Mrs Eva Reichmann 223; Royal Holloway College, University of London 164; Edwin Smith (photographer) 74, 171, 185; Snark International 42; Sir John Soane Museum, London 152; Lady Stair's House Museum, Edinburgh 231; The Tate Gallery, London 26 t, 37, 49 r, 121, 150; Ullstein Bilderdienst, Berlin 94; Wales Tourist Board (Bwrdd Croeso Cymru) 82; Simon Wingfield Digby Esq. 18 r.

For permission to publish extracts from poems in this book, acknowledgement is made to the following:
For W. B. Yeats, extract from 'Sailing to Byzantium' from the Collected Poems of W. B. Yeats, to M. B. Yeats, Macmillan and Co. Ltd, and The Macmillan Company, New York (copyright 1928 by The Macmillan Company, renewed 1956 by Georgie Yeats).

Eadwine, from the *Eadwine,* or *Canterbury Psalter, c.* 1150 A.D. Many of the early Anglo-Saxon manuscripts were made by monks and preserved in their monasteries

Chapter 1

Before the Conquest

ENGLISH literature is often described as beginning with Chaucer. This would give England six centuries of literature. Actually there were more than six centuries of literature before Chaucer was born. The modern reader can make out the meaning of a page of Chaucer, but if he looks at our earliest literature he finds that it reads like a foreign tongue.

The two most important events in the history of England took place before the Norman Conquest. It was then that the Angles, Saxons and Jutes came to England in marauding bands and made English history possible. From all accounts they were respectable gentlemen when at home, but they changed their manners when they were looking for *Lebensraum*. They were heathen, and the second great event is the conversion of the English to Christianity. In 597 Augustine had come from Rome and begun to convert the Jutes in Kent, while about the same time monks from Ireland set up monasteries in Northumbria. Most English poetry in this Anglo-Saxon period is associated with these two events. Either the stories are brought over by the invading tribes from their Germanic homes, or they show a keen interest in Christianity.

Literature in this period was recorded in manuscripts, and the life of a manuscript is a hard one. Our knowledge of Anglo-Saxon poetry depends on four groups of manuscripts. These are: the manuscripts collected by Sir Robert Cotton, now in the British Museum; the *Exeter Book* given to Exeter Cathedral by Bishop Leofric, sometime after 1050; the *Vercelli Book*, found at Vercelli near Milan in 1822 (and no one knows how it got there); and finally the manuscripts in the Bodleian Library at Oxford, given by the Dutch scholar Francis Dujon or Junius, Librarian to the Earl of Arundel. In Sir Robert Cotton's collection is the manuscript of *Beowulf*, the most important poem of the period, and its history shows how everything seems to fight against the survival of a manuscript.

As a result one cannot assess Anglo-Saxon literature or medieval literature from the extant manuscripts. Anglo-Saxon jewellery and other objects of art testify that there existed a far richer and more sophisticated civilization than the surviving remains indicate. One might suppose that there was an early tradition of lyrical poetry, and yet no poems are extant before the thirteenth century, and then mostly religious verse survives, for kept in monasteries, it had a better chance of preservation than secular lyrics. There are twelfth-century records at Ely, suggesting that lyric poetry was extant there at that time and giving to Canute the credit for being one of the earliest of medieval poets. There are references to early popular lyrics, some of which scandalized the more respectable. In this lost Anglo-Saxon and medieval literature there was, to quote a single instance, Bede's vernacular lyric. We learn of this from his disciple Cuthbert describing his death: 'in our language, skilled in our poetry', he spoke of the terrible parting of the soul and the body.

The Angles brought the story of *Beowulf* to England in the sixth century, and there after A.D. 700 the poem was made. This was about seventy years after the death of Mohammed and in the same age as the beginning of the great T'ang Dynasty in China. Three hundred years later, about the year 1000, the manuscript, which still survives, was written down. What happened to it for the next seven hundred years is unknown. In 1706 it was recorded as being in Sir Robert Cotton's library. Only twenty-six years later a disastrous fire broke out which the *Beowulf* manuscript narrowly escaped. The charred edges of its leaves can still be seen in the British Museum. Two fragments of another poem *Waldere* were found as recently as 1860 in the binding of a book in the Royal Library at Copenhagen.

Beowulf is the first long poem in English, some three thousand lines. Yet the hero and the setting have nothing to do with England. Though the Angles brought the story to England, it is not even about the Angles, but about the Scandinavians. The German tribes, though they warred with each other, and with anyone else within reach, had a 'free trade' in stories. Their poets, at least, believed in 'Germania', the single German people. So it is that our first English poem is a Scandinavian story, brought over by Angles, and made into a poem in England. The story of *Beowulf* is of a monster named Grendel who is disturbing Hrothgar, king of the Danes, in Heorot, his great hall. A young warrior called Beowulf comes with a group of comrades to the rescue. He overcomes Grendel and then later in a dwelling at the bottom of a lake he fights Grendel's mother, a sea monster. In the second part of the poem Beowulf is a king, and as an old man he has to defend his country from a fiery dragon. The poem closes with an account of his funeral rites. The weakness of the poem, to some critics, lies in the story. They say it is only a fairy story of monsters and dragons. But in those early days the monster was real. Any man might meet him in an untrodden path on a dark night. He was there, huge, bestial, evil, waiting for you, and the hero was the man who could kill him. More recent criticism suggests that the story is more than just a story. It is implied that it has symbolic,

An Anglo-Saxon banquet. The exchange of gifts and of meat and drink is a theme much celebrated in early English poetry

religious, and perhaps even mythological values. With the story there is a picture of society at the Court of a warrior, the courtesies, the beer-drinking, the exchanges of gifts, and the poet present among the warriors, chanting his verses of the deeds of fighting men. It is in some of these interludes that the poem displays strength, beauty of style and the dignity of an aristocratic and civilized world.

Like all Anglo-Saxon poems it is written with a long line. The lines do not rhyme, but each line has alliteration, and the poet has a special and extensive vocabulary. He uses 'picture-names' for the things and people he has to describe, so the 'sea' is the 'swan's road' and the 'body' is the 'bone-house'. The story belongs to the pagan life of the Germanic tribes, but the poem itself was set down after the conversion of the English to Christianity. The new worship and the old heroic virtues mingle. But the values of the poetry belong to the earlier pagan age with a sense of endurance, of fate, and of unfailing courage revealing a spirit that is never again recaptured. How strong was the old heroic spirit can be seen in the short poem 'Maldon' written soon after the Battle of Maldon in 993:

> *Thought must be the harder: the heart, the keener,*
> *Courage must be greater as our strength grows less.*

Here the poet recaptured the values of an earlier heroic age and the epic way of writing. To write thus about a contemporary battle was, for poetry in any age, a rare achievement.

Nothing in Old English literature can compare with *Beowulf*; it has the size and dignity of a classical epic. Possibly its author had read Virgil. A number of shorter poems survive which belong like *Beowulf* to the stories of the Germanic peoples. 'Widsith' (the Far Traveller) describes the wanderings of a poet through the courts of Germanic kings. In the *Exeter Book*, there are seven short poems of great human interest. Life in all these poems is sorrowful, and the speakers fatalistic, though courageous and determined. The mood is found in one of these poems, 'Deor', where the poet, unhappy because estranged from his lord, reminds himself of sorrows in the past and adds:

> *That grief passed away: so may this sorrow pass.*

The religious poetry uses the same verse and vocabulary as the stories of the heroes. The Church was using the old pagan poetry in the new fight for Christianity. The Christian missionaries saw that they could not destroy the old stories, so they told the new biblical stories in the old way. Further, many of the Christian monks enjoyed the old pagan stories, sometimes enjoyed them too much. This mixture of Christian and pagan can be seen in *Andreas* (St Andrew), a religious poem and yet an adventure story with all the old atmosphere of the heroic tales of warriors.

Of named poets in this Christian tradition we know only two. The first, Caedmon, has something recorded of his life but next to nothing of his work. Of the second, Cynewulf, we know nothing of his life but

Saxon women weaving, ignorant of the screams of the tortured souls in Hell. Religious and domestic themes were often closely related in Old English literature

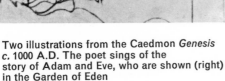

Two illustrations from the Caedmon *Genesis*
c. 1000 A.D. The poet sings of the
story of Adam and Eve, who are shown (right)
in the Garden of Eden

(through the runic 'signature' in several poems) we can identify at least some of his poems. Caedmon was a shy and sensitive cowherd employed by the monastery at Whitby. He became a poet, as Bede says, after a visit by an angel. Caedmon is said to have rendered Old and New Testament stories into English verse. These probably do not survive, but someone did make poems out of parts of *Genesis, Exodus* and *Daniel*.

There are three other outstanding religious poems. One is part of the Genesis story, the account of the Fall of the Angels. The English poet has made a vivid rendering of the story which Milton was later to tell in *Paradise Lost*. The second is *The Dream of the Rood*, by far the most imaginative of the Old English poems. The Cross appears to the poet in a dream and describes the unwilling part it played in the Crucifixion. The third is the story of *Judith*, the most exciting narrative in Anglo-Saxon poetry, of how Judith slew the tyrant Holofernes. No other Anglo-Saxon poetry approaches *Judith* in its dramatic quality or in the sense it gives of genuine human characterization.

The Anglo-Saxon prose writers can be seen more clearly. The earliest definite figure is Aldhelm (d. 709) bishop of Sherborne who wrote in praise of virginity in an ornate Latin. The greatest is the Venerable Bede (673–735) who spent nearly all his life of intense study in the monastery at Jarrow. He never travelled farther than from Jarrow to York, but his mind travelled over all the studies then known, history, astronomy, and the lives of saints and of martyrs. Foremost among his works is his great *Ecclesiastical History of the English Race*. He made his monastery at Jarrow a great centre of religion and study in that troubled century when the Christian civilization of Europe was threatened with destruction.

His own life seems to have had a beauty and simplicity such as the Irish monks had brought into their settlements in England; but in him this simplicity was combined with an outstanding greatness of mind. Bede wrote in Latin and the excellence of his work gave him in his own lifetime a European reputation.

In the century after Bede, the Danish invasions broke up a nascent civilization in England. One after another the great abbey houses were destroyed. It is strange how often a nation's hour of trial produces a great figure. Such was England's fortune when, in 871, a young man of twenty-two became king. Alfred (849–899) deserves to be remembered as an outstanding figure – soldier, strategist, scholar, educator, administrator, above all a great personality, who played appeasement with the Danes until he was ready to meet them. He had a zest for knowledge and its distribution. Much of his work was translation and much he only directed, but in all, his was the guiding spirit. For the clergy he prepared a translation of the *Pastoral Rule* of Gregory the Great, rendering the original, as he tells us, 'sometimes word for word and sometimes sense for sense'. So that his people might know their own country better he translated Bede's *Ecclesiastical History* and *The History of the World* by Orosius. Alfred touched up Orosius with the accounts given him by two travellers, Ohthere and Wulfstan, of 'Germania' and the countries beyond its boundaries. Boethius's *Consolation of Philosophy* he rendered to please himself. Writing in prison Boethius had proved that the only

By the late ninth century most of England was in Danish hands. The Danes crossed the North Sea in their longships which were often intricately decorated, with carved animal heads mounted on the prow

genuine happiness comes from the spirit, from an inward serenity, and Alfred found something in his own life to answer this mood. Out of the notes of events kept by the monasteries he conceived the idea of a national history, and this for a time was achieved in the *Anglo-Saxon Chronicle*. The work is by a number of hands of varying skill, but it is the first great book in prose in English. It continues after Alfred's death, and the Peterborough version has records to the year 1154. The account of the war with the Danes shows how many suffered in that age, how bitter, insecure, and cruel life was. When one thinks of Alfred with that background, his stature as a man increases, until he towers up as one of the great figures in English history.

In the century after his death much of the work he had begun was lost, but two writers wrote a religious prose which has been preserved. Outstanding was Ælfric, the greatest writer of English prose before the Conquest. He was a pupil of the monastery school at Winchester, where scholarship was cherished, but his aim was to make Christian documents available to those who did not understand Latin. He composed two books of *Homilies* in a language that simple uneducated people could understand. Later Ælfric translated the *Saints' Lives*, concentrating on themes which, as he states in his preface, are 'suitable for narration to the lay attendants at monastic services'. He is the first man in England to be working consciously at prose style. With him, though to many he is now an unknown name, rests the honour of being the first writer of English prose conscious of the fine and variable medium of the English language, and determined that the vernacular should flourish with the dignity that he rightly associated with Latin, still the language of Christendom as a whole.

The other memorable name in this difficult period was Wulfstan, Archbishop of York (d. 1023) whose *A Sermon of the Wolf* is addressed to the English when the Danes were persecuting them most severely in 1014. Wulfstan makes a flaming indictment of Aethelred, a weak and cowardly king, accusing him of unpreparedness in defence, of villages destroyed, of moral and national disintegration. He confirms the accounts in the *Chronicle* of the cruelty and hopelessness of the years of the Danish invasion, and all this is more vivid and realistic for the Christian exhortation to 'creep to Christ, and call upon Him unceasingly with trembling hearts and deserve his mercy'. It was a hard and a cruel time, and with only a little imagination one can realize the stature of these men who worked and spoke as they did.

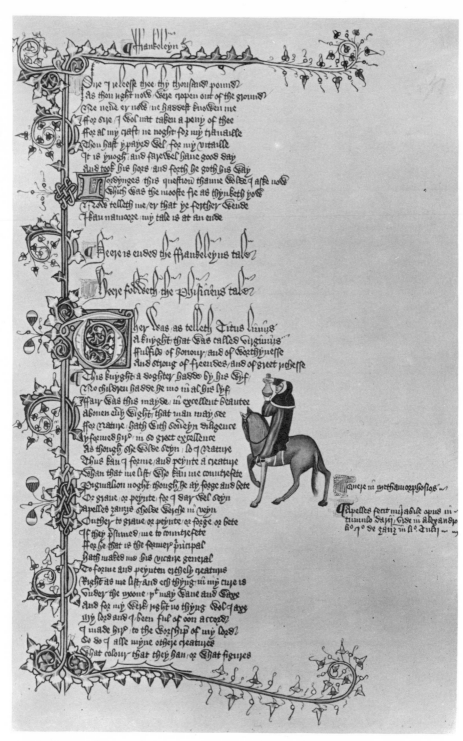

The Doctor of Physic; from the fourteenth-century Ellesmere manuscript of the *Canterbury Tales*

Chapter 2

English Poetry from Chaucer to John Donne

MODERN POETRY begins with Geoffrey Chaucer (*c.* 1340–1400), diplomat, soldier and scholar. There was a long controversy in criticism as to whether there was a 'continuity' between the Old English poets, Chaucerian and post-Chaucerian verse. Sir Arthur Quiller-Couch ('Q'), writing in the early twenties, implied that the early poetry was altogether different, and could without much harm be neglected. The modern view has restored the faith in tradition. It is true that the early poets are unintelligible to the modern reader without preparation. But this is no argument, for even the early seventeenth-century verse of Shakespeare is not intelligible unless the reader is prepared for a certain amount of preliminary labour. It is the same language and intelligibility is all a question of degree. Poets such as Gerard Manley Hopkins and Auden have been able to find suggestion and inspiration in the early poets.

Chaucer was a bourgeois who understood the Court, but he had a keen eye for the ordinary man and he was a reader who had studied most of the available literature. He profited by his French and Italian journeys to study the more ambitious ways of Continental poetry. Like every scholar of his time he knew medieval Latin, and he had read diligently some of the Latin classics, especially Ovid and Virgil. He wrote because he must have been aware of his own genius. His audience was necessarily a small one, and in his own lifetime could not have been more than a few thousand people, comprising courtiers and members of the rising professional and merchant classes. Small though it may have been numerically, when one realizes the degree of literacy it was considerable and composed of important people, with a spread over different social groups.

Much of his work shows his taste for medieval literature, particularly as it was found in France. He delighted in allegory, and in the elaborate sentiments of courtly love. It was C. L. Kittredge in his *Chaucer and his Poetry* who indicated how 'vastly fortunate it was that Chaucer was born high enough in the social scale not to need holy orders as a means of escape from warping circumstances. Otherwise a great poet would have been spoiled to make an indifferent parson.' He adds that it was equally fortunate that Chaucer was not an aristocrat, 'he would not have understood the lower orders, but would have lived and died the poet of chivalric love'.

As Chaucer tells us in the *Prologue* to *The Legend of Good Women* he laboured at the translation of *The Romance of the Rose* of Guillaume de Lorris and the satirical Jean de Meung, and he had studied their poem closely. Guillaume had treated woman with adoration, and Jean with mockery, and Chaucer remembered both ways in his own verses. His more completely medieval poems are represented by *The Book of the Duchess* (1369), an allegory on the death of Blanche, wife of John of Gaunt, and *The House of Fame*, a dream medley with some classical memories but full of intricate and sometimes rambling medieval lore. These, with his lyrics, the ballads and rondels, would have made him a considerable poet for his century, but three others works set him apart as a great poet in the history of poetry in general: *Troilus and Criseyde* (1385-7), *The Legend of Good Women* (1385) and the unfinished *Canterbury Tales*.

Of these, the most ambitious as a complete work is *Troilus and Criseyde*. The story, which Shakespeare later used in the most difficult of his plays, Chaucer had found in Boccaccio's *Il Filostrato*. It was a

A portrait of Chaucer from an early fifteenth-century manuscript of Thomas Occleve's *De Regimine Principum*, painted, as Occleve says, 'to putte othir men in remembraunce of his persone'

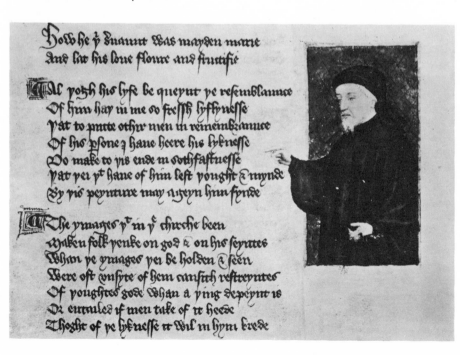

medieval addition to the classical theme of the Trojan Wars, the story of Troilus's love for Criseyde and of her faithlessness. The story would do for a novel, and in some ways Chaucer has made a great novel in verse, with characters intelligible in any age, and with a full movement of life surrounding the main theme.

In comparison *The Legend of Good Women* seems a slight piece, with its brief narratives of the unhappy fates of Cleopatra, Thisbe, Philomela and others, who suffered in the cause of love. In the *Prologue* to this poem Chaucer returned to allegory, to the medieval *Garden of the Rose*, and embedded in this part of the poem is the most beautiful of all his lyrics: 'Hide, Absalon, thy gilte tresses clear'.

It is for the *Canterbury Tales* that Chaucer's name is best remembered, the unfinished collection of stories told by the pilgrims on their journey to Canterbury, with the *Prologue*, the clearest picture of late medieval life existent anywhere. His quick, sure strokes portray the pilgrims at once as types and individuals true of their own age, and still more, representative of humanity in general. The idea of a collection of stories Chaucer may have had from Boccaccio's *Decameron*, but he borrowed

An illustration from a 1509 edition of Boccaccio's *Decameron*. It is highly probable that Chaucer met Boccaccio on his travels abroad, and he was later to base his *Troilus and Criseyde* on the Italian poet's *Il Filostrato*

little more than the initial idea. He keeps the whole poem alive by interspersing the tales themselves with the talk, the quarrels, and the opinions of the pilgrims, and here the Wife of Bath, with her detailed comments on marriage and the treatment of the male sex, is supreme.

How great was Chaucer's art can be seen by comparing his work with that of John Gower (*c.* 1325–1408), who shared many of Chaucer's interests. If Chaucer had not lived, Gower would be one of the outstanding poets remembered from this century. Like Chaucer he read French and Latin as easily as he read English, and he composed poems with equal fluency in all three languages.

In Chaucer's age the English language was still divided by dialects, though London was rapidly making East-Midland into a standard language. In the West there lived on, or came to life, a poetry which has little in common with that of Chaucer, and which he seems to have actively disliked. Outstanding is *The Vision of Piers the Plowman*, by William Langland, probably a priest of one of the lowest orders. His poem may have circulated among clerical or semi-clerical audiences. The number of extant manuscripts shows that the poem was popular. In a long and complicated succession of scenes he portrays almost every side of fourteenth-century life. He sees the corruption of wealth and the inadequacies of government. To him the only salvation lies in honest labour and in the service of Christ. If he were not a mystic he would be a revolutionary. He is the nearest approach to Dante in our poetry, for despite his roughness, and his bleak atmosphere he has written the greatest poem in English devoted to the Christian way of life.

Nor was Langland's poem the only one which came out of the West Country. A single manuscript preserves four poems written in the North-Western dialect. *Pearl, Purity, Patience* and *Sir Gawain and the Green Knight* have sufficient similarities to lead some to the belief that they were all the work of one group. *Pearl*, the outstanding religious poem of the group, tells of a father who has lost his child, and the mystical language describing his vision has the glamour and fervour of the Revelation of St John. Of the others *Sir Gawain* is impressive. The story is a romance based on an ancient legend of a Green Knight who challenges Arthur's Knights, and who having had his head cut off, picks it up, rides away and reminds his opponent of his promise to face him in return at the Green Chapel in a year's time. The charm of the poem, and there is nothing apart from Chaucer to match it in the whole of English medieval verse, lies in the poet's feeling for contemporary life, in the descriptions of dress and armour and in the details of the hunting scenes. *Sir Gawain* is the most subtle verse romance in English medieval literature. The romances, the stories of Arthur, of Charlemagne and of the Trojan Wars, and the more native stories of *King Horn* and *Havelok the Dane*, are among the most typical products of medieval literature, but not now the most interesting.

Compared with the romances, the life of the medieval lyric has been strong and enduring. The tunes and the phrasing of many of the lyrics which survive, especially those in the famous Harleian Manuscript 2253, come to the ear with an unsullied freshness:

> *Betwene March and Averil*
> *When spray beginneth to spring.*

Best of all medieval lyrics is 'Alysoun', which survives every change in the language, and remains today perfect and unmatchable.

With the lyrics may be remembered the ballads, for the ballads were lyrics in which a story was told in one particular way. Possibly the ballads are the part of medieval literature which has survived the best. 'Sir Patrick Spens' and 'The Mill Dams of Binnorie' have all the magic which later generations were to associate with the Middle Ages. Further, they possess a way of verse, subtle and allusive, which is not to be found elsewhere.

Chaucer as a poet is so good that he makes the fifteenth century appear dull. His imitators are brought on to the stage of literature only to receive cat-calls. So it is with Thomas Occleve and John Lydgate,

Sir Gawain rides through the forest on his horse, Gringolet.

> *He had death-struggles with dragons, did*
> *battle with wolves,*
> *Warred with wild trolls that dwelt*
> *among the crags . . .*
> *And ogres that panted after him*
> *on the high fells . . .*
>
> *Sir Gawain and the Green Knight*

A labourer digging with a metal-tipped spade, from a manuscript of *The Vision of Piers the Plowman*, 1427

though the latter at least cannot be accused of indolence. Actually no one did imitate the best in Chaucer. The more elaborate poets seem imitative and repetitive. One feels that poetry must have some new voice, however sharp and discordant. The situation is not unlike that at the end of the Victorian age. One tradition has gone on too long. Of this older tradition the allegories of Stephen Hawes, especially *The Pastime of Pleasure*, are typical. They seem to belong to a dead past. One poet in this age by his rude originality served to emphasize this wraith-like quality of Hawes and the courtly imitators of Chaucer. John Skelton (*c.* 1460–1529) wrote a ragged, uncouth line, broken, irregular, but compact with meaning and brutal in its directness:

> *Though my rime be ragged,*
> *Tatter'd and jagged,*
> *Rudely rain-beaten,*
> *Rusty and moth-eaten,*
> *If ye take well therewith,*
> *It hath in it some pith.*

In satire he is pungent, foul-mouthed, but he employed his irregular verse in another way in *The Boke of Phyllyp Sparowe*, a lament on a pet sparrow killed by a cat. The poem has speed and liveliness, and this and much else in Skelton's verse has survived in the memories of poets even to the twentieth century.

'Phillyp Sparowe's tombe'; an illustration from the first edition of Skelton's *The Boke of Phillyp Sparowe*, 1550, a lament over a tame bird murdered by a cat

In Scotland, Chaucer's influence fared better than in England, with Robert Henryson's *Testament of Cresseid* and with a royal supporter in King James I of Scotland's *Kingis Quair*. William Dunbar belonged to the same school, but he was too original to be described as an imitator; the colour and elaborate device of his verse seem like some medieval tourney come to life again, or like a heraldic device set into words. The best known of his poems, 'The Lament for the Makaris',* dealt with the favourite medieval theme of the uncertainty and brevity of human life. With these poets the text-books have always put Gavin Douglas, and so that the four may not be separated his name is added here. If his own verse is unexceptional, he is remembered for his rendering of Virgil into English verse.

The new way in English poetry came mainly through the imitation of Italian models and it brought difficulties of its own. The early stages of this Italian influence can be found in poems by Wyatt and Surrey published in 1557 in an anthology generally known as *Tottel's Miscellany*. Sir Thomas Wyatt was a courtier and diplomat who kept his head, in more than one sense,' in the troubled Court of Henry VIII, and the Earl of Surrey was a nobleman who went to the scaffold at the age of thirty. Wyatt, who could write graceful and sad-toned lyrics successfully, when he was not thinking of Italian models, struggled to render into English the fourteen-line Italian form of the sonnet. He succeeded, but the marks of his painful labour are upon his verses. Surrey, who seemed to compose with less effort, also practised the sonnet, though the most important of his experiments was the translation of the second and fourth books of Virgil's *Aeneid* into English blank verse. Surrey can little have guessed how honourable would be the heritage of the measure which he was employing. Introduced here for the first time into English as a medium for translating from the Latin, blank verse was to become, through Marlowe's employment, the great measure of English poetic drama, to be used by Shakespeare, and by other verse dramatists to the present day. In non-dramatic verse the lineage was no less noble: Milton chose it for *Paradise Lost*, Keats for *Hyperion* and Tennyson for the *Idylls of the King*.

Nor could Wyatt and Surrey have known how often the sonnet form would attract later poets. They themselves, influenced by Petrarch, used the sonnet for love poems of a particular type: the lover is dutiful, anxious, adoring, full of wanhope, and of praises for his mistress; the mistress is proud, unreceptive, but, if the lover is to be believed, very desirable. Throughout the Elizabethan age poets imitated these Petrarchan moods of love, and used the sonnet to express them. Some saw through the artificialities of the sentiment, which Shakespeare mocked with the speeches of Mercutio in *Romeo and Juliet*. Sir Philip Sidney, in *Astrophel and Stella*, jested at the fashion, and yet half succumbed to it:

*Makers=poets.

some of his sonnets plead for realism, and others luxuriate in the baroque devices which the convention allowed. Shakespeare, though he satirized sonnet-writing, was himself a sonneteer, but as always, Shakespeare is different. Some of his sonnets are addressed not to a woman but to a young man, and they are in the terms of warmest affection. Others are written not with adoration but with an air of disillusioned passion to a 'dark lady'. His power over words, from the play of the pun to the very transmutation of speech, marks them all. The pretty things are there, but with them in the graver sonnets a profound moral vision. The most profound of the sonnets reads:

> Th'expense of spirit in a waste of shame
> Is lust in action, and till action, lust
> Is perjured, murderous, bloody, full of blame,
> Savage, extreme, rude, cruel, not to trust,
> Enjoyed no sooner but despised straight.
> Past reason hunted, and no sooner had
> Past reason hated as a swallowed bait
> One purpose laid to make the taker mad;
> Mad in pursuit and in possession so,
> Had, having, and in quest to have, extreme,
> A bliss in proof and proved a very woe;
> Before, a joy proposed; behind, a dream.
>   All this the world well knows yet none knows well,
>   To shun the heaven that leads men to this hell.

The sonnet outlived the Elizabethan period. Milton used the form, not however for amorous dainties, but to define moments of auto-biography, and for brief, powerful comments on public events. To the sonnet Wordsworth returned to awaken England from lethargy, to condemn Napoleon and to record many of his own moods. Keats, who had studied Shakespeare and Milton to such purpose, discovered himself as a poet in his sonnet, 'On First Looking into Chapman's Homer'. In the nineteenth century Meredith in *Modern Love* showed how a sixteen-line variant could be made a vehicle of analysis, and D. G. Rossetti in *The House of Life* came back, though with many changes, to the older way of Dante and Petrarch.

Wyatt and Surrey were succeeded by Edmund Spenser (c. 1552–99), who was a master of the poetic art, and was acknowledged by his contemporaries as such. Of his life little is known. He was an undergraduate at Cambridge and liked by the elegant and the clever, including Gabriel Harvey, whom the young men of those days regarded as the wisest of their elders. No one in the family could help him on the painful road that led from University to the Court. His art made him some friends, and his intelligence others. The Earl of Leicester may have encouraged

An illustration from the first eclogue of Spenser's *The Shepherd's Calendar,* 1579. Colin Clout, the Shepherd boy, has broken his pipe in a fit of despair because Rosalind will not return his love

him. He went to Ireland and, except for two visits to England, there remained reluctantly until he was driven to London in distress to die and by the Earl of Essex's benevolence to be buried in Westminster Abbey. Among his poems, two volumes will always be remembered, *The Shepherd's Calendar* of 1579 and *The Faerie Queene,* which began publication in 1590.

His early work, *The Shepherd's Calendar,* read for the first time, is an odd, difficult and old-fashioned work. It cannot be judged straight from human experience, as can Chaucer's *Troilus and Criseyde.* Like a museum piece it needs a reference to the catalogue before its beauties can be appreciated. Spenser has written twelve 'eclogues' or shepherds' poems, one for each month of the year, and in the manner of the classical and renaissance eclogue-writer he has permitted himself a variety of themes, from church satire to praise of the Queen. The title promises a simple rustic book but the poems are clever, mock-simple, courtly pieces.

The final effect of *The Faerie Queene* is of a wash made from the brightest pigments with little to arrest the intellect or astound the imagination as in Shakespeare, with strange and incongruous passages of satire and allegory but with magnificence continually breaking in. The stanza, which Spenser invented for *The Faerie Queene,* has this miraculous power of gathering words up into itself, caressingly, and so adorning them with its music that they become more notable than they were before.

Spenser, like all great artists, felt the form and pressure of his time conditioning his writing. He was aware of a desire to make English a fine language, full of magnificent words, with its roots in the older and popular traditions of the native tongue. He had the ambition to write English poems which would be great and revered, as the classical epics of Homer and Virgil had been, or the new ambitious romantic poetry of Ariosto and Tasso. He was aware of the popular stories and myths, which had lingered on from the Middle Ages, the Arthurian tales, the allegories, the giants and enchanters. He knew, no less, the nobly fashioned heroic tales from the classical world, of Hector and Achilles, Ulysses and Aeneas. Somehow he would make a poem in which the medley of native story joined with a classical ambition in presentation. Double, even treble, motives crossed within his mind, all ultimately controlled by the fact that his surest audience lay within the Court, his most treasured auditor, if only she would listen, the Queen herself, Gloriana, the Faerie Queene. His mind looked out beyond the Court to the people, to their superstitions and faiths, and he had even the grave moral aim of improving the England which he loved, but the Court and the Queen were in the forefront of his vision. In him the medieval and Renaissance met, the modern and the classical, the courtly and the popular. Whatever may have been the complexity of these aims he remained superbly an artist.

It is doubtful whether the modern reader will make his way joyfully through *The Faerie Queene* as Keats did, going excitedly right through to the end and then returning to read again. But it is a poem in which

The Redcross knight subdues Sans Joy the Sarazin, who is saved by Duessa, from Spenser's *The Faerie Queene*. Right: The Faerie Queen herself, Elizabeth I, is carried in procession by her courtiers. (Detail from a painting attributed to Robert Peake)

one can read for pleasure the splendid passages, with their sustaining music. Such is Spenser's description of the 'Bower of Bliss', in Book II, Canto xii:

> There, whence that Music seemed heard to be
>   Was the fair Witch herself now solacing,
>   With a new Lover, whom, through sorcery
>   And witchcraft, she from far did thither bring:
>   There she had him now laid a slumbering,
>   In secret shade, after long wanton joys:
>   Whilst round about them pleasantly did sing
>   Many fair Ladies, and lascivious boys,
> That ever mixed their song with light licentious toys.
>
> And all that while, right over him she hung
>   With her false eyes fast fixed in his sight
>   As seeking medicine, whence she was stung,
>   Or greedily depasturing delight:
>   And oft inclining down with kisses light,
>   For fear of waking him, his lips bedewed,
>   And through his humid eyes did suck his spright,
>   Quite molten into lust and pleasure lewd;
> Wherewith she sighed soft, as if his case she rued.
>
> The whiles some one did chant this lovely lay;
>   'Ah see, who so fair thing dost fain to see,
>   In springing flower the image of thy day;
>   Ah see the Virgin Rose, how sweetly she
>   Doth first peep forth with bashful modesty,
>   That fairer seems, the less ye see her may;
>   Lo see soon after, how more bold and free
>   Her bared bosom she doth broad display;
> Lo see soon after, how she fades, and falls away.

The best poetry of the Elizabethan age went into drama and, apart from Spenser, no one can compare with Marlowe and Shakespeare as writers of verse. The dramatists proved themselves poets outside the drama: Marlowe with *Hero and Leander*, Shakespeare with *Venus and Adonis*, *Lucrece* and the *Sonnets*, and Ben Jonson with numerous lyrics, including the well-known 'Drink to me only with thine eyes'. Poetry flourished in that time, and the poems varied from long Colossus-like pieces to the most delicate songs and lyrics. The work of Michael Drayton (1563–1631), a representative poet, is a museum of most of the ways in which poetry could then be written. He could erect poetic Leviathans and he could turn a lyric as light as a feather blown into the sunlight. His historical poem, 'The Barons' Wars' (1603), moves at a steady pace. Its sluggish treatment of the material illustrates by contrast what a powerful imagination Shakespeare employed when he converted history into genuine poetic drama. But Drayton could turn from ponderous works to compose *Nymphidia*, one of the happiest of English fairy poems; the compact and stirring 'Ballad of Agincourt'; and that admirable sonnet 'Since there's no help, come let us kiss and part'.

Samuel Daniel (1562–1619) had something of the same energy in composition, combined with the same absence of dominating diction. Like Drayton, he attempted to write history in verse with *The Civil Wars between Lancaster and York* (1595; revised edition, 1609), but his most genuine talent lay in reflective poetry, which, in poems such as his *Epistles*, was later to attract Wordsworth's attention.

The longer poems of the Elizabethan age demand concessions from the reader. He must approach them with a historical interest, or his taste will be offended and his attention diverted. But the songs and lyrics, in which the age delighted, have ever given a spontaneous pleasure to posterity. Shakespeare, in *Twelfth Night*, shows how in the house of the Duke Orsino the song was a ready and acceptable entertainment. So it was in the great houses of the Elizabethans and in the Court. Many of the poets of that age knew the art of wedding verse and sounds, and in the song-books of the period can be found the lyrics of Thomas Campion and others who delighted the audiences of their day.

One has to stretch across the years to reach Drayton and Daniel, but John Donne (1572–1631) seems often to stand before us as a contemporary. His life was adventurous – a gallant, a courtier, a member of Essex's Cadiz expedition, secretary to the Lord Keeper, a prisoner for his runaway match with his master's niece, and at last the Dean of St Paul's. His mind was restless and adventurous: he read widely, treasuring the most recondite forms of knowledge. Some intense nervous excitement marked all that he thought, all that he did. He had the power of experiencing keenly, and of reviewing the experience against the background of quite contrary moods. He is the lover and the sensualist, but his mind reviews his love in the terms of philosophy or explores it with the images gathered in his scientific and theological reading. So it is in his poem 'The Good-Morrow':

> *I wonder by my troth, what thou, and I*
> *Did, till we lov'd? were we not wean'd till then?*
> *But suck'd on country pleasures, childishly?*
> *Or snorted we in the seven sleepers den?*
> *T'was so; But this, all pleasures fancies be.*
> *If ever any beauty I did see,*
> *Which I desir'd, and got, t'was but a dream of thee.*
>
> *And now good morrow to our waking souls,*
> *Which watch not one another out of fear;*

For love, all love of other sights controls,
And makes one little room, an everywhere.
Let sea-discoverers to new worlds have gone,
Let Maps to other, worlds on worlds have shown,
Let us possess one world, each hath one, and is one.

My face is thine eye, thine in mine appears,
And true plain hearts do in the faces rest,
Where can we find two better hemispheres
Without sharp North, without declining West?
Whatever dies, was not mixed equally;
If our two loves be one, or, thou and I
Love so alike, that none do slacken, none can die.

He can perceive beauty, but at the very moment of that perception he sees the corpse, the cerement clothes, the skeleton. He knows passion, but he can mock at the physical body through which passion is transmitted. This restlessness brings his mind and his body very close to each other. His thought is ever at the service of his passions; his passions enter into his thought. Contraries exist in his mind, but they are ever moving one into the other. He is the young gallant who ends his life as Dean of St Paul's.

This frankness in passion, this despair of making a unity out of the broken images of life, have brought him close to some contemporary poets. He was naturally impatient of the conventional verse forms, of the regular rhythms, the well-worn similes. Instead of the accepted catalogue of comparisons used by the Petrarchan sonneteers, he sought out the strangest images. Dr Johnson was later to name him and his school the 'metaphysical' poets, because they yoked ideas which no one had yet seen together. That Donne did this is true, but often he can achieve his effects in another way, by the most brief and simple statements.

A 'school' of poets Donne certainly created, and much of the history of poetry in the seventeenth century could be written in the terms of loyalty or antagonism to his manner. His most interesting followers were religious poets. George Herbert (1593–1633), compared with Donne, has a simple and unimpeded devoutness. Yet the lyrics in *The Temple* successfully employ an unusual, often a homely, imagery, to give expression to religious experience. Henry Vaughan (1621–95), who was influenced by Donne and Herbert, had a mysticism which is recorded in poems such as 'The Retreat', and in 'I saw Eternity the other Night', but not all his work reaches this high level. The third of this group was Richard Crashaw (*c.* 1612–49), the Roman Catholic poet, whose *Steps to the Temple* (1646) shows the influence not only of Donne but of Marino, the Italian poet, who used similarly elaborate forms.

Among the poets who had written verses lamenting the death of Donne had been Thomas Carew (1598–1639), one of the earliest of the 'Cavalier' poets. His verses had grace and wit, and his love lyrics and madrigals have found a place in the anthologies. His long poem, 'The Rapture', has not been similarly honoured, for, whatever may be its poetical merit, it has a licentiousness of which anthologists do not normally approve. Carew was the most careful of the 'Cavalier' lyrists, some of whom appear to be brilliant amateurs in verse. Sir John Suckling (1609–42), though he wrote often and sometimes seriously, seems to have been improvising in some of his light and cynical love lyrics. Richard Lovelace (1618–58) had probably a less sustained poetic gift than either Carew or Suckling, but he had the good fortune to make some happily turned lines, including 'Stone walls do not a prison make', by which his name will be remembered. A little apart from these 'Cavalier' lyrists is Robert Herrick (1591–1674), a disciple of Ben Jonson, who spent his exile as a cleric in Devonshire in the composition of verses. His poems were collected in 1648 as *Hesperides*, a volume which contains over a thousand pieces, both secular and divine. Less conscious in his verse than Ben Jonson, he had learnt from his master the art of brief expression, and to this he added his own lyrical gift, and his power of seizing upon the illuminating but unexpected word. The whole of the English countryside in its Maydays and fairings and its half-pagan rustic ritual comes to life in his poems. The lyrics are often of love, fanciful, light-hearted, but with a gentle melancholy as he remembers how swiftly the joys of the earth disappear. While Herrick lived in retirement, Andrew Marvell (1621–78) was close to the great life of his country in the troubled days of the Commonwealth and the Restoration. His earliest poems are quiet, reflective pieces based on rural life and include his well-known poem 'The Garden'. He became tutor to Cromwell's ward and wrote in praise of the Protector poems such as the 'Horatian Ode upon Cromwell's Return from Ireland'. With the Restoration of Charles II his poems were satiric and filled with an angry bitterness; poems such as his attack on the incompetence of the country in 'The Last Instructions to a Painter' are a complete contrast to his earlier work.

'Death and the Lovers', an engraving by Albrecht Dürer.

> *Alas, as well as other Princes, we*
> *(Who Prince enough in one another be)*
> *Must leave at last in death these eyes and ears,*
> *Oft fed with true oaths, and with sweet salt tears*
> John Donne, *The Anniversary*

'Newton', by William Blake. Sir Isaac Newton, among other scientists of the seventeenth and eighteenth centuries, revolutionized man's concept of the laws of nature

English Poetry from Milton to William Blake

THE SEVENTEENTH century is in many ways the century of transition into our modern world. The Civil Wars separated men from the older ways of living, and the religious controversies killed much that had remained lively in the national imagination since the Middle Ages. Science and, with Science, rationalism were growing in power, and much of that power was to be used to destroy man's capacity for myth-making, to remove from the arts much of the authority they had once possessed. Donne's restlessness seems the anticipation of a sensitive personality, feeling not so much with his mind as with the 'tips of his fingers' the world which is to arise around him. A few of his followers, such as Abraham Cowley, accepted the new situation with a facile optimism, believing that somehow science and poetry could be employed each in the service of the other.

It was in this period, when the position of the poet had been made difficult, that John Milton (1608–74) wrote in a manner that recalled poetry to the most elevated and regal conception of its function. His early work was written before the Civil Wars, and included *Comus* (1634) and many of the minor poems which were first collected in 1645. In the national upheaval he was occupied as a controversialist and Latin Secretary, and those who know Milton only from his verse may well be surprised to discover the vituperation and abuse which he dealt out to his opponents in the pamphleteering warfare. In the Civil Wars Milton supported what was ultimately the losing side, and the disappointment was the more severe as the cause of Cromwell had awakened in him high hopes for the future of humanity. A gesture of the heroic marks his closing years, when blind, half-fugitive, old, hope-shattered, he turns to compose the great poetic works which from his youth had haunted his imagination. *Paradise Lost* was published in 1667; *Paradise Regained* and *Samson Agonistes* in 1671.

Of Milton's works *Comus* is probably the most popular and intelligible today. Those who have seen the piece played will not be led away by the text-book disquisitions on its dramatic ineffectiveness. Like some other plays, it reads as if it had little dramatic content but it acts well,

A scene from Milton's *Comus*, by C. R. Leslie (1794–1859), and the manuscript of the concluding lines of Milton's 'Lycidas'

*Thus sang the uncouth swaine to th'oakss & rills
while y⁸ still morne went out with sandals gray
he taucht the tendr stops of various quills
with eagr thought warbling his Dorick lay
and now the Sun had stretcht out all the hills,
and now was dropt into the wester'n bay
at last he rose and twitcht his mantle blew
To morrow to fresh woods and pasturs new*

and the fact that it is not very like a masque need trouble only the pedant. As far as *Comus* has a story it tells of the temptation of the chaste maiden by the enchanter Comus, and of the power which her virtue gave her to resist him. Almost all the ideas that govern Milton's later poetry are already here. He saw life as a struggle, the Puritan struggle, for the survival of the good and the virtuous. So Eve and Adam were told to contend in *Paradise Lost*, so does Christ struggle against Satan in *Paradise Regained*, and Samson against false counsels in *Samson Agonistes*. For Milton this struggle is never easy, for his mind is aware of the attractions of the earth and the pleasures of the body; to Comus he gives a magnificent plea that all the pleasures of the earth should be enjoyed.

While the Puritan ideal was not easy, still less was it negative. It is regrettable that he composed his later and mature works when circumstances had cast such a black shadow across his path. No one who moves among these later poems can fail to feel the chill which blows around their massive colonnades, inducing a sense of loneliness, and a desire for ordinary human companionship. Yet they are amongst the greatest of our non-dramatic poems. The classical epic of Homer and Virgil, on whose design Milton had based his poems, is now little read at least in the original languages. The story of Adam and Eve may have ceased to have much importance for most minds, and this also tells against Milton; but nothing can destroy the picture of Satan's rebellion, half-heroic, half-evil, or the language which seeks, over human experience and past literature, for parallels to describe his cosmic action. Such is the verse which Milton gives to Satan in his address to the Fallen Angels:

> *What though the field be lost?*
> *All is not lost; the unconquerable Will,*
> *And study of revenge, immortal hate,*
> *And courage never to submit or yield:*
> *And what is else not to be overcome.*
> *That Glory never shall his wrath or might*
> *Extort from me. To bow and sue for grace*
> *With suppliant knee, and deify his power*
> *Who from the terror of this Arm so late*
> *Doubted his Empire; that were low indeed,*
> *That were an ignominy and shame beneath*
> *This downfall; since by Fate the strength of Gods*
> *And this Empyreal substance cannot fail,*
> *Since through experience of this great event*
> *In Arms not worse, in foresight much advanc'd,*
> *We may with more successful hope resolve*
> *To wage by force or guile eternal War,*
> *Irreconcilable to our grand Foe,*
> *Who now triumphs, and in th'excess of joy*
> *Sole reigning holds the Tyranny of Heav'n.*

Milton had from the first a sense of dedication to poetry, as he has himself expressed in 'Lycidas', and his whole mental life became a discipline so that he might achieve the great poems which in his youth he had outlined in his imagination.

If Milton exposes Puritanism at its best, Samuel Butler (1612–80), in his satire *Hudibras*, showed all the hypocrisies of Puritanism, and its cramping of the human spirit. In this burlesque poem, through which moves the spirit of Cervantes, he shows great comic invention in displaying the Presbyterian knight Sir Hudibras and his squire, Ralph, in action. Beneath the comedy and the coarseness there seems to dwell a cynical, perhaps a sceptical, mind. The poem was popular at the time, and it can be still enjoyed. The contrast of this intelligent buffoonery with Milton's grand manner is complete.

The legend that Milton was an unpopular poet has lived so long that probably it will never be destroyed. The facts cry out against the legend; he was read in his own age, and throughout the eighteenth century he was imitated widely though never very intelligently. He has always been read since by that minority which finds pleasure in poetry as an art. For a time in the twentieth century his poems were ungenerously judged. These false critics may have set many readers against the poet, but anyone who acquires his poems and reads them has at hand an enjoyment more varied and profound than any anticipation could conceive. It is true that in his own age he stood somewhat apart, and that poetry followed other ways, The clearest 'movement' in Milton's age came from those who desired a greater simplicity in verse, with the employment of contemporary and intelligible themes. Those who believed in this manner came to use one particular form of verse known as the heroic couplet. It is the type of verse which later Pope was to make famous:

> True ease in writing comes from art, not chance,
> As those move easiest who have learn'd to dance.*

Neat, measured, exact, regular, the heroic couplet was like a rococo façade, and the complete contrast to the twisted, agonized lines in which Donne tortured himself into expression. The beginning of this 'regular' movement has always been associated with the names of Edmund Waller (1606–87), and Sir John Denham (1615–69). That the changes which they made in poetry were recognized by their contemporaries can be seen in Dryden's praise of Waller, 'he first made writing easily an art'. Dryden was praising the lucidity both of subject and treatment, such as were to be found in Denham's 'Cooper's Hill'. Four often-quoted lines in that poem became the insignia of the new group:

> O could I flow like thee, and make thy stream
> My great example, as it is my theme.
> Though deep, yet clear; though gentle, yet not dull;
> Strong without rage; without o'erflowing, full.

John Dryden (1631–1700), who discovered so much to praise in the new school, was himself one of its chief exponents. Dramatist, critic, translator, Dryden was foremost a poet, and, in poetry, he was primarily a craftsman. The 'man of letters', whose life was largely controlled by economic exigencies and dependence on the Court, cherished as his first ambition as an artist the making of good verses. He has been widely

*An Essay on Criticism.

read and admired, but the English have not taken him to their hearts as they have done many a lesser man. In the *Annus Mirabilis* (1667), he wrote of the Dutch War and the Fire of London: this is a most unusual feat in transferring almost immediately contemporary events into poetry. In *Absalom and Achitophel* (1681), he exposed the politics of Shaftesbury's intrigues and Monmouth's disloyalty, and produced the best of his satires. His description of Shaftesbury as Achitophel is particularly effective:

> *Of these the false Achitophel was first:*
> *A Name to all succeeding ages cursed.*
> *For close Designs and crooked Counsels fit;*
> *Sagacious, Bold, and Turbulent of wit,*
> *Restless, unfixed in Principles and Place,*
> *In Power unpleased, impatient of Disgrace.*
> *A fiery Soul, which working out its way,*
> *Fretted the Pigmy Body to decay:*
> *And o'er informed the Tenement of Clay.*

As a translator, he rendered Virgil, Juvenal, Ovid and Chaucer, and the best of his prose is the preface of 1700 to the *Fables*, in which, in the

The execution of the Duke of Monmouth, July 1685. The events of the Monmouth Rebellion were described by Dryden in his poem *Absalom and Achitophel.* Shaftesbury (Achitophel) was attempting to stir up sentiment in favour of declaring Charles II's Protestant but illegitimate son, the Duke of Monmouth (Absalom), heir to the throne

Alexander Pope, in his grotto at Twickenham. As an artist he studied perfection with a rare singleness of purpose

year of his death, he introduced some of his translations to the public. His range cannot be estimated without a consideration of his criticism and his plays in verse. The plays contain many of his most delightful and sometimes amusing lyrics. A number of his contemporaries among the courtiers of Charles II wrote light amorous lyrics of great charm: often it seemed the more dissolute the man the more delicate and charming the songs and lyrics: such were those of Sir Charles Sedley (1639–1701) and the Earl of Rochester (1648–80).

The career of Alexander Pope (1688–1744), in many ways Dryden's successor, has been more hotly and more frequently debated than any other in English literature.

As often, some confused the man and the poet. He was puny, ill-made, venomous, unjust, splenetic, and his enemies have found occasion to emphasize each item in the inventory of defects. As an artist, he studied perfection, with a rare singleness of purpose, and he is the nearest approach to a classical poet in our language. It is true that his vision had limitations: the ardours and endurances of romantic poetry he avoided, nor had he the sense of dedication and high purpose of Milton or Words-worth. In the *Essay on Man* he expressed a philosophy in verse, but rather as moral precepts than as a vision. Superficially his teaching may seem optimistic, but beneath the surface can be seen the alert mind, perceiving the pride of man, his high-vaunting ambitions, and, in contrast, the inadequacy of his faculties. If Pope ever forgot that inner vision, he had his friend Swift, close at hand, to remind him.

Thus it was as a satirist that Pope was most effective. At his best, in *The Rape of the Lock*, he was able to mock at the whole of the fashionable society of the eighteenth century, while showing that he had some passionate attachment to its elegance. *The Dunciad*, in which he abused dullness in general, and the contemporary dunces in particular, is more ephemeral until one approaches the magnificent conclusion on Chaos, undoubtedly the most profound passage in Pope's work:

> *Thus at her felt approach, and secret might,*
> *Art after Art goes out, and all is Night,*
> *See skulking Truth to her old Cavern fled,*
> *Mountains of Casuistry heap'd o'er her head!*
> *Philosophy, that lean'd on Heav'n before,*
> *Shrinks to her second cause, and is no more.*
> *Physic of Metaphysic begs defence*
> *And Metaphysic calls for aid on Sense!*
> *See Mystery to Mathematics fly!*
> *In vain! they gaze, turn giddy, rave, and die.*
> *Religion blushing veils her sacred fires,*
> *And unawares Morality expires.*
> *For public Flame, nor private dares to shine;*
> *Nor human Spark is left, nor Glimpse divine!*
> *Lo! thy dread Empire CHAOS! is restor'd;*
> *Light dies before thy uncreating word,*
> *Thy hand, great Anarch! lets the curtain fall,*
> *And Universal Darkness buries All.*

Not all Pope's work is satiric. He began with nature poems of an elegant kind, the *Pastorals* and *Windsor Forest*, and the great labour of his middle age was his translation of Homer. This work has often been abused, but, from its own day to this, it has been one of the most widely read volumes of verse in the language. Homer it may not be, but it is a poem, and one which has given a genuine enjoyment. A floridness of diction mars some of the effects of two poems, 'Eloisa to Abelard' and the 'Elegy to the Memory of an Unfortunate Lady', where the gentler and more romantic sides of his nature struggled for expression.

Criticism sometimes speaks of the age which followed Pope as if it were dominated by his example. Nothing could be less true. John Gay (1685–1732) used the couplet in his *Fables* and other poems, but the best of his talent went into the lyric and *The Beggar's Opera*. Pope had only two genuine followers, Samuel Johnson and Oliver Goldsmith, and they both differ from him widely. Johnson devoted only a small part of his time to the writing of English verse. Lexicography and the prose works occupied much of his time. Often he wrote verses in Latin but he had a great command of the couplet, as appears in his two satires, 'London' (1738), and 'The Vanity of Human Wishes' (1749); both based on Juvenal, these show what his powerful mind, his grave moral outlook and his incisive phrasing could achieve. The graces of Pope are absent, the mockeries, and the stifled gaiety of Pope's humour, but in their place there is a heavier tread, regular and resounding.

In *The Traveller* (1764) and *The Deserted Village* (1770), Johnson's contemporary, Oliver Goldsmith (1728–74), the son of an Irish clergyman, depicted the social and economic evils of his time in both England and Ireland. He has a wider understanding of contemporary problems than Pope, but that, of course, does not of itself make him a better poet. The couplet form for his verse he had adapted from Pope, but he wrote in an easier, more Chaucerian manner.

If Goldsmith, who was also a novelist, essayist and historian, had only had a greater capacity for taking pains he would have been one of the foremost figures in our literature.

While Pope kept the reader's attention fixed on society, there was growing up in the eighteenth century an interest in nature for its own sake. Nature had always been a theme in English poetry, from Anglo-Saxon times to Shakespeare and Milton, but in the eighteenth century

'Autumn', an illustration to James Thomson's *The Seasons.* Thomson was one of the first poets of the eighteenth century to celebrate the theme of nature in its more wild and rugged aspects.

Crown'd with the sickle and the wheaten sheaf, Comes Autumn, nodding o'er the yellow plain

it becomes an independent theme. Such an interest appears in James Thomson's (1700–48) *The Seasons*, which began publication in 1726. The poem was immediately popular, and though it circulated among the wits, it also had an audience among ordinary people to whom Pope's elegant satires never penetrated. Thomson was too diffuse to be a great artist. Yet for over a century he was one of the most widely read poets in England. His sympathy with ordinary life, and for poverty, combined with his generous sentiment, made him acceptable to many who could not tolerate the hard brilliance of Pope. Also his treatment of nature was original, even if ponderous, and it was a theme growing in popularity.

What this increased interest in nature signified is difficult to record. Part of it was a delight in 'prospects', in scenes such as a painter might use. Now that roads were improving, gentlemen and ladies could look out from their carriages on the views, and much of what they saw pleased them. Some even constructed 'views' on their own estates and parklands. The delight was often not for the pretty and regular design, but for the more wild and rugged aspects of nature. It was as if the human mind were in revolt against the increasing rationalism of the century. Much of this interest was linked with a generous sentiment towards humanity, and towards movements, such as Methodism, which drew attention to the great gulf between the wealthy and elegant society of the century and the condition of those who lived in abject poverty. William Cowper (1731–1800) gathers up many of these contemporary interests into his work. He is most widely known for 'John Gilpin', a good jest, but actually the jest of a mind fretful and tormented, fighting in secret for its sanity. His most successful poem, *The Task* (1785), moves freely amid rural scenes and describes them in a manner less heavy and pretentious than that of Thomson. Behind all of Cowper's varied moods there lingers the dread that reason might one day retreat, and this led to the most poignant of his poems, 'The Castaway', where, more clearly than in any other poem in English, is shown the fear of approaching insanity.

Morbidity, which threatened Cowper, seemed to hover near a number of creative minds in the eighteenth century. It was as if the sensitive mind in that robust age was driven in upon itself into self-laceration and anguish. Some of this melancholy may have been a fashion, a delight in ruins, spectres and midnight walks among the tombs, but it was real enough to colour the whole life of Thomas Gray (1716–71), the author of the 'Elegy'. Gray as a young man had seen the gay and elegant life of Europe in the company of Horace Walpole, the brilliant, dilettante son of Sir Robert Walpole, one of England's most formidable Prime Ministers. But his long years were spent in the enervating life of an eighteenth-century don in Cambridge. Some sadness of spirit within him paralysed action, and made creative work

almost impossible. He was among the most learned men of Europe in his day, yet his poems are a thin sheaf, a few odes and the 'Elegy'. He brought into his poems new interests, medieval in 'The Bard' and Scandinavian in 'The Descent of Odin', but with the whole of the classical and medieval world within his grasp it is sad that some melancholy or inertia held him from composition. A taste for Gray's odes is a cultivated one: the reader must delight in ornate words, often chosen for the memory of their employment by earlier writers. Of the 'Elegy' successive generations of Englishmen have already given their judgement, and this can be summarized in Dr Johnson's memorable words: 'Had Gray written often thus it had been vain to blame and useless to praise him.'

Gray's depression is genial and controlled compared with that of his contemporary, William Collins (1721–59), whose brief life was marked by penury and bouts of insanity. Collins was not unaware of the life of his time, as poems such as 'How Sleep the Brave' show. But the most distinctive side of his mind lived in shadows where the shapes of magic could form themselves. This is found most openly in his 'Ode on the Popular Superstitions of the Highlands', but it is present in 'Ode to Evening' and in the 'Dirge in Cymbeline'.

The untidy and largely disreputable life of Christopher Smart (1722–71) culminated not merely in morbidity but in the madhouse-cell. There he composed the 'Song to David', written, so the legend runs, 'partly with charcoal on the walls, or indented with a key on the panels of his cell'. The 'Song' has had its extravagant supporters and the most sober judgement cannot miss the spiritual vision and the singing quality, rather like a clanging of bells or the sound of trumpets.

One poet rose against all the pressure of the material world, and though men might call him insane, it was an exulting insanity, the divine frenzy of vision and prophecy. William Blake's (1757–1827) work stands alone in our literature, for no one saw life in the same way as he did. He was aware of the material world, of the 'dark Satanic Mills', but in his own exulting way he overcame them.

He was a poet and a painter of a genius wholly individual. If he is to be believed, he actually saw the angels and strange figures which his pictures portray. They sat beside him in the garden, or in the trees, gathering around him as naturally as a group of friends. These visions loosened him from the material world, in which so much of the eighteenth century was stuck fast as in a slough of mental despond. He liberated the human soul from its slavery to matter, and in his more

Left: Thomas Gray, author of the popular *Elegy in a Country Churchyard*.

There at the foot of yonder nodding beech
That wreathes its old fantastic roots so high,
His listless length at noontide he would stretch,
And pore upon the brook that babbles by

energetic moments saw a life beyond good and evil, a white, burning image of pure energy. His *Auguries of Innocence*, is, with his lyrics, one of his most simple, poetical statements:

> *To see a World in a Grain of Sand*
> *And a Heaven in a Wild Flower,*
> *Hold Infinity in the palm of your hand*
> *And Eternity in an hour.*
>
> *A Robin Red breast in a Cage*
> *Puts all Heaven in a Rage.*
> *A dove house fill'd with doves and Pigeons*
> *Shudders Hell thro' all its regions.*
> *A dog starv'd at his Master's Gate*
> *Predicts the ruin of the State.*
> *A Horse misus'd upon the Road*
> *Calls to Heaven for Human blood.*
>
> *Each outcry of the hunted Hare*
> *A fibre from the Brain does tear.*
> *A Skylark wounded in the wing,*
> *A Cherubim does cease to sing.*
> *The Game Cock clip't and arm'd for fight*
> *Does the Rising Sun affright*
> *Every Wolf's and Lion's howl*
> *Raises from Hell a Human Soul.*

Repression he regarded as evil, though freedom from repression he interpreted not psychologically, as is the contemporary manner, but mystically. Much of his thought seems to have sprung fully formed out of his own intuitions, though his reading was wider than is often imagined, and the influence of some mystics, particularly of Swedenborg, is strong upon his work.

As a prophet, and a liberator of the human spirit, Blake is of first importance, but as an artist he is limited by his arbitrary methods, and by an absence of discipline. To disregard tradition completely is the most dangerous course any artist can pursue. Whatever has been gained by our predecessors has been hardly won, and the mental anarchy, which lays it in ruins in order to build the new Jerusalem in its place, smacks of the sin which Lucifer shared with little Bethel. In his later *Prophetic Books*, Blake is in this danger. He uses a symbolism of his own invention, a secret language, bewildering to the reader, and destructive of the unity of his poems as works of art. As a poet Blake is at his best in his simplest poems, in the early *Songs of Innocence and Experience*, where wisdom speaks with the voice of a child. Here and in some later poems such as *The Everlasting Gospel* he wrote with those fragrant intuitions which awaken the human mind to the best and most innocent vision of

'Satan in his original glory' by William Blake

itself. Only one side of him is shown in his poetry and his letters; as a painter his art has a brilliance of imagination which is compelling and often leads the observer to total surrender. The appeal to the eye is ever more immediate and consuming than verbal communication.

Almost contemporary with Blake is Robert Burns (1759–96). So much that is false has been written about Burns, particularly in his own country, and sometimes in moments of induced exuberance, that the truth is worth recording. The best of his work appears in the satires, most of which were written while he was still farming at Mossgiel. Many of these appeared in 1786 in the Kilmarnock edition of his poems, and it is in this volume that his genius announced itself at its best, though some of his greatest satires including 'Address to the Unco' Guid', 'Holy Willie's Prayer', and 'The Jolly Beggars' did not appear in it. This volume opened for him the doors of fashionable society in Edinburgh where, for a season, as the untutored ploughman poet, he was a lionized curiosity. No journey was ever more fateful to a poet, no people more unwittingly unkind to genius. His moral nature, always susceptible, particularly to amorous and alcoholic adventures, suffered, and farming had lost some of its attractions after the elegances of the capital. His Edinburgh friends found him a post as 'gauger' in the Excise which was henceforth his main means of support.

His reputation as 'untutored', which he himself helped to create, is false, for he had read widely both in earlier Scottish poetry and in Pope, Thomson, Gray and Shakespeare. When he wrote in English, he wrote as a cultivated English poet would write, and his Scottish poems are not naïve dialect pieces, but clever manipulations of language varying from Ayrshire to standard English. Nor was he, as sometimes represented, a child of the French Revolution. He was a 'Pittite up to a point', and a strong navy man, whose best work was written before the French Revolution. He is rightly judged not against the wide expanse of European politics but against his own narrow Scottish background. He revolted against the sanctimonious hypocrisy of the religious, and against the social barriers that divided man from man. This egalitarian philosophy he discovered, not in the text-books of political theory, but from his own observation, and he expressed it admirably, even recklessly, in one of the greatest of all his poems, 'The Jolly Beggars'. After his journey to Edinburgh he composed only one poem, 'Tam o'Shanter', which can match these early pieces. The rest were mainly sentimental songs and lyrics, of the type of 'John Anderson my Jo'. It is of interest that both his best poems concern taverns. To the tavern he was attracted for reasons which were obvious, and beyond that, they alone were egalitarian institutions in his age, more so than the Church, and certainly more so than any social institutions.

The forms of poetry were changing at the close of the eighteenth century, but this did not deter George Crabbe (1754–1832) from returning to the couplet of Pope and Johnson. So successful was his work that he had a steady following of readers even in the age of Byron. Those who have not read his poems always consider him a dull writer. His themes, it is true, were the grim, realistic incidents of rural life, seen without romantic illusion. But his sincerity in recording life as it was, and his eye for detail, have given *The Village* (1783), *The Parish Register* (1807) and *Tales in Verse* (1812) an attraction for anyone who may submit himself to it. Some have thought it easy to write like Crabbe, as unfortunately did Crabbe sometimes, and this has led to the banal lines which the satirists have attacked. At his best, he was a realist in verse, no mean achievement, and his poem on Peter Grimes inspired Benjamin Britten in the libretto of the most distinguished English opera of our century.

If Crabbe shows that the older manner in poetry still had a fresh life, Thomas Chatterton (1752–70) in his imitations of medieval poetry gave evidence of that awakening of wonder which led to romantic poetry. Chatterton's story has passed into legend, but whether the boy who committed suicide at eighteen would have developed into a great genius must remain unknown. He had an arrogant nature and wit, and had he lived he might have produced verse very different from the sham medieval pieces with which he tried to deceive the learned world of his day.

'Kindred Spirits', by Asher B. Durand. The poets of the 'Romantic Revival' all had a deep interest in nature, not only as a source of beautiful scenes, but as an informing and spiritual influence

Chapter 4

The Romantic Poets

THE FIRST thirty years of the nineteenth century are distinguished by a cluster of poets whose work has been as much discussed as that of any group of writers in the English language. 'Romantic revival' is the label that has been attached to them, though they themselves might not have understood what it meant and certainly did not use it. It is only an attempt to show how their work differed from that of their predecessors. They all had a deep interest in nature, not as a centre of beautiful scenes but as an informing and spiritual influence. It was as if, frightened by the coming of industrialism and the nightmare towns of industry, they were turning to nature for protection. Or as if, with the decline of traditional religious beliefs, men were making a religion from the spirituality of their own intuitions.

These personal experiences they all valued to a degree which is difficult to parallel in earlier poets. Spenser, Milton and Pope make verse out of legend or knowledge which is common to humanity. The first generation of romantic poets look into themselves, seeking in their own lives for strange sensations. With Wordsworth such sensations have a moral value and are often associated with simple and human objects. They were largely based on his own life and he made an epic of personal experience in *The Prelude*. With Byron the creative impulse arises from the exotic pursuit of some mood, or adventure, which man has seldom exploited before. With Coleridge, the stimulus leads to the dream territories of Xanadu. The younger generation employ classical mythology as with Shelley in *Prometheus Unbound* and Keats in *Hyperion*, but even here the ancient figures and stories are modified to illustrate their own life. In the poetry of all of them, there is a sense of wonder, of life seen with new sensibilities and fresh vision. This strangeness of the individual experience involves each of the romantics in a spiritual loneliness. They are keenly aware of their social obligations, but the burden of an exceptional vision drives them into being almost fugitives from their fellow-men. This sense, present in them all, can be found most strongly in Shelley, who seems even more content amid the dead leaves, the moonlit water and the ghosts, than in the places where men inhabit, though theoretically he is deeply involved in the ultimate potentiality of man. The romantic poets lead the reader to strange areas of human experience, but seldom welcome him in the language of ordinary conversation or even with the currency of normality. To this generalization Wordsworth must be quoted as the major exception.

William Wordsworth (1770–1850) is at once the oldest, the greatest and the most long-lived of the group. He died in 1850, but poetry died in him in about 1815, only to return fitfully, almost painfully. As a young man he had high hopes for humanity: he had been nurtured in the Lake District, where everything had led him to think well of man. The teaching of Rousseau and his own experience convinced him that man was naturally good. In the French Revolution he saw a great movement for human freedom, welcoming it as many young men of a certain generation welcomed in the twentieth century the coming of the Union of Soviet Republics. Wordsworth himself confessed that the greatest moral shock of his life came when England declared war in 1792 on the young French Republic. In the years which followed he had to endure an agony of spiritual disillusionment. He saw that the France of the young Bonaparte was following, not the vision of the liberties of man, but the path of Charlemagne.

Louis XVI was executed in January 1793, less than a year after England had declared war on France. Both Wordsworth and Coleridge had welcomed the French Revolution as a great movement for human freedom, and both were to be profoundly disillusioned when the years of revolutionary fervour resulted in nothing more than a military dictatorship

Partly under Burke's influence, he came to regard England as the protector of freedom against this new Napoleonic imperialism. For the best twenty-five years of Wordsworth's life England was at war, and when peace came it found him a man from whom the uniqueness of his earliest experience had passed. Many of his critics see him as a bitter reactionary. There is an element of justice in this estimate, though it is far from the whole truth. He followed his beliefs honestly to the end, and if he distrusted reform, one of his reasons lay in the fear that the England he loved, particularly rural England, would be destroyed by the hand of the rising industrialists.

His early life had been a dedication to poetry, storing his mind with the experience in nature which later he was to recall in verse. This period of intense living culminated in his presence in France during the early stages of the Revolution. All that his personality felt from the excitement of public events was accentuated by his love for Annette Vallon. The biographers seem to have given a shout of exultation on discovering that Annette became the mother of a Wordsworthian daughter, and that he left her to return to England. In the years that followed, under the influence of his sister Dorothy, he recovered a spiritual vision and a unique poetic way of recording it.

His love for Dorothy was the most deep and passionate experience of his whole life and during the winter that they spent in Goslar in Germany their intimacy seems to have been absolute.

The most memorable account of his own mind in those years Words-worth has written himself in his autobiographical poem, *The Prelude*, which was not published until 1850. This is the greatest poem of the modern period in English, the spiritual record of a single mind, honestly recording its own intimate experiences, and endowed with a rare capacity for making the record intelligible. There can be few poems to which the modern reader, harassed by personal distress, or troubled by the movement of world events, can return with such certainty of reward. It would have been well for Wordsworth's reputation if *The Prelude* could have been published immediately on its completion.

No poem in English offers a parallel. In scale it is epical, and is composed in blank verse as was Milton's *Paradise Lost*, but instead of dealing with world events or the adventures of heroes, it outlines the development of one single, and from all outward considerations, unimportant personality.

In his own lifetime Wordsworth was first known through the *Lyrical Ballads* (1798), in which S. T. Coleridge collaborated with 'The Ancient Mariner'. The volume was an experiment, for Wordsworth was attempting to make verse out of the incidents of simple rustic life, in a language that was a selection from the phrases of ordinary speech. Coleridge in his poem was endeavouring to employ poetry to give credibility to the miraculous. Wordsworth's experimental pieces are only half-successful, but in 'Michael' he showed how tragic dignity could be given to the story of a shepherd and his son.

In 'Tintern Abbey' he returned to the recollections of his own childhood, and demanding a more liberal vocabulary than the theory of the *Lyrical Ballads* had prescribed, showed, as in *The Prelude*, how a unique experience could be brought within the reader's understanding by bold and imaginative language.

After the *Lyrical Ballads*, Wordsworth held less closely to poetic theory. He used the sonnet, as Milton had done, to arouse England to a sense of her responsibility in international affairs and to express poignant moments in his own experience. Many of the most famous belong to the year 1802, when his thoughts were much with France and her desertion under Napoleon of her role as a liberating force (*I griev'd for Buonaparte with a vain And an unthinking grief*): to the same year belonged the most famous of the sonnets, 'Composed upon Westminster Bridge' (*Earth has not anything to show more fair*). His skill in the sonnet remained, even when much of the rest of his verse showed a decline: so as late as 1822 he wrote 'Inside King's College Chapel, Cambridge':

> *Tax not the royal Saint with vain expense,*
> *With ill-matched aims the Architect who planned –*
> *Albeit labouring for a scanty band*
> *Of white-robed Scholars only – this immense*
> *And glorious Work of fine intelligence!*
> *Give all thou canst; high Heaven rejects the lore*
> *Of nicely-calculated less or more;*
> *So deemed the man who fashioned for the sense*
> *These lofty pillars, spread that branching roof*
> *Self-poised, and scooped into ten thousand cells,*
> *Where light and shade repose, where music dwells*
> *Lingering – and wandering on as loth to die;*
> *Like thoughts whose very sweetness yieldeth proof*
> *That they were born for immortality.*

In the 'Immortality' Ode, he recorded a mystical intuition of a life before birth, which dying out in this material world can be recovered in a few fortunate moments in the presence of nature. In the 'Character of the Happy Warrior' the deaths of his brother, Captain Wordsworth, and of Nelson, led him to a noble summary of the life of action. In the 'Ode to Duty' he composed in a mood of more classical severity than was his custom. He describes the more sober moral faith of his middle years, and the same new-found austerity is present in 'Laodamia', one of his rare classical poems. Probably few poets, Shakespeare alone apart, can give more to the reader in the twentieth century than Wordsworth. It may be that his vision of nature was an illusion, but in recording it he

Inside King's College Chapel, Cambridge

pursued many experiences into the secret corners of man's nature, so that few sensitive minds will fail to discover in his poems some answers to their own intuitions.

Wordsworth's most intimate friend was S. T. Coleridge (1772–1834), and their influence on one another was most productive. Wordsworth had a profoundly moral nature, capable of deep feeling, but controlled by a stubborn Northern austerity. Also he had great endurance, and the tasks he undertook he achieved. Coleridge, on the other hand, saw all knowledge as his province, but it was a province which he seemed never to conquer. One of his contemporaries said that he 'spawned plans like a herring' but that they were never completed. The early biographers treated him with scant justice, assigning his weakness solely to an indulgence in opium. It is true that he was an opium addict, but he took the drug first to relieve the acute pain of illness, and ill-health pursued him throughout his life. The whole conception of his achievement has been changed since Kathleen Coburn has been permitted, as late as 1957, to publish his notebooks. They reveal Coleridge as one of the most learned and industrious men of his century, a view some have tried ineffectively to refute. When all that he wrote has been digested his true stature as one of the great seminal figures of the nineteenth century will emerge. His mind read, digested, made notes, but so often stopped short of publication. Once he had mastered an idea himself his desire to reveal it to others diminished. He lived so much in thought and contemplation that he may not at first sight seem a sympathetic character. In his own personal life he could indulge in the meanest of emotions, that of self-pity. To his friends, and to his obtuse wife, he acted with a scant regard for responsibility, yet all who met him fell under the charm of his personality, and the brilliance of his conversation.

Thus, though he occupied much of his time with poetry, it is not as a poet alone that he should be remembered but as a critic and a philosopher. In a period when science, religion and politics were at variance he aimed at bringing them into unity. His attempt is puzzling and ultimately and inevitably inadequate, but it anticipates a modern need, still unsolved. In his literary criticism, particularly in *Biographia Literaria* (1817), he has anticipated the modern philosophical and psychological criticism of the arts. He defined the nature of Wordsworth's poetry. Further, he attempted the far more difficult task of exploring the nature of poetry as a whole.

In a more strictly philosophical sphere his *Aids to Reflection* had a wide popularity in the nineteenth century: he attempted to distinguish between *understanding* which gives us a knowledge of the ordinary world and *reason* which guides us towards the ultimate spiritual truths. Ernest Hartley Coleridge edited in 1895 a selection of aphorisms from his notebooks as *Anima Poetae*, but, as already suggested, it is only recently that his industry and the range of his knowledge and reflective capacity have been confirmed in definitive editions of his notebooks and letters. All this should be remembered when the attempt is made, as so often, to judge Coleridge solely from three poems, 'The Ancient Mariner', 'Kubla Khan' and 'Christabel', composed during the period of his closest association with Wordsworth.

From the admirable poem written to Wordsworth after reading *The Prelude*, it is clear that Wordsworth wrote the poetry which Coleridge most admired. He would have liked to have been himself such a poet, gathering the meaning of life as he saw it. A poet cannot write the poetry he wants to write but only the poetry that is within him. Within Coleridge there was a strange territory of memory and dream, of strange birds, phantom ships, Arctic seas, caverns, the sounds of unearthly instruments and of haunted figures, flitting across a scene where magic

One of Gustave Doré's illustrations to Coleridge's poem *The Ancient Mariner*

The ice was here, the ice was there,
The ice was all around:
It crack'd and growl'd, and roar'd and howl'd,
Like noises in a swound!

At length did cross an Albatross,
Through the fog it came;
As if it had been a Christian soul,
We hail'd it in God's name

reigned in a world beyond the control of reason. Some have sought for a moral in 'The Ancient Mariner', and for such as must have these props, Coleridge attached a lesson at the end of the narrative, but the poem itself is like some Arabian tale, where all moves in a weird and un-expected sequence. It is a poem unique in English; something is derived from the ballad, but the whole is nourished by the lavish resources of Coleridge's own subconscious. The poem creates from the first a world of its own, with the storm sequence, the shooting of the Albatross and the weird way in which the bird is avenged.

'Kubla Khan', though sometimes judged as a fragment, is best con-sidered as a complete poem and almost as a definition of this magical element in Coleridge's poetry, the song of the Abyssinian maid called up by a magician. These poems are far removed from the gravity and 'high seriousness' of Spenser, Milton or Wordsworth. The poet in them is no longer the arbitrator of life, but the controller of a dream-territory, called out of the subconscious. Much modern poetry has followed Coleridge in this manner, removing verse from its older and more normal purposes. The strange thing is that Coleridge should have given this lead, for it is one of which Coleridge as critic would have little approved.

Though all their work is often grouped as 'romantic', Wordsworth and Coleridge had little in common with their popular contemporaries, Sir Walter Scott (1771–1832) and Lord Byron (1788–1824). Scott, in a series of poems, beginning with *The Lay of the Last Minstrel* (1805), was continuing the interest in medieval ballad and romance which had been popular in the eighteenth century. The interest was genuine and had originated in his antiquarian study. After his 'raids' into the Highlands he had prepared a collection of ballads and romances entitled *The Minstrelsy of the Scottish Border* (1802–3). From collection he was led to invention and a series of poems followed which included *Marmion* (1808) and *The Lady of the Lake* (1810). After the success of *Waverley*, his first novel, in 1814 his main energies were devoted to prose fiction, but he continued writing verse romances to 1817. In substance and range they cannot compare with the novels, but they use all the romantic resources of chivalry, warfare, pathos, sentiment and the glamour of an imagined past. They have had a certain survival value and they are better than most critics, and even the author himself in his engagingly modest moments, considered them to be.

Lord Byron has been overdiscussed as a man and underestimated as a poet. Even in his boyhood days at Harrow he had the desire to write, though his first volume, *Hours of Idleness*, is a sorry collection of maudlin lyrics. When this was abused he replied with a wholesale attack on critics and poets alike, *English Bards and Scotch Reviewers* (1809). The poem was unwise, unjust and impertinent, but it had spirit and a flair for satire. From 1809 to 1811 he travelled abroad and returned to take his seat in the House of Lords and to publish the first two cantos of *Childe Harold* (1812). Apart from his verse, Byron had already a reputation as a madcap and romantically sinister personality. The impecunious schoolboy at Harrow, with the lame foot, had grown into the English 'milord', proud, contemptuous, lionized, the Napoleon of the London drawing-rooms. That his mind had a more profound mood can be seen from his speech in the House of Lords against the death-penalty for the Nottingham frame-breakers. Had he followed the direction of that speech he might have become a great national leader in an age when England cried out for leadership. But the romantic within him demanded the exploitation of his sensations, not the dreary and exacting labours of politics.

Already he had travelled widely, and his romances had an added excitement of revealing countries that his audience had never been able to visit for themselves. He gave an air of authenticity to his adventures, with even the suggestion that he had himself indulged in similar exploits. These romances, which began with *The Giaour* (1813), captured the taste of his generation. They made his reputation not in England

Byron, as he appeared after his daily ride during his stay in Northern Italy, from a silhouette by Mrs Leigh Hunt

Below: Turner's painting of 'Childe Harold's pilgrimage'. Byron's Romances, based on his travels in Italy and Greece, had the added excitement of revealing countries that his audience had not been able to visit for themselves

alone, but throughout Europe from France to Russia. More ambitious was *Childe Harold* (1812–18), in which the autobiographical elements are only thinly disguised, and there are many contemporary scenes, as in his famous description of the Ball in Brussels on the eve of Waterloo.

Byron's greatness as a poet lies, however, not in these poems, nor in his sombre and self-conscious tragedies such as *Manfred* and *Cain*, but in the satires which begin with *Beppo* (1818) and include *The Vision of Judgement* (1822) and *Don Juan* (1819–24). Unfortunately, the prudery of the Victorian critics obscured these poems from the public, and they have never received their due esteem. *Don Juan* is one of the great poems in our language, a performance of rare artistic skill. Humour, sentiment, adventure and pathos are thrown together with that same disconcerting incongruity as they are found to have in life. The autobiographical elements still remain as in the account of Don Juan's approach to England:

> At length they rose, like a white wall along
>   The blue sea's border; and Don Juan felt –
> What even young strangers feel a little strong
>   At the first sight of Albion's chalky belt –
> A kind of pride that he should be among
>   Those haughty shopkeepers, who sternly dealt
> Their goods and edicts out from pole to pole,
> And made the very billows pay them toll.
>
> I've no great cause to love that spot of earth
>   Which holds what might have been the noblest nation;
> But though I owe it little but my birth,
>   I feel a mix'd regret and veneration
> For its decaying fame and former worth.
>   Seven years (the usual term of transportation)
> Of absence lay one's old resentments level,
> When a man's country's going to the devil.

His spirit might have flourished better in some world other than the heavy Georgian society in which he grew up. The last episode in Greece showed that he had leadership and courage. In his marriage he appears at his worst, and then, for a short time, he seems to have been insane. The world of sentimentality and self-conscious moral rectitude, in which Lady Byron lived, tormented him. He knew freedom of spirit only in Italy, whether amid the wild female creatures whom he gathered around himself in Venice or in the gentle ministrations of Countess Guiccioli. The admirable *Letters* and *Journals*, many unfortunately destroyed, show how easily his whole nature flowed in this Italian period, and the result was the three satires through which his name as a poet is best remembered.

If Byron exposes the diablerie of romanticism, P. B. Shelley (1792–1822) shows its idealism. To some critics he is irritating and ineffectual, yet considered more profoundly he is, with Blake, the nearest example of poet as prophet. In his life he suffered more than Blake, and certainly made others suffer more. There was a time when he would, confidently, be described as a greater poet than Blake, as indeed he is, but recent criticism, even when not hostile, has dealt very severely with his work. This declension has been particularly marked in the middle decades of the twentieth century, when romantic poetry has generally been at a discount.

An unimaginative father forced the routine of Eton upon him. Later he escaped from Oxford by expulsion, for circulating his views on Atheism to Heads of Colleges and others. From then to the end there is no steady track to his life; he seems hurried from one situation to another by some power beyond his will, though in every new crisis he maintains his integrity. His early, rash marriage to Harriet Westbrook can be blamed upon neither of them. That she suffered is obvious, and so everyone was to suffer who encountered Shelley's ecstatic and uncompromising nature. That he should leave her was inevitable, but to attach to him any responsibility for her suicide would be unjust. His nearest approach to happiness came from his association with Mary Godwin, and after Harriet's death she became his wife. With Mary his life was spent mainly on the Continent, in Switzerland and Italy, and there he was drowned in 1822 during a storm in the Gulf of Spezia.

Before he was a poet Shelley was a prophet, and his poetry is largely the medium for his prophetic message. He refused to accept life as it is lived, and tried to persuade others of the absence of any necessity for so doing. If tyranny were removed, and cruelty, and the corruption of man

A sketch by Shelley. Often in his verses Shelley returns to the image of a boat upon a moonlit sea. He was drowned in 1822 during a storm in the Gulf of Spezia, off the Italian coast

through jealousy and the exercise of power, life would be beautiful, and an experience governed by love. This message to humanity he had derived in part from the *Political Justice* of his father-in-law, William Godwin, though much of it came from his own reading of the words of Christ and the teaching of Plato. His most ambitious work as a poet lay in his attempt to transmute his teaching into poetry. After such comparative failures as *Queen Mab* and *The Revolt of Islam*, he succeeded ultimately in incorporating his message in *Prometheus Unbound*. In this lyrical drama he takes the tragedy by Aeschylus as a model, with the story of how Prometheus was bound to a rock by Jupiter. He modifies the legend to glorify the spirit that man might have if he would take love as his guiding law and refuse to tolerate any tyranny, even though the name of a god were summoned as the sanction.

The theme of *Prometheus Unbound* is the great one of the moral salvation of man, and the verse has a lyrical quality unsurpassed in modern literature. Yet many readers find Shelley's poetry unsatisfactory. He had no sense of humour, and little contact with ordinary life. Neither the Chaucerian nor the Shakespearian quality is there, despite his success as a dramatist in *The Cenci*. Nor is this all, for he lacks the grip upon the solid material world which Milton retained. The images which he employs are of insubstantial things, winds, dead leaves, sounds, colours, waters. He seems sometimes more of a disembodied spirit than an ordinary human being. Often in his verses he returns to the image of a boat upon a moonlit sea; or the crescent moon itself, shaped like a boat, burning in the clear Italian night. Some such image dwells in the mind even after his verses have been forgotten: an ethereal form in a boat upon a lake, and in the boat a light burning always. If his verses are less read than once they were, and even if he is remembered by that ode 'To a Skylark', the least characteristic of his poems, he has had some permanent influence on life, for with his translucent spirit he has touched the philosophy of progress until it has become vision, and from vision, life may come.

John Keats (1795–1821), the last-born of the romantics, and the first to die, has a story as miraculous as any in English literature. The son of a stable-keeper, he spent the best years of his youth in training to be a doctor, though early in his career as a medical student a devotion to poetry occupied him intensely. With very little help from any formal education, and with none from his family circle, he gathered around himself a world of beauty in which he could believe. Out of dictionaries and reference books he discovered the classical fables and legends; from Spenser and Shakespeare he learned the magic power of words, and from the Elgin Marbles and the paintings of his friend Haydon he explored statuary and pictorial art. He was genius self-taught, and the rapidity with which he sprang to mature stature is astounding. His *Letters* are not only a brilliant record of his critical opinions, but show his tormented love for Fanny Brawne, his wide capacity for friendship, and the tragedy of his journey to Italy in a vain endeavour to recover health. The impact of the *Letters* has done much to sustain his popularity in the twentieth century. He wrote to his friends many passages which have remained memorable as literary criticism. So he wrote in one of his letters to his brothers on 21 December 1817:

> It struck me what quality went to form a Man of Achievement, especially in Literature, and which Shakespeare possessed so enormously – I mean *Negative Capability*, that is, when a man is capable of being in uncertainties, mysteries, doubts, without any irritable reaching after fact and reason . . . This pursued through volumes would perhaps take us no further than this, that with a great poet the sense of Beauty overcomes every other consideration, or rather obliterates all consideration.

The whole of his letters are strewn with such reflections, showing how his mind concentrated continuously on the problems of poetic creation.

He followed his first volume of poems with a long romance entitled *Endymion* (1818) which led to the vicious diatribe of J. G. Lockhart in *Blackwood's Edinburgh Magazine*: 'It is a better and wiser thing to be a starved apothecary than a starved poet; so back to the shop, Mr John, back to plasters, pills and ointment boxes.' Admittedly, the poem is over-exuberant and entangled. The first man of letters to encourage Keats was Leigh Hunt (1784–1859). As a radical Leigh Hunt was fearless, and as a critic he had vision for he early recognized the genius of both Shelley and Keats. But his verse had a lush and exuberant quality which Keats imitated, though in justice it must be admitted that it was present in Keats's poetry before he met Leigh Hunt. Despite these failings *Endymion* has individual passages which yield a peculiar quality of beauty, as if Keats knowing all the effects which the painter and the sculptor cannot achieve had brought them all into his verses. The savage attacks on Keats naturally wounded him, and some, erroneously, thought they were the ultimate cause of his death.

He showed in the poems published in 1820, with 'Lamia', 'Isabella' and 'The Eve of St Agnes', that he could present stories in verse, creating for each an appropriate background rich in colour and detail. Into the middle of 'Isabella' where, employing Boccaccio's simple and romantic narrative, he re-told of how Isabella's brothers put her lover to death and how he appeared to her in a dream, he inserted a savage passage of realism as if moving from his romantic world to an awareness of the injustices of his own time. G. B. Shaw has described this as his only passage of social realism. In 'Lamia' he suggested a philosophy along with the story, in the belief that the knowledge gained by the imagination was truer than that derived from argument.

The theme of these poems he explored in the 'Odes', which are his most complete and flawless work and show with what unparalleled rapidity he was maturing. Probably the 'Ode to Psyche' was his first and it was a poem to which he himself attached major importance. He

An illustration by Holman Hunt to Keats's poem *Isabella*, the macabre story of how Isabella discovers the body of her murdered lover and buries his head in a pot of basil.

For seldom did she go to chapel-shrift,
And when she left, she hurried back, as swift
As bird on wing to breast its eggs again;
And, patient as a hen-bird, sat her there
Beside her basil, weeping through her hair

returns to the old legend of Cupid and Psyche, which he had long known. Cupid 'the winged boy' can claim no particular attention: he is already a god, and adequately attended to by the Muses. But surely Psyche should be a goddess, though she came a little too late for the Greeks to deify her. Keats will himself act where the Greeks failed and so he brings the Ode to its triumphant, if elaborate, conclusion:

> Yes, I will be thy priest, and build a fane
>   In some untrodden region of my mind,
> Where branched thoughts, new grown with pleasant pain,
>   Instead of pines shall murmur in the wind:
> Far, far around shall those dark-cluster'd trees
>   Fledge the wild-ridged mountains steep by steep;
> And there by zephyrs, streams, and birds, and bees,
>   The moss-lain Dryads shall be lull'd to sleep;
> And in the midst of this wide quietness
> A rose sanctuary will I dress
>   With the wreath'd trellis of a working brain,
>   With buds, and bells, and stars without a name,
> With all the gardener Fancy e'er could feign,
>   Who breeding flowers, will never breed the same,
> And there shall be for thee all soft delight
>   That shadowy thoughts can win,
> A bright torch, and a casement ope at night,
>   To let the warm Love in!

There followed the other Odes, most notably the 'Ode to a Nightingale', 'Ode on Melancholy', 'Ode on a Grecian Urn' and the 'Ode on Indolence'. The lines 'To Autumn' are not entitled an 'Ode' in 1820 and the structure is descriptive rather than organic as in the Odes. While the 'Grecian Urn' expresses most clearly the thought underlying the series, a thought central to his whole position as a poet, and often reported in the *Letters*, it is in the 'Ode on Melancholy' that he most fully defines the life of imagination which endows moments of beauty wherever perceived with an eternal life as real as, even more real than, the life of fact.

Much in Keats's verse seems to imply that the life of the sensations, and the contemplation of beauty, are in themselves enough. His two unfinished drafts of a poem on the theme of *Hyperion* suggest that had he lived he might have grown beyond this into a great philosophical poet. It is idle to speculate what a poet may do, but in estimating Keats's achievement in his brief years it may be remembered that he was born in the same year as Carlyle but he died sixty years before Carlyle's death.

I hate the ~~~~ hollow ~~~ 'the little ~~~

Tennyson reading *Maud* aloud. From a sketch by Dante Gabriel Rossetti, 1855.

Mr and Mrs Browning being then for a while at No. 13, Dorset Street, London, invited a few friends to hear Tennyson read 'Maud' as he had undertaken. . . . My brother, unobserved by Tennyson, made a pen-and-ink sketch of him . . .

From *Pre-Raphaelite Diaries and Letters,* edited by W. M. Rossetti

Chapter 5

English Poetry from Tennyson

THE ACCIDENT of death makes a break in poetry about the year 1830: Keats died in 1821, Shelley in 1822, Byron in 1824 and Coleridge and Wordsworth were poetically 'dead' by 1830. A new poetry came with Tennyson and Browning, though readers at the time were slow to recognize it. The popular poets in 1830 were still Scott and Byron and others who catered for similar tastes: Samuel Rogers with his *Italy*, Thomas Moore with his Irish lyrics and with the incredibly popular Eastern romance of *Lalla Rookh*, and Thomas Campbell, who was in many ways superior to either of the others. Among minor poets John Clare (1793–1864), a self-taught farmer poet, published a series of volumes beginning with *Poems Descriptive of Rural Life* (1820). Interest was reawakened in his verse in the twentieth century by the autobiography of his tormented life. The twentieth century has also retained an affection for Thomas Lovell Beddoes (1803–49), whose *Death's Jest-Book* (1825, and often revised), a play in the Elizabethan manner, has some memorable lyrics.

The tradition of Scott and Byron, as it was understood in 1830, was one of poetry made easy. Tennyson and Browning were to restore to poetry something of a higher function, though Tennyson was charged with sometimes having one eye on the audience and, after he was made Laureate, with having both eyes on the Queen. They succeeded in retaining a large audience for poetry in an age when the novel had become the popular form of literature.

Tennyson (1809–92) was so much abused in the generations after his death that it is well to see his performance with justice. Fortunately, since the sixties, much in this direction has been achieved. His biography has been more fully presented and he has emerged as a sympathetic figure even though complex and certainly less stable than his Victorian image. The becloaked Laureate, or the talkative figure sitting late over his dinner table with his over-filled pipe and his port represents less the truth than the high-strung, nervously susceptible introvert. His poems have been brilliantly re-edited by Christopher Ricks. Even in the decades when Tennyson was under attack no one denied him a most perfect control of the sound of English, an impeccable ear and a consummate choice and taste in words. Indeed, his early lyrics seem to exist only to weave patterns of words, like tapestries, or to create tunes and verbal rhythms, delicate and faultless. The charge could be made that the words were too good for the meaning which they contained. Compared with any one of his predecessors in the Romantic period, he lacked originality and depth, and many of the poems in the volumes of 1830 and 1833 have a certain vacuity. The charge would not be equally just if made against the *Poems* of 1842, for here in poems such as 'Ulysses' he combined all his early felicity with a theme symbolizing the romantic conception of the heroic spirit.

Tennyson's genius lay in the lyric, the dramatic monologue, and the short poem, 'Oenone', 'The Dream of Fair Women' or 'The Palace of Art'. His skill is apparent at its most distinguished in his dramatic monologue on 'Tithonus', the legendary classical figure condemned to an arid immortality.

His ambition called him forth to a longer and grander work. Thus he occupied himself at intervals throughout his career with the *Idylls*, his Arthurian poems, picturesque, romantic, but also allegorical and didactic. The *Idylls* have many virtues, and to hear again isolated passages is to recall how sensitive was his ear, how fastidious his taste. Yet once one recalls Chaucer or Spenser or Donne, the virtues of the *Idylls* seem unimportant. Tennyson has reduced the plan of the Arthurian stories to the necessities of Victorian morality. He has failed to look upon his own age with unabashed, far-seeing eyes. The vision of life itself he has rejected and instead made these faultless verses, melodious, decorative, and, judged by the great standards, false. The *Idylls* are ultimately the poem of the Laureate; but *In Memoriam* is the poem of the poet himself, and, since it is so genuinely his, it becomes at the same time the great poem of his age. He records the death of his friend Arthur Hallam and his thoughts on the problems of life and death, his religious anxieties, and his hard-won faith in an eternal life. The rather fretful mystic, the child before God, terrified of this Universe and distrustful of the growing evidence of Science, the infant crying for Divine guidance, such is the poet of *In Memoriam*, and the portrait, if not always attractive, is ever truthful.

Tennyson commanded a very wide audience and his imitators were numerous. It was not unnatural, then, that opposition to his verse should grow. He had in many ways been representative of his age, and like Kipling, had to suffer when society took to new traditions. Further, he had pursued the romantic way of writing as far as it would go, and it was only natural that adventurous young poets should look in different directions. Now we can judge his poetry, as we do that of Kipling, without prejudice and distortion. The beauty of his verse can only be appreciated by turning to it once again. He made poetry the description of a beautiful and antique world, as if deliberately closing his eyes to the ugly industrialism of his own century. Poetry, conceived in this way, would not be an interpretation of life, but a charmed and distant illusion. Often Tennyson seems to have been aware of the danger, and 'Locksley Hall' and *The Princess* and 'Maud' touch upon his own time. Unfortunately, the mind which he brought to these problems was often dulled, and 'Locksley Hall' shows that he could be deluded by the mirage of progress which the material prosperity of the nineteenth century seemed to offer. *In Memoriam* alone goes farther and gives not the voice of the preacher, but vision, and the strange anomaly is that while the preacher's voice was commanding and resonant, the voice of the vision was like the voice of a little child.

The moral and religious problems which occupied Tennyson are the main theme of Robert Browning (1812–89). Like Tennyson, his work suffered a period of disparaging criticism in the nineteen-twenties and thirties and indeed there was a time when he was better known for his rescue of Elizabeth Barrett (1806–61) from her home in Wimpole Street than as a poet. Fortunately an ample number of biographies in the fifties and sixties have re-established his position. The mid-twentieth century views of his poetry have become increasingly favourable, indeed more generous than that expressed in this text. Of his elopement only two things need be said. First, the lady herself was a poet in her own right, as her *Sonnets from the Portuguese* and *Aurora Leigh*, which just misses real greatness, amply show, and in their early married years she was far more popular than Browning. Secondly, Browning in his adventure had, as usual, all the luck. If only Elizabeth had died on that flight to the Continent, Browning would have been the ogre of the piece instead of the romantic hero. This must be remembered, for it may in part explain why he believed so optimistically that everything in life did ultimately turn out well. Even in the years when his verse was discounted he always had vigorous supporters.

In pursuing his study of the human mind, Browning drew upon a wide and unusual reading, which easily baffled the reader by its remoteness. Already in *Sordello* (1840) he had employed a knowledge of medieval Italy with an allusiveness which no reader could hope to follow. He had developed also an independence of style, with an assumption of unusual, even grotesque rhymes, and abrupt, broken phrasing. At its best this gave to his verses a virility which contrasts pleasantly with the over-melodious movement of much nineteenth-century poetry. That he was a master of verse can be seen from the easy movements of his lyrics, but his special effects, though they gave realism to his poems, were in danger, in his later works, of becoming a mannerism.

The appearance of realism through a medium which was dramatic was what he most attempted to attain. In drama itself he was only moderately successful, though Macready was persuaded to play in

Strafford in 1837. He was happier in using drama without much thought of practical application to the theatre, as in *Paracelsus* (1835), a brilliant expression of his philosophy, or in *Pippa Passes* (1841), where his ideas are simply but aptly shown through a series of human actions. He was interested not so much in the conflict of a group of characters, as in the fortunes of a single mind, and so he evolved the 'dramatic monologue'. It was in this form that many of his best-known pieces were composed, 'Andrea del Sarto', 'Fra Lippo Lippi','Saul', and 'The Bishop orders his Tomb'. Their appearances in a series of volumes, which included *Dramatic Lyrics* (1842), *Men and Women* (1855) and *Dramatis Personae* (1864), gave him in the latter half of the century a reputation second only to that of Tennyson. They remain his outstanding achievement.

He put his method to the greatest test in *The Ring and the Book* (1868–1869), where a series of dramatic monologues is woven to make one of the longest poems in the language. Browning selected a sordid Italian crime, which Carlyle sardonically described as an Old Bailey story that could have been told in five minutes. He so examined the minds of all that not only their motives, but the whole of his philosophy become apparent. After *The Ring and the Book* his poetry develops in obscurity, though some of these later pieces have a subtle interest quite distinct from anything in the earlier work.

He remains one of the most difficult poets to assess. His poems are crowded with memorable characters, and the whole of Renaissance Italy comes to life. At first he seems to have created a world of living people as Shakespeare had done, but a closer inspection shows that Browning's men and women are not free. They live in a spiritually totalitarian state in which Browning is Chancellor and God is President, always with the proviso that the Chancellor is the President's voice on earth. His own life had been, in the best sense, fortunate so that he knew little of evil and yet, evil fascinated him. Had he known more of life he might have come to realize evil as a fierce and positive corruption in human life, and that realization would have deepened his poetry.

The poetry of the later nineteenth century is far more varied than is sometimes allowed. If Tennyson's was the voice that most people heard, there were many others unlike his. Matthew Arnold (1822–88), who gave to the Board of Education and the necessities of a regular income years which might have been devoted to verse, yet produced such poems as *Empedocles on Etna*, 'The Forsaken Merman', 'Thyrsis', 'The Scholar Gipsy' and 'Dover Beach'. Arnold, who was a son of Dr Arnold of Rugby, was over-educated for the well-being of his imagination. He had a Messianic complex, and in his prose took upon himself the whole burden of the problems of life. He had, like some others in his age, a restlessness in belief, as if he were perpetually crying over spiritual spilt milk. As a literary critic his keen intellect, high seriousness and wide learning led him, as is suggested later, to make a permanent

Matthew Arnold, gentleman, scholar and civil servant, but 'conscious of a strange aching in his heart'

and major contribution. But all this did not help him as a poet. He would have been better either as a revolutionary or a vagabond. He was neither, but a gentleman, a scholar and a civil servant, conscious of a strange aching in his heart. Often he wished to write poems that would illustrate his theories about poetry, and such a dull poem as *Merope* or such a coldly efficient narrative as 'Sohrab and Rustum' is the result. But when he listened to that aching in his heart, he was able to convey his longings, his sadness, even his frustration, in poems which had a quiet and classical perfection. All that he felt is brought to its greatest perfection in his lyric of 'Dover Beach', where he contemplates on listening to the spray and the roar of pebbles sucked in by the waves:

> *Sophocles long ago*
> *Heard it on the Aegaean, and it brought*
> *Into his mind the turbid ebb and flow*
> *Of human misery; we*
> *Find also in the sound a thought,*
> *Hearing it by this distant northern sea.*
>
> *The sea of faith*
> *Was once, too, at the full, and round earth's shore*
> *Lay like the folds of a bright girdle furl'd;*
> *But now I only hear*
> *Its melancholy, long, withdrawing roar,*
> *Retreating to the breath*
> *Of the night-wind down the vast edges drear*
> *And naked shingles of the world.*
>
> *Ah, love, let us be true*
> *To one another! for the world, which seems*
> *To lie before us like a land of dreams,*
> *So various, so beautiful, so new,*
> *Hath really neither joy, nor love, nor light,*
> *Nor certitude, nor peace, nor help for pain;*
> *And we are here as on a darkling plain*
> *Swept with confused alarms of struggle and flight,*
> *Where ignorant armies clash by night.*

Arthur Hugh Clough (1819–61), who was at Rugby under Matthew Arnold's father, had a brief and restless career which did not fulfil his early high promise. In the middle of the Second World War he gained a sudden moment of fame when Churchill quoted to Roosevelt 'Say not the struggle nought availeth' with its final line 'But westward, look, the land is bright'. The fifties brought a fine definitive edition of his poems and readers discovered, hidden often within his use of the unpopular hexameter, much originality in his verse-narrative *The Bothie of Tober-na-Vuolich* and the poem in letters *Amours de Voyage*.

Edward FitzGerald (1809–83) certainly did not share Arnold's conception of duty. He lived an incredibly indolent life, but his taste for literature, and his intelligent criticism of it, were his two most consistent pursuits. In 1859 he published his free version of the work of a Persian poet, Omar Khayyám, as *The Rubáiyát of Omar Khayyám*. At first the little volume was unnoticed, but once attention had been drawn to it, the public never allowed it to fall into neglect, and it has been read and enjoyed by many who have read no other poem. The gentle melancholy of the verse, and the romantic style, were, as has often been pointed out, FitzGerald's addition to the original. So freely has he handled the medieval Persian poet, so fully has he placed into his lines the sad longing which his century knew so well, that though his work is a translation he must be considered as an artist, and a considerable one, among the figures of his century.

One of the earliest poets to discover FitzGerald had been D. G. Rossetti (1828–82), and the attraction was not unnatural. Tennyson, Browning and Arnold were engaged in the problems of their age, Rossetti rejected them. This son of an Italian political refugee shut out from his work all the moral, political, and religious interest with which so much Victorian literature is concerned. For him life existed only to

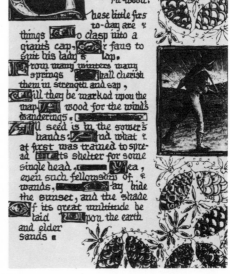

A contemporary illustration to Edward FitzGerald's translation of *The Rubáiyát of Omar Khayyám*, and (right) a page from Dante Gabriel Rossetti's sonnet sequence *The House of Life*.

supply the images of art. Primarily a painter, he had encouraged a group of young men, including Holman Hunt, Millais and Ford Madox Brown, to abandon formalism in painting and, with the example of the primitive Italian painters, to execute their works with independence and truth. In poetry, Rossetti had set before himself similar ideas, though his mind, visionary and symbolical, combated the realism which his principles suggested. His early poem, 'The Blessed Damozel', best represents the conflicting sides of his mind: the detail is material, the theme mystical, but the ultimate motive sensual. Whatever his theory may dictate, his mind searches out a world of symbols, winds, dim moonlit waters, strange rich colours, seen in a half-light, not the material world at all, but a dream-world where nothing is tangible:

> Groping in the windy stair,
> (Darkness and the breath of space,
> Like loud waters everywhere).

Such was the atmosphere of the lyrics and ballads in his *Poems* (1870) and *Ballads and Sonnets* (1881). Love was the main theme pursued with this strange combination of the mystic and the sensual, in a sequence of sonnets entitled *The House of Life*. The vocabulary and phrasing were devised in part from his reading of the early Italian poets whose verse he translated in *Dante and his Circle*.

Egotistical and in many minor ways dishonest, Rossetti's sombre and intense personality had a magnetism which attracted young men. Among them was Algernon Charles Swinburne (1837–1909), who, after a troublesome career at Eton and Oxford, and a number of experiments in verse, startled London in 1866 with *Poems and Ballads*. Victorian poetry had been guarded in its themes and Swinburne, in deliberate revolt, wrote of a love passionate, cruel, often perverted and sadistic. Instead of delicate sentiments and adorations, there is frenzy, ruthlessness and satiety. It was as if a satyr had been let loose in a Victorian drawing-room. His lyrical verse never reached a higher quality than in 'Itylus' nor is his imagination ever more alert. He transfigures the crude legend of incest and murder, and the mythical revenge by which one sister is turned into a swallow, and the other, Philomela, into a nightingale. From the sordid debris of the old legend Swinburne seizes upon a single moment and converts it into lyrical beauty:

> O sister, sister, thy first begotten!
> The hands that cling and the feet that follow
>   The voice of the child's blood crying yet,
> 'Who hath remembered me? Who hath forgotten?'
> 'Thou hast forgotten, O summer swallow,
> But the world shall end when I forget.'

The verse with its heavy alliteration and its swaying rhythms enhances the effect of the sensual. Most of this knowledge of the darker places of passion came not from his own experience but from his reading, which included Baudelaire, whose death he commemorated prematurely in 'Ave atque Vale'. In one way he was reasserting Keats's plea for the pagan ideal of beauty as it could be discovered in Greek literature. His knowledge here was wide and led not only to one of the most impregnable of all his lyrics, 'Itylus', but to two lyrical dramas, *Atalanta in Calydon* (1865) and *Erechtheus* (1876).

Swinburne continued to be occupied with poetry, and with the criticism of the Elizabethan drama, for over forty years after the publication of *Poems and Ballads*, but the full, overpowering force of that volume never returned. His career has sometimes been described as that of a tropical bird displaying for a while its gaudy wings in the damp and foggy air of London and then, since it did not die, being nursed and carefully housed for the rest of its days. In some of the later volumes, in *Songs before Sunrise* (1871), with its praise of the cause of Italian independence, and in *Tristram of Lyonnesse* (1882), with its re-telling of the tale of Tristram and Iseult, a new strength waywardly appears. But it is forced, and soon overclouded by a medley of melodious words. His early themes had been exceptional, limited, sexual, and once he had exhausted them, he lost strength. 'Dolores', 'Laus Veneris' and 'Faustine', the poems in which he exploited these early attachments unrestrainedly, were the places where his genius stood revealed, unabashed, even if decadent. A few quieter poems, such as 'Itylus' and 'The Garden of Proserpine', accompanied that central mood and gained an expression equally strong. But when later he wrote of wider and more normal subjects, poetry gave way to rhetoric, and the words swayed into labyrinthine melodies where sound exceeded sense.

Rossetti attracted one other poet, in most ways as much unlike Swinburne as possible. William Morris (1834–96), bluff, energetic and outspoken, counted poetry as only one of his many activities. He touched upon the life of his age first as a craftsman, a designer of furniture, wallpapers, fabrics, and later as a social revolutionary and a communist. If Rossetti was one of his teachers, Ruskin was another, and from Ruskin he learned that there was no room for the genuine craftsman in a capitalist world that thought only of quick production and large profits. Rossetti wished to make beautiful things in an ugly world. Morris, under Ruskin's discipline, wished to remake the world so that all manufactured things might be beautiful. As an influence upon his century the later period of social activity is the more important, but the poetry belongs largely to the early period.

His early volume, *The Defence of Guinevere* (1858), shows him following Rossetti into a medieval world, and, with Malory and Froissart to guide him, he makes poems either human and tense, or

Edward Burne-Jones (left) and William Morris, two members of the Pre-Raphaelite Brotherhood

dream lyrics, beautiful without weight or substance. In his longest work, *The Earthly Paradise* (1868–70), he goes back to Chaucer's way of using verse for story-telling. He misses Chaucer's humanity, and he has neither his cunning in language nor his vivid power in character. In *The Earthly Paradise*, Morris is still closing his eyes to the world around him; 'poor idle singer of an empty day', as he describes himself, he is peddling his beautiful wares through an ugly world.

With the completion of that poem he came to the period of his life when the more immediate task of reform called to him irresistibly. The penalty he had to pay was that he had less leisure to pursue his poetical work. Fortunately, it did not cease entirely. His visits to Iceland filled him with an admiration for the Sagas, and *Sigurd the Volsung* (1876), inspired by his Northern reading, is one of his most successful achievements. Along with verse he continued to write prose: *A Dream of John Ball* (1888) and *News from Nowhere* (1891). These stories of the redeemed world of the future have had the widest currency of all his work. To some, the imaginative prose stories of his last period have a value beyond anything in his poetry, and it is true that in *The Well at the World's End* (1896) he has conjured up a world not to be found elsewhere.

Two other poets are connected with Rossetti's name, though their manner of life differed widely from his. His sister Christina Rossetti (1830–94), though she admired her brother, lived a devout and religious life. Her early fairy poem, 'Goblin Market', shows a rich and coloured imagination, which became subdued later as her religious loyalties increased. In Coventry Patmore (1823–96), on the other hand, the increase of spiritual attachment led to an increase of poetical power. *The Angel in the House* (1854–6), a novel in verse, showing that domestic virtue was a poetical theme, has boldness in using poetry for everyday, realistic effects. The more philosophical portions of the poem already revealed Patmore's mysticism, and in *The Unknown Eros*, a series of odes, he developed this with great boldness in language. As a Catholic poet he far exceeds in power Francis Thompson (1859–1907), whose ornate poetry proved more attractive to some readers. Thompson's legend of poverty and distress has added to the appeal, and though his advocates have been over-ambitious, it may be conceded that in 'The Hound of Heaven' he described an experience which all mystics have undergone, in an imagery which many readers, who are not mystics, seem to have understood.

It would be interesting to know how much nineteenth-century poetry lost because of the dominance of the novel as a literary form. Two novelists at least, George Meredith and Thomas Hardy, began as poets and continued as poets in the intervals of writing novels. George Meredith (1828–1909) began by writing delightful and easily intelligible lyrics of which the most memorable is *Love in the Valley*. This answers the lyrical mood to be found in some of the early scenes of his novel, *The Ordeal of Richard Feverel*. The complex analysis of mood, characteristic of the novels, has also a poetical counterpart in *Modern Love* (1862). Behind the novels one is aware of a philosophy, and this gains fuller and more explicit expression in his later poetry than in any of his prose. These philosophical poems, such as *Poems and Lyrics of the Joy of Earth* (1883), in their hard and cramped language, attempted to reconcile morality and the teachings of biology.

Bestiality and sentimentalism were always attempting to curb man in his upward struggle towards the normal life, or, as Meredith described it, the life of 'common-sense'. The novels suggest Meredith's belief that comedy could show man's weaknesses and the poems express that faith more openly. As poems they are difficult but the ground-work of their thought is solid, and rewarding. Both his poetry and his novels have found very little acceptance in the mid-twentieth century. But they will be re-discovered.

Thomas Hardy (1840–1928) was not a philosophical poet as was Meredith, though a settled belief in the cruelty of life and in the pathos of men and women who are tormented by it lurks behind all his work. In his many short lyrics, he showed men and women, caught in the tragic irony of circumstance, inflicting cruelty on one another, or pursued by a malign destiny. The brevity with which these clear-cut pictures were controlled is evidence of his individual poetic art. Sometimes it reached the heights of a strange and dominating imagination, as in 'Nature's Questioning':

> *Has some Vast Imbecility*
> *Mighty to build and blend*
> *But impotent to tend,*
> *Framed us in jest, and left us now to hazardry?*
> *Or come of an Automaton*
> *Unconscious of our pains? . . .*
> *Or are we live remains*
> *Of Godhead dying downwards, brain and eye now gone?*

In the years when his work as a novelist was over, he composed his epic-drama of the Napoleonic wars, *The Dynasts* (1904–8). The range of the poem, with its Overworld and its widely extended human scene, was held within Hardy's control as completely as the brief, human incidents of the lyrics. He created a drama too elaborate for the stage, but one arousing many clear and moving scenes in the theatre of the mind.

At a time when the vogue of the long poem was declining, Hardy boldly fashioned his great work. Two poems only of the same period can stand in comparison. C. M. Doughty (1883–1926), the explorer, whose prose records of travel, *Arabia Deserta* (1888), influenced T. E. Lawrence, published in 1906 the beginning of his long poem, *The Dawn in Britain*. So different was this from the tradition of poetry that it has seldom had its due. None of the obvious charms is here, nor the softer graces, but in language robbed of all rhetoric, and with incident firmly, even gauntly, described, he built up a vision of the early days of our civilization. The only other poem of similar ambition was Robert Bridges's *The Testament of Beauty* (1929), which had great popularity. Bridges (1844–1930) had been writing verse for over fifty years before he came to define his faith in Reason and Beauty in this philosophical poem, which is written in a free measure that sometimes runs a little too close to the harmonies of prose.

As one approaches the poetry of one's own age the task of criticism becomes more difficult, for contemporary or near-contemporary work arouses enthusiasm or antipathy more easily than the poetry of the past. The modern period in England has certainly not escaped the atmosphere of controversy. All that can be done here is to outline what poets have attempted, knowing that in later decades the judgement will be modified. As the nineteenth century closed, so romanticism closed with it. A group of poets captured its last phase in lyrics which have a melancholy beauty. It was as if they knew that the words and symbols which they were using would soon be put away as old-fashioned things. From their lyrics they excluded the problems of morality and philosophy which troubled the Victorians, and in brief, poignant lines they found images for their own moods, their loves and the moments in experience that had affected them. Oscar Wilde (1854–1900), as a poet, was among the less important of these writers, except in *The Ballad of Reading Gaol*, though his work as a dramatist and the notoriety attaching to his name, gave his verses a considerable reputation. Also, as in his drama, he was improving so rapidly that had he continued to write his contribution might have been a memorable one. Far more effective was Ernest Dowson (1867–1900), the bohemian and poet vagrant of the decade, who existed somehow by his translations. He is best known for his lyric 'Cynara', which seems to add a new rhythm to English poetry:

> *Last night, ah, yesternight, betwixt her lips and mine*
> *There fell thy shadow, Cynara! thy breath was shed*
> *Upon my soul between the kisses and the wine;*
> *And I was desolate and sick of an old passion,*
> > *Yea, I was desolate and bowed my head:*
> *I have been faithful to thee, Cynara, in my fashion.*

With a more classical severity Lionel Johnson (1867–1904) built quiet, ordered lyrics, with a calm and reserved beauty. Like Dowson he cultivated the bohemian life of the nineties poets, and drank excessively. There is an orderliness in his verse far removed from the disorderliness of his life. Its quality can be seen in such a lyric as 'By the Statue of King Charles at Charing Cross'.

Removed from these writers by his manner of life but not unattached to them in mood was A. E. Housman (1859–1936), Professor of Latin at University College, London and later at Cambridge. A classical scholar of the highest order, seemingly a remote and authoritative personality, yet sensitive in one friendship to an extent that affected his whole life. He produced two volumes of verse, *A Shropshire Lad* (1896) and *Last Poems* (1922), which though they have had a few severe critics have become among the best-known verses of the period. To these must be added his lecture on *The Name and Nature of Poetry* (1933) where he confounded the more theoretical Cambridge critics by claiming Dr Watts's 'Soft and easy is thy cradle' was 'bad rhyme and all, poetry beyond Pope'. All his verse was composed in short lyrics, delusively simple in vocabulary, with quick dramatic themes, as in a ballad, and often with a tragic emphasis. The verses are full of cunningly contrived memories of other poets and the vocabulary, when seemingly it is the plainest English, has Latin recollections. So the Latin *summa rerum* gives the ultimate effect of the concluding lines of his 'Epitaph on an Army of Mercenaries':

> *What God abandoned, these defended,*
> > *And saved the sum of things for pay.*

For the Shropshire poems, a Shropshire which he never visited, many influences combined, Shakespeare's songs, Scottish border ballads, Heine, Kipling, memories of Wilde's trial and many others. It all combined into lyrics of poignant urgency. He was a poet who, like Gray, might have been with the greatest had he chosen to stretch his talent more fully.

Rudyard Kipling (1865–1936) broke into English verse with an entirely new manner as early as 1886 with *Departmental Ditties*, followed by *Barrack Room Ballads* (1892); *The Seven Seas* (1896); *The Five Nations* (1903). As with his fiction the impact was enormous; the novelty of the Indian background, the uninhibited patriotism, the doctrine of work, the interest in machines, had a topical appeal. In addition there was technical excellence. Much of what Kipling believed in politically has disappeared. He envisaged imperialism as a civilizing force, but continuing interest in a poet does not depend on his politics, as Dryden's reputation shows. That Kipling has remained deservedly popular can be seen in T. S. Eliot's *A Choice of Kipling's Verse* (1941) with its appreciative introductory essay, and Charles Carrington's biography (1978). It is not often remembered that Kipling left India when he was twenty-four. Much of his thought is based on South Africa rather than India. T. S. Eliot defines the inimitable quality of Kipling's verse in a revealing passage: 'An immense gift for using words, an amazing curiosity and power of observation with his mind and with all his senses, the mask of the entertainer, and beyond that a queer gift of second sight, of transmitting messages from elsewhere, a gift so disconcerting when we are made aware of it that henceforth we are never sure when it is *not* present: all this makes Kipling a writer impossible wholly to understand and quite impossible to belittle.'

Of the lyrical poets of the early twentieth century some have been severely criticized. They were known as the 'Georgian' poets (George V and not George VI), because their verse was represented in Sir Edward Marsh's *Georgian Anthologies*. They were said to lack profundity and to play with artificial emotions. Harold Monro (1879–1932) created a centre for them with his Poetry Bookshop. John Drinkwater was the most typical, with smooth, gentle lyrics of rural life. Sir John Squire was a lyric writer and a critic esteemed after the First World War; his taste was traditional, but his enthusiasm and his journal *The London Mercury* added to the liveliness of the literary scene. Though much of the attack on the 'Georgians' was just, it has been overplayed. D. H. Lawrence (1885–1930), for instance, had lyrics of subtle competence in the Georgian books. Among the poets still remembered are W.H. Davies (1871–1940), whose prose *Autobiography of a Super-Tramp* appeared in 1908, and who composed nature and love lyrics of a compelling intensity; and Edmund Blunden (b. 1896), an editor of John Clare, whose poems were a detailed study of rural life. In prose he wrote *Undertones of War*, one of the best personal narratives of the First World War. A more

Wyndham Lewis, 'A Battery Shelled, 1919'.

From gloom's last dregs these long-strung creatures crept,
And vanished out of dawn down hidden holes.
Wilfred Owen, *The Show*

vivid talent for a time sustained Ralph Hodgson, whose vision of nature was compared with that of Blake. James Stephens (1882–1950), though Irish, was associated with the group; his lyrics now seem less memorable than his prose phantasy, *The Crock of Gold* (1912). His fellow countryman George William Russell ('A.E.') (1867–1935) wrote lyrics which have a mystical effect. Robert Graves (b. 1895) has had a more massive career. Beginning with the ballad and imitations of Skelton, he survived the First World War and with Laura Riding became a 'modernist', only to return to earlier forms, though with much self-criticism. He has continued in the sixties and seventies with a series of volumes which have much poetic liveliness. Graves also made a contribution to English fiction with his historical novels. W. W. Gibson belonged to the 'Georgians', though his typical poems were of industrial England and the lives of working men. Edward Thomas (1878–1917), who wrote nature poems in the intervals of enforced journalism, has survived better than most.

The major attack concentrated on Rupert Brooke (1887–1915). His *Poems* (1911) were followed by *1914 and Other Poems* published in 1915 after his death at Skyros. In a group of sonnets he evoked the patriotism and idealism of that strange and tragic year of 1914. Brooke saw war as a purifying, romantic experience, and death as heroic. A generation living to experience the sordid reality of trench warfare turned against him. Whatever criticism may assert, his poems are read and new editions published continually.

Outside the controversies Walter de la Mare (1873–1956) was welcomed by his contemporaries, and always will be wherever English lyric poetry is appreciated. The elusive features governing his verse are found in his prose fiction of *Memoirs of a Midget* (1921). James Elroy Flecker (1884–1915) also remains a rewarding poet. His early verse, *The Bridge of Fire* (1907), showed the influence of the French Parnassians, but his distinctive contribution came after his study of oriental languages and residence in the East, with *The Golden Journey to Samarkand* (1913), a poem of new long exciting rhythms and a fresh exotic imagery.

The acceptance of these and other poets was disturbed by two events. T. S. Eliot's (1888–1965) *Prufrock* in 1917 marked a new way in poetry as assuredly as Donne did in his day. Further, the war itself was such a scarifying experience that the earlier romanticism became repellent. The change appears in the war poems of Siegfried Sassoon (1886–1967), who moved from the country-gentleman scenes of his prose *Memoirs of a Fox-Hunting Man* (1928), to bitter satiric poems giving the realities of the war. Yet this was not the final mood. Wilfred Owen (1893–1918), killed a week before the Armistice, saw through the bitterness to 'passivity'. In 'Strange Meeting' he described two soldiers, who have killed each other, meeting and recognizing 'the pity of war'. The publication of his complete poems and his letters established him as the major poet of the First World War.

Even writers who began with melodious verse felt the necessity for an expression closer to life. John Masefield (1878–1967) moved from the lyrics of *Salt-Water Ballads* (1902) to the uncompromising realism of *The Everlasting Mercy* (1911) and *The Widow in the Bye Street* (1912). His later series of vigorous narrative poems had a more generous selection of theme: in *Dauber* (1913) he returned to the sea, and in *Reynard the Fox* (1919), with some Chaucerian reminiscences, gave a vivid account of fox-hunting.

Others found more complex paths to new ways in poetry. The earliest was Gerard Manley Hopkins (1844–89), a Roman Catholic convert and a Jesuit. Few of his poems appeared until Robert Bridges published a volume in 1918 and even then recognition was slow. In the thirties Hopkins became a major influence, and his notebooks and correspondence increased the impression of strong originality. Hopkins's letters show how deeply he had thought about poetry and he gave a profounder expression to religious experience than any poet since the seventeenth century. With technical audacity he had deviously returned to the traditions of Anglo-Saxon poetry, employing a specialized and ingeniously invented vocabulary. By 'sprung rhythm' and stress he varied the number of syllables within the unit of verse and contrived surprising rhythmical effects of brilliance. He sought to make a poem as unified as a tune, and words and grammar were subordinated to that effect. Outstanding among his poems was *The Wreck of the Deutschland*, composed as early as 1875, and written when he was deeply affected by the death of five Franciscan nuns on board the Deutschland. Younger writers found in him a model for expressing the complexity of modern experience. Hopkins himself used his verse in other ways, to speak of the glory of God in nature and to explore his own self-tormented mind:

> *I am soft sift*
> *In an hourglass – at the wall*
> *Fast, but mined with a motion, a drift,*
> *And it crowds and it combs to the fall;*
> *I steady as a water in a well, to a poise, to a pane,*
> *But roped with, always, all the way down from the tall*
> *Fells or flanks of the voel, a vein*
> *Of the gospel proffer, a pressure, a principle, Christ's gift.*

W. B. Yeats and T. S. Eliot dominated the first half of the century. It is revealing of the modern literary scene that neither of them was English. In W. B. Yeats (1865–1939), the Irishman, two generations of poetry

Gerard Manley Hopkins, drawn by himself, aged twenty. He used his verse to speak of the glory of God in nature

The Isle of Innisfree, County Sligo.

I will arise and go now, for always night and day
I hear lake water lapping with low sounds by the shore;
While I stand on the roadway, or on the pavements grey,
I hear it in the deep heart's core.

W. B. Yeats, 'The Lake Isle of Innisfree'

met. The earliest verse, *The Wanderings of Oisin* (1889), employed Irish legend, while later, in London, he grew decorative, in a Pre-Raphaelite manner, though he always remained conscious of his Irish background. How well he wrote in that romantic manner can be seen in the survival of 'The Lake Isle of Innisfree' with something of its original freshness. Yeats realized that poetry had to be adjusted to the changes of his time, and this he achieved in an individual way. Through Blake and Swedenborg he found a metaphysical approach. Some of the sources he employed, magic and the like, seemed unworthy, but the poetic results were of profound beauty. Apart from this philosophical change, much else was happening. He was profoundly moved by the 'troubles' in Ireland, which resulted in the Easter rebellion, as is seen in poems such as 'Easter 1916'. Swift had now replaced the Pre-Raphaelites as a master. Yeats did not turn resentfully on the past but out of his own need made verses, often austere yet always beautiful. At times severity is cast aside for a masterful magnificence, as in 'Sailing to Byzantium':

> That is no country for old men. The young
> In one another's arms, birds in the trees
> – Those dying generations – at their song,
> The salmon-falls, the mackerel-crowded seas,
> Fish, flesh, or fowl, commend all summer long
> Whatever is begotten, born, and dies.
> Caught in that sensual music all neglect
> Monuments of unageing intellect.
>
> An aged man is but a paltry thing,
> A tattered coat upon a stick, unless
> Soul clap its hands and sing, and louder sing
> For every tatter in its mortal dress,
> Nor is there singing school but studying
> Monuments of its own magnificence;
> And therefore I have sailed the seas and come
> To the holy city of Byzantium.

In such verse he showed a dominant, even arrogant control of his medium, using simple phrases with a mastery that equalled that of Wordsworth. This is seen at its best in *The Wild Swans at Coole* (1919), *Michael Robartes and the Dancer* (1921), *The Tower* (1928) and *The Winding Stair* (1933). To his poetry must be added his moving autobiographical studies and essays. He stands out as the greatest poetical figure of the first half of the twentieth century, of a stature beyond controversy. Out of fables and strange beliefs he made images to hold beauty together in a world where so much conspired for its destruction.

In the twenties and thirties a number of poets extracted themselves from what had been a dominant insular form of romanticism and re-established international contacts. Outstanding in this development was T. S. Eliot, born in 1888 in St Louis, Missouri, who resided in England, entered the Anglican Church and adopted British nationality. He was encouraged and his imagination stimulated by another American, Ezra Pound (1885–1972).

It is difficult to know how much American poetry to include in a history of English literature. Despite American memories in his verse, Eliot is an English poet. Ezra Pound, from Idaho, was an American exile, becoming a European, spending his active years in England, Paris and Italy. In London in 1914 Pound launched the 'Imagist' movement, emphasizing the use of common speech, new rhythms and clear images, There were English and American adherents, including T. E. Hulme. H. D. (Hilda Doolittle), Amy Lowell, F. S. Flint and Richard Aldington. Eliot was influenced by T. E. Hulme (1883–1917), who attacked romanticism for its sentimental and illusory faith in man's ability to develop, and urged a classicism which would adequately define human imperfections. Pound's early poetical pseudo-autobiography *Hugh Selwyn Mauberley* (1920) had the witty and complex intelligence, the agile and multifarious reference, which English poets sought in the following decades. Later he concentrated on the *Cantos*, his major poetical work.

T. S. Eliot, both by verse and prose essays, made a revolution in the taste of his generation. His early poems in *Prufrock* (1917) were satiric, sometimes comic, always dramatic and impersonal, with an underlying disparagement of the so-called benefits of civilization. The title piece, begun at Harvard in 1910 and finished in Germany in 1911, is remarkable when the dates are realized. The major influences were to be Donne, the later Elizabethan and Jacobean dramatists, and Laforgue, with Dante also frequently present.

In *The Waste Land* (1922) Eliot viewed the post-war disruption of the European civilization that had so long sustained the Western world. Some find a sense of hope and Christian reconciliation, but this is not the main impression gathered from this 'heap of broken images'; rather it shows the bare emptiness of life without belief. The brilliant transitions of theme and the multiple reminiscence have been much admired, yet the poem was originally much longer, for Eliot allowed Pound to remove nearly half the text before publication. The influence of *The Waste Land* has been immense: no poet, in his own life-time, has seen erected such a verbal monument of criticism. The meaning has complex references often half-concealed, which lead to commentary, yet the poem is best read without the notes for the effect made on the imagination. Involved and erudite as the references are, the poem has also some of the most naturally idiomatic passages in contemporary verse. There followed in 1925 an edition of *Poems* including 'The Hollow Men', which is closely related to *The Waste Land*.

In 1927 Eliot joined the Anglican Church and in the same year wrote the moving religious poem, 'Journey of the Magi'. He had already drafted as early as 1924 a strange but absorbing dramatic piece about Sweeney, which organized itself into *Sweeney Agonistes* (1932). In these experiments he discovered himself as a verse dramatist, and despite some important volumes of verse including *Ash Wednesday* and *Marina* (1930), he concentrated in the following years on drama. From his success in the theatre he returned, after much thought on technique and life, to the contemplative poem of 'Burnt Norton' to be followed by 'East Coker', 'The Dry Salvages' and 'Little Gidding', all published together in 1943 as *Four Quartets*. These poems may yet remain the most durable element in his achievement. They arise from Eliot's interest in F. H. Bradley's philosophy and from his knowledge of the Catholic mystics. The major theme was time, experience and the possibilities of reconciliation. 'Burnt Norton' has quiet confident verses with reflections in a rose-garden ('Only through time, time is conquered'). 'East Coker' was the Somerset village from which his family emigrated to the United States and the poem dwells in the past. In 'The Dry Salvages' (a group of rocky islands off the coast of Massachusetts) he deals with his own past in America. In 'Little Gidding' the war years with the bombing of England are related to the past of the village which had held a religious community in the seventeenth century and had its church sacked by Cromwell's soldiers. Eliot is too close for any certain estimate. His vision of the tragic half century in which he lived still works too powerfully amongst us. It is enough for the time being that he was the major influence on his own generation and that he created a poetic revolution.

Eliot had many imitators but no direct successors, yet in the thirties writers who felt his influence dominated the poetical scene. At the centre were W. H. Auden (1907–73), Stephen Spender (b. 1909), Cecil Day Lewis (1904–72) and Louis MacNeice (1907–63); with Auden as the leader and poetically the most versatile. Their impact was considerable, though it did not always arise from what was most permanent in their work. For a time they dedicated themselves to employ poetry in social and political problems. Middle-class, public-school Englishmen, ashamed of their privileges, they viewed England's economic depression and despaired of the future. Auden expressed this forcefully, if crudely, using the old fifteen syllable line, the line of Tennyson's 'Locksley Hall':

Smokeless chimneys, damaged bridges, rotting wharves, and choked canals,
Tram lines buckled, smashed trucks lying on their sides across the rails.

To them all, the Soviet Union was a sytem of construction and hope, and behind the Soviet Union lay Marxism, to their minds a stronger and more consistent doctrine than anything suggested by the English leaders. Neither attachment was profound or formal. Freud, in a general way, was an influence, and D. H. Lawrence; both of whom had hoped

Poets' corner, 1960: From left to right; Louis MacNeice, Ted Hughes, T. S. Eliot, W. H. Auden and Stephen Spender

for a society where human contact would be full and complete. Poetically *The Waste Land* was a powerful influence, but they lacked Eliot's astringent qualities and did not follow Eliot in his Christian loyalties. When Auden arrived at Christianity it was by another route. C. Day Lewis summed up their view: 'Post-war poetry was born among the ruins. Its immediate ancestors were Hopkins, Owen and Eliot.' This attitude was complicated by another factor with which Eliot as an American had no concern. They judged that the public school and its empire-making loyalties were anachronistic and yet they had an atavistic nostalgia for the junior common-room, shown in their private jokes and the pervading atmosphere of intimate male friendship, all of which constituted their most insular element. Their loyalties coalesced in defence of the Republican side in the Spanish Civil War. The issues of that tragic engagement are now known to be complex, but for these English poets here was the last heroic cause. If there was failure here, nothing could be retrieved. Auden defined it in the chorus to his 'Spain', and Cecil Day Lewis in one of his most effective poems wrote of how the Basque trawlers fought a rebel cruiser:

> *Freedom is more than a word, more than the base coinage*
> *Of statesmen.*

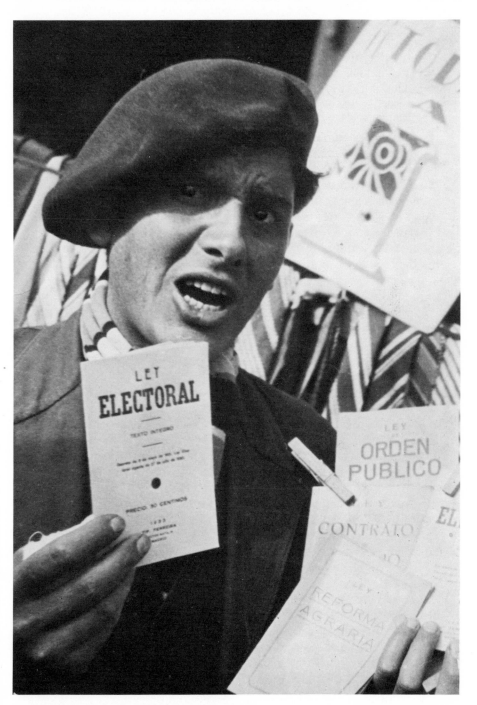

The Spanish Civil War presented the last heroic cause for the English poets of the 1930s

An even younger generation concentrated on the Spanish issue and the young communist John Cornford wrote some moving lyrics.

While the Spanish Civil War began the break-up of the group, the war and the alliance of Germany with the Soviet Union signalled its end. They lived to write other poems, but the sharp impact they made in the thirties was over. Auden emigrated to America in 1939, and one who had been a leader and a very English poet spent more than half his poetic life in New York.

The total assessment of Auden is difficult. Not all his verse is easily available and his views and loyalties so changed during his life that some of his poems were drastically revised. He found his way first from Marx to humanism and then by 1939 adopted Christianity 'without its myth-ology'; by 1941 came a complete acceptance of the Christian revelation. He remained a lyric poet, with an ear as keen as Tennyson's for what is subtle in English rhythms. The political poems had an immediate impact, but they will not compare with the outstanding lyrics, such as the well-known 'Lay your sleeping head, my love'. Nothing of this could be learned from Eliot. In addition to the lyrics there was irony, satire and wit, as if Skelton were alive again. The American poems, the work of a poet in isolation, are not sufficiently known: *Another Time* (1940) with the effective poems on the death of Yeats and Freud; *New Year Letter* (1941); *The Age of Anxiety* (1948); *Nones* (1951); *The Shield of Achilles* (1955). Here a Christian theme recurs with influences from Kierkegaard, a selection of whose works he edited in 1955, and of Niebuhr. A new development in his later work was marked by his libretti in which he was associated with his friend Chester Kallman. These included the *Rake's Progress*, the music for which was composed by Stravinsky. Though he remained an American citizen he returned to Europe before his death, to Oxford and to his house in Austria. The obituaries rated him as the major poet of his generation. He will be difficult to assess, particularly in his rejection of much in his earlier works.

While Eliot, Auden, and their associates drew the main critical attention, many poets in the thirties and the forties chose different ways. Edith Sitwell's (1887–1964) earliest work appeared during the First World War. She wished to break through 'the rhythmical flaccidity, the verbal deadness' that preceded her and she succeeded in *Façade* (1922), *Bucolic Comedies* (1923) and *Gold Coast Customs* (1929). She and her brothers (Sir Osbert and Sacheverell) were interested in the ballet and the quick precision and alertness of dance music entered her verses. The three Sitwells worked in close association, particularly to produce a periodical, *Wheels*, which conducted revolt in a sprightly manner. They all represented, perhaps for the last time, an aristocratic mood in English literature. Sir Osbert (1892–1969) later developed an individual satiric style, as in *Argonaut and Juggernaut* (1920). He was also a short story writer of an entertaining distinction, as in *Triple Fugue* (1924); and a novelist, particularly in his novel of Scarborough, *Before the Bombardment* (1926). His main work in his later years, to which reference is made elsewhere, was his autobiography, which is a major period piece. Sacheverell (b. 1897) is best known as an art historian and a writer of landscape in prose in volumes such as *Southern Baroque Art* (1924). His poetry had the same evocative qualities as his prose, as in *The Thirteenth Caesar* (1924). Edith Sitwell's later poems were different. A Christian element prevails and tragic moods occur, as in *The Song of the Rose* (1945) and *The Canticle of the Rose* (1949).

Roy Campbell (1901–57) showed that not all poetry had a left-wing angle: a South African, he enlivened the scene with *The Flaming Terrapin* (1924), and after numerous volumes, his *Collected Poems* appeared in 1949. Other poets, despite social and political pressures, sought an introspective exploration of the individual life. Kathleen Raine (b. 1908) in *Collected Poems* (1956) had this self-inquiring talent, with a mystical overtone, derived from her study of Blake. George Barker (b. 1913), whose *Collected Poems* appeared in 1957, had since 1933 published verse, which, while showing an awareness of his age and its predicament, yet was more personal in approach than that of Auden and his group. Hugh MacDiarmid (1892–1979) showed that there was an independent tradition in Scottish poetry, with his broadly based human sympathies; while Edwin Muir (1887–1959), also a Scot but in an international tradition, wrote with impressive sincerity in his contemplative and philosophical poems, published as *Collected Poems* (1952). Henry Treece and G. S. Fraser were among those wishing to move into a freer world of the imagination. The dominant voice here was that of Dylan Thomas (1914–53). His beautiful voice was well known to radio audiences to whom he read not only his poems but essays especially prepared, such as *Quite Early One Morning* (1954). Shortly before his death he wrote a play for radio, *Under Milk Wood* (1954), which was also widely performed in the theatre. He became a legend in his own life-time, and this makes it difficult to reduce him to the size in which posterity will see him. He began with *Eighteen Poems* (1934) and concluded with *Collected Poems* (1953). From the first his work was resented by Auden's group. It was more complex and ignored the temporal to deal with elemental things. Some English critics failed to realize that Thomas was Welsh, a non-Welsh-speaking Welshman from Swansea, but aware of Welsh poetic traditions, which are enigmatic and full of metrical and verbal complexities. His verse was seldom without a meaning, but there was a business on foot to make the reader work and to introduce concealments that would puzzle the critics. Thomas's fanciful village of 'Llareggub' is quoted in learned works without realization of what happens when the word is spelled backwards. Whatever his ultimate position, his lyrics have the enduring qualities of simplicity and unageing themes: 'And death shall have no dominion'; 'A Refusal to Mourn the Death, by Fire,

When Dylan Thomas died in New York in 1953 at the age of thirty-nine he was already a legendary figure. Since his death his reputation, and his audience, have grown. This photograph shows an exhibition at the Boat House, Laugharne, where Thomas used to work, with his daughter in the foreground (with shawl)

of a Child in London'; 'Do not go gentle into that good night'; and others.

Poetry in the middle of the twentieth century was not a popular art. Most of the respected poets had but a small audience, and their work was 'difficult'. Thus Herbert Read (1893–1968) exacted much from his readers if they were to enjoy his closely intellectual lyrics, and this was true of many of his contemporaries. Read had much influence as a critic of art and literature, and, like Blunden, he achieved possibly his most lasting success in a prose narrative of the First World War, *In Retreat* (1925). One poet broke through to the sort of popularity that Tennyson had once possessed: John Betjeman (b. 1906) made a special position for himself as a defender of the Victorian Age in architecture, and of the shape of things past in general. He succeeded Day Lewis as Poet Laureate and it was a popular choice. His *Collected Poems* (1958), published by Murray, Byron's publisher, had a large audience. This was followed by his verse autobiography *Summoned by Bells* (1960) and *High and Low* (1966). Many say that he is far from greatness, but, at least, he is a reminder that in the past poets dealt with intelligible human themes and were widely read. In the middle of the twentieth century one leaves the poetic scene without any major figure and with the sense that poetry has no dominating place in the mind of England. There were some poets, who for a time had prestige, who concentrated on the brief and complex lyric, as if they were reflecting the intricacies of Sir William Empson. By common consent Philip Larkin was the most enduring. Yet it may be in some irrational way consoling to recall that such was the mood of critical comment just before the beginning of the great age of Elizabethan poetry.

In this portrait of the whole of English poetry from Anglo-Saxon times onwards it would be foolhardy to make any assessment of immediately contemporary work. As has been suggested the poet has largely lost his audience, or at least he has lost a national audience such as Scott, Byron and Tennyson commanded. The media, which have been able somewhat to accommodate drama, though not without some corruption of the art, have done nothing effectively for poetry. At one period radio did a little, but mainly by encouraging the past, not by exploring contemporary achievement. No writer can now regard poetry as a profession. Even Roy Fuller, who has published consistently and with distinction since 1939 and has been Professor of Poetry at Oxford, still pursued his profession as a solicitor until his recent retirement. Government agencies such as the Arts Council give grants. Such bodies can encourage the executive artist, the dancer or the actor, but it is the audience alone that can encourage the creative artist.

Here begynneth a treatyse how the hye fader of heuen sendeth dethe to somon euery creature to come and gyue a counte of theyr lyues in this worlde and is in maner of a morall playe.

Everyman.

The frontispiece to an early edition of the late fifteenth-century 'Morality' play, *Everyman*

Chapter 6

English Drama to Shakespeare

THE BEGINNINGS of drama in England are obscure. There is evidence that when the Romans were in England they established vast amphitheatres for the production of plays, but when the Romans departed their theatre departed with them. The earliest records of acting in the Middle Ages are concerned not with plays but with individual players, jesters, clowns, tumblers and minstrels. Of these the most important is the 'minstrel', who is a link with the Anglo-Saxon 'scop', who sang the long poems of heroes. Throughout the Middle Ages, in his multi-coloured coat, the minstrel must have been a familiar and welcome figure. He could be found at the King's court, in castles, at tournaments and weddings or in the market-places, gathering a crowd and speaking or singing his stories. It is recorded that in the army of William the Conqueror, the minstrel Taillefer died reciting the lay of Roncesvalles. On occasion the minstrel could grow rich under wealthy patronage. Yet the life of the humbler minstrel was at best a hard one, tramping the roads, exposed to the weather and relying upon the generosity of such audiences as he could find. Officially, the hand of the Church was against him, and there was little hope that his soul would be saved from damnation. At the same time the Church must have seen that the minstrels encouraged pilgrims in the more weary stages of their journeys. Some clerics even imitated the methods of the minstrels, and stood in public places mingling words of religious guidance with secular stories. Monks, too were human after all, and enjoyed the minstrel's stories, and sometimes an unfrocked cleric would himself turn minstrel.

If the Church did not look kindly upon the minstrels and their less reputable companions, it was the Church itself that brought back drama into England. The Church had condemned the theatre of the Roman Empire, and its spectacles and themes gave every reason for such an attack. Yet the ritual of the Church had itself something dramatic within it, and by the tenth century that ritual extended into the rudiments of a play. During the Easter celebrations, such a biblical incident as the visit of the three women to the Empty Tomb was simply presented by priests, with accompanying words, chanted in Latin. One group of

priests or choir-boys would represent the Angels guarding the Tomb.
Three other priests would approach them. The first group chanted in
Latin:

Whom are you looking for in the sepulchre, ye women who follow Christ?

The others would chant in reply:

Jesus of Nazareth, who was crucified, O Heavenly beings.

Then the first group replied again:

He is not here: He has arisen as he said he would do.
Go! Announce it, since he has arisen from the sepulchre.

A similar set of words and actions was devised to present the visit of the
shepherds to the infant Christ. How the Church came to countenance
these dramatic representations is unknown. They seem a natural development of church services, and possibly it was hoped that they would
counteract the village celebrations of May Day and Harvest time.
Though their origin is uncertain, it is clear that these liturgical dramas
developed in a way which the Church could not have anticipated.

At first, the liturgical play was merely a part of the church service,
but by the thirteenth century it had grown until every part of the
church was used in an action which converted the whole edifice into
one stage, with the audience present amid the actors. Such a liturgical
play on the birth of Christ is recorded at Rouen. The three kings enter
at the east, north and south of the church and proceed until they meet
at the altar. They chant words descriptive of their actions and then sing
an anthem. A procession forms and moves towards the nave while the
choir chants. A star is lit over the altar, and the kings approach it. A
dialogue follows, and then the kings sleep, to be awakened by an angel
telling them to proceed home another way. The procession re-forms,
and the Mass follows.

Such a spectacle was witnessed by many for the sake of the spectacle
alone, and there were signs that the higher ecclesiastical authorities were
disquieted. The Church, which had reintroduced drama, was discovering
that the dramatic element was growing stronger than its religious
purpose. What happened cannot be traced in an orderly fashion, though
the results are clear enough. Between the thirteenth and fourteenth
centuries drama became secularized. The ecclesiastical authorities when
they found what they had created was an embarrassment, removed it
from the church itself to the precincts. There, by a number of changes, it
became elaborated and secularized. The words themselves were no longer
spoken in Latin, but in English, and instead of the brief liturgical
speeches, a longer dramatic script was invented around the biblical
narratives. The actors were no longer the clergy, but members of the

'Christ Harrowing Hell', from an early engraving, after a manuscript of the Chester Mystery Plays. The porter of Hell is blowing on a trumpet to arouse the fiendish hosts

medieval guilds, with each guild usually responsible for one play. The guilds, as a co-operative effort, prepared for certain Feast Days, notably for the festival of Corpus Christi, a series of biblical plays to be performed at various 'stations' in a town. Each play would be mounted on a platform, fitted with wheels, and so could be drawn from one 'station' to another. These religious plays, important solely in the history of drama, are also important in themselves. Here was drama as a genuinely social activity, a co-operative enterprise, maintained by guilds of craftsmen, employing their own members as amateurs.

Records show that such drama was widespread. The number of plays which has survived is limited, though probably representative. Four main cycles have been preserved, those of Chester, York, 'Towneley' or Wakefield and Coventry. Of these the York is the most complete: in a series of plays it presents the Bible story from the Creation to the Day of Judgement. The plays in the four surviving cycles vary in dramatic skill, though they all show sincerity and independence, with pathos present at times, as in the play of Abraham's sacrifice of Isaac. They have a frequent intrusion of homely and comic characters, as in the treatment of Noah's wife as a shrew. One writer of these religious or 'Miracle' plays stood out from all the rest, and he was responsible for five plays in the 'Towneley' or Wakefield cycle. In one of his plays, the *Secunda Pastorum*, depicting the visit of the shepherds to the infant Christ, he shows his independence of the biblical narrative by introducing a sheep-thief named Mak, and his wife, and by giving some realistic discussion on the shepherd's life and its hardships. It is difficult now to recapture the minds of the audiences who saw these plays. The main comic incident in *Secunda Pastorum* shows how Mak and his wife dress up a stolen sheep as a baby and hide it in a cradle, where finally it is discovered by other shepherds. Could the dramatist have been unaware of the contrast that this grotesque visit to a cradle would have with the other visit, with which this play concludes, where the same shepherds visit the infant Christ? These religious plays formed a great national tradition, which possibly we have never fully appreciated, and England was duller when Puritanism eradicated these pleasures from the people.

Later than these religious dramas were the 'Morality' plays, in which the characters were abstract vices and virtues. At first sight these seem less lively entertainments than a play of Noah's wife or a sheep-thieving Mak. Some of the authors of the 'Morality' plays were, however, able to make real and contemporary characters of the vices and virtues. So in a play entitled *Mankynd*, the hero is attacked by three rascals, Nought, New-gyse and Nowadays, and, though this assault has its moral purport, it is presented on the stage as a comic and realistic attack by a trio of gangsters. The possibilities of the 'Morality' play are best proved in England by the effectiveness and the long-continued success of the late fifteenth-century play of *Everyman*. Death summons Everyman to God; his worldly companions gradually forsake him, until Good Deeds alone is left to accompany him on his last ordeal. Though the characters are abstractions, they have relationships which are human, and though the whole action is controlled by the lesson which is to be taught, the play has a natural development, often a genuine realism, with a pathos direct and sincere.

It is difficult to trace the development of drama at this period, because so much of the evidence is missing, and the historians, who have presented a connected narrative, have achieved a show of order only at the sacrifice of truth. A variation developed in the morality itself with John Skelton's *Magnificence*, for this has a secular theme.

It is clear that, apart from the 'Morality' plays, there existed short plays named 'Interludes'. These were not popular pieces like the religious plays, nor were they allegorical as were the 'Moralities'. They were mainly performed in the houses of the more intelligent Tudor gentry. It is known that Sir Thomas More enjoyed them. One of the best is Henry Medwall's *Fulgens and Lucres*, which was discovered only in recent years. The plot shows Lucres hesitating between a high-born and low-born suitor and finally giving herself to the second. No other 'Interlude' is so advanced in its structure.

Many other 'Interludes' gave entertainment, with some instruction, to Tudor gentlemen and ladies. Often the humour was crude, the action clumsy and the road back towards moralizing and allegory ever open. Development in literature is seldom at an even pace, but sudden and unexpected. It is difficult to realize that these 'Interludes' were written in the century which was to see the production of some of our greatest plays. Further, the 'Miracle' plays, the 'Moralities' and the Interludes remained popular even when the new, ambitious drama had captured the stage. How the change from rudimentary drama to the great achievement that ended in Shakespeare came about has naturally been a matter for speculation. While nothing can explain the genius of Marlowe or Shakespeare, the changes in the form of drama can be in part explained by the revival of interest in classical drama. The classical example gave dramatists a boldness and elevation of purpose, which native drama had nowhere achieved. In Kyd and Marlowe and Shakespeare, this sense of the high potentiality of drama contrived to reunite itself with much that was valuable in the older native tradition.

Classical drama gave examples both for comedy and tragedy, and as far as England is concerned these models were, with negligible exceptions, Latin. George Gascoigne, on the title-page of his *Jocasta*, affirms that he is rendering from a Greek play by Euripides, though actually he was translating from the Italian. English comedy might well have developed without any Latin intrusion, and what is best in it remains native to the end. Tragedy, on the other hand, could not well have grown out of the 'Miracle' plays and the 'Moralities', and here a new start is made in the sixteenth century with the help of Latin models. The Latin models for comedy were Terence and Plautus and some of their influence can be seen in Nicholas Udall's *Ralph Roister Doister* (about 1553) which was performed by Westminster boys. This is a play on the theme of the boasting character, the *miles gloriosus* of Latin comedy, and though much of its humour parallels the 'Interludes', the classical model has helped Udall to build a full-length play, instead of a comic dialogue dependent on a few tenuous situations. How strong is the native element can be seen in *Gammer Gurton's Needle* (about 1550, printed 1575), a play which is a little earlier than *Roister Doister*, and can claim to be the first extant English comedy. The central situation in the play is trivial and farcical – the loss and discovery of a needle – but the dramatist had a gift for dialogue, a knowledge of rustic life and a distinct power in creating characters which include the farm labourer, Hodge, a firmly drawn, comic figure, natural and lifelike.

In tragedy, the problem was more severe, and it is still difficult to realize the strength of genius which allowed Kyd, Marlowe and Shakespeare to solve it. The main model was Seneca, a philosopher of Nero's time, whose moral discourses were known in antiquity, and who was also the author of a series of 'closet' dramas. He had employed the Greek mythological stories, and much of the outward semblance of Greek drama. But it was as if a romantic had re-written classical drama to

A woodcut made for the 1633 edition of Kyd's *The Spanish Tragedy*. Horatio is found by his father, murdered in the garden

answer his own mood, and a romantic with a taste for atrocities and for moralizing. Seneca was a dangerous model, and yet this strange combination of interests was not unsuitable to the Elizabethan mind. Here they found in the Latin language what they might presume to be the form and themes of the Greek stage, and all this without the embarrassment of the Greek language, which few of them understood. Their own interest in crime, violence and atrocity was confirmed fully in this classical authority. The moralizing speeches might at first seem more difficult to assimilate; but the 'Morality' plays, and indeed the main tradition of medieval literature, had accustomed them to moral discourse. As for rant and rhetoric, they could enter easily into any contest with their Latin preceptor.

Seneca's own plays were translated, published and five of them performed between 1559 and 1581. Meanwhile in 1562 there was acted, before Queen Elizabeth in the Inner Temple, the first extant tragedy in English, *Gorboduc*, by Thomas Sackville and Thomas Norton. Though Senecan in manner, the play has an English theme, and its main motive, of the dangers that follow an unsettled succession, would be of topical interest in Elizabeth's reign, to an audience of lawyers and courtiers.

The English desire for a play with a more vigorous action is shown in the early popularity of chronicle or history plays, which are a peculiarly native production. The extant examples are probably not among

A woodcut made for the frontispiece to an early edition of Christopher Marlowe's tragedy, *Dr Faustus*, showing Edward Alleyn as the doctor who sells his soul to the devil

the earliest of the type. They are mainly remembered because some of them presented an outline plan for Shakespeare in a number of his plays: they include *The Famous Victories of Henry the Fifth* (about 1588), *The Troublesome Raigne of John, King of England* (about 1590) and *King Leir* (*c.* 1594). These and other chronicle plays have action in plenty, but they are formless. The problem, if drama was to develop, was to combine the vigour of this native tradition with the ambition in style and arrangement of Senecan tragedy.

The solution of the problem was the outstanding achievement of two dramatists, Thomas Kyd (*c.* 1557–*c.* 1595) and Christopher Marlowe (1564–93). Kyd, who was probably writing a little before Marlowe, gave the theatre, in *The Spanish Tragedy*, the play that it wanted. He accepted as much of the Senecan tragedy as was convenient, and on this basis constructed a well-designed popular tragedy. He discovered how easily blank verse might be converted into a useful theatrical medium. He used horrors and crimes and the Senecan motive of revenge, but his characters are distinct, his situations theatrically effective and his play a united design. The central theme in an elaborate plot is the revenge of Hieronimo for the murder of his son Horatio, and the dramatic interpretation of the old man is the most human and skilful portrayal which the English stage had seen up to this time. Kyd was the author of a play on the Hamlet theme of which no copy is extant, but it is clear from *The Spanish Tragedy* that Shakespeare was deeply indebted to the older dramatist.

Christopher Marlowe was a young Cambridge dramatist of wide reading, whose life was tempestuous and whose death tragic. Apart from his brief career as a dramatist, he seems to have been involved in political intrigue as an agent, or spy, and there is some evidence that his opinions on philosophy and religion were considered dangerous. His most important work is contained in four tragedies, composed between 1587 and 1593: *Tamburlaine the Great*, in two parts; *Dr Faustus*; *The Jew of Malta*; and *Edward II*. *Tamburlaine* gives best the quality of Marlowe's imagination. As his hero, he chooses a fourteenth-century Tartar herdsman, whose conquests outrival those of any of the heroes of antiquity. Fantastically ambitious, Tamburlaine is also grotesquely cruel. Marlowe delights in these excesses, until sometimes he seems to be satirizing his own manner, and the scene in which Tamburlaine harnesses his chariot with kings of Asia became a stock incident for parody in Elizabethan drama. Marlowe is not content to portray Tamburlaine merely as a master of cruelty and conquest. Tamburlaine's lust for power is given a philosophical sanction: he is the single human personality, alone under the vault of the heavens, challenging men and gods with his strength. No enemy overcomes him, except Death, the same enemy that *Everyman* had to encounter. The difference between Marlowe and the author of that 'Morality' play illuminates the contrast between the medieval and the Renaissance outlook. The author of *Everyman* was conscious of life in the world as a spiritual journey, in which the only hope of success lay in a devout acquiescence in God's will. Marlowe, though he knows Death to be lurking in the shadows, challenges the divine rule, believing that the ecstasy of earthly glory is its own reward, whatever may happen:

> *Ah! Faustus*
> *Now hast thou but one bare hour to live,*
> *And then thou must be damned perpetually:*
> *Stand still you ever moving spheres of heaven,*
> *That time may cease, and midnight never come:*
> *Fair Nature's eye, rise, rise again, and make*
> *Perpetual day, or let this hour be but*
> *A year, a month, a week, or natural day,*
> *That Faustus may repent, and save his soul*
> O lente lente currite noctis equi.*
> *O, gently gently run you horses of the night.

In *Tamburlaine* this quest of material glory is unembarrassed by conflicting values of a Christian world. This problem Marlowe faces in *Dr Faustus*, by employing the German legend of the magician who for the sake of universal knowledge sells his soul to the devil. If *Tamburlaine* shows the will to power in the face of material obstacles, *Dr Faustus* examines the inner, more introspective, and spiritual consequences of such a quest. The play is not wholly successful. The opening scenes, in which Faustus barters his soul, are magnificent, and the closing presentation of the final hour of retribution reaches a depth of pathos which Marlowe never again equalled. The weakness lies in the middle scenes, some of which are crude, grotesque and even farcical – so inadequate, indeed, that some have doubted Marlowe's authorship.

The Jew of Malta misses the high poetry of the earlier plays, nor has it their grandeur in the conception of character. It descends to melodrama, while it is so extravagant that Marlowe might well have been satirizing his own earlier work. Barabbas, the Jew, has been unjustly treated by the Christians, and in revenge applies a Machiavellian attitude to mankind, which Marlowe interprets as the perpetration of a series of crimes, so wild and incredible that it is difficult to realize that even an Elizabethan audience, with its taste for these delights, could treat them seriously. *Edward II* is, in comparison, a sober play, far more carefully balanced in its structure than any of Marlowe's other works, and, though it misses the fire and glamour of *Tamburlaine*, it has a more varied interpretation of character. Marlowe has converted a theme of English history from the formlessness of the old chronicle plays into genuine tragedy. The central figure, Edward II himself, instead of being aggressive and overpowering, as are Tamburlaine and Faustus, is sentimental and weak.

While tragedy developed in the hands of Marlowe and Kyd, comedy had also proceeded beyond the rustic humours of *Gammer Gurton's Needle*. The most brilliant intelligence to practise comedy before Shakespeare was John Lyly (1554–1606), who was also the author of the novel *Euphues*. Lyly looked to the Court for his audience, and his players were child actors. It is difficult to realize that the finely drawn sentiment of his comedies, their delicacy and their elaborate mythological themes belong to the same age as the loud ranting of Tamburlaine, and the blood-drenched stage of *The Spanish Tragedy*. Yet the final attractiveness of the Elizabethan theatre lay in its power of incorporating all these elements sometimes within the confines of a single play. A number of Lyly's plays have been preserved. They were produced at approximately the dates which follow, and published normally a few years after the first performance: *Campaspe* (1584), *Sapho and Phao* (1584), *Gallathea* (1585), *Endimion* (1588), *Midas* (about 1589), *Mother Bombie*, *Love's Metamorphoses* (both about 1590) and *The Woman in the Moon* (about 1594). All of these plays are in prose, except *The Woman in the Moon*, which is a verse play, and a satire on women. They all use mythological subjects, except *Mother Bombie*, which is a modern comedy. Lyly has seldom had full justice given to his achievement, for he is followed so soon by Shakespeare. His originality and invention are remarkable. He combined the realistic farce, the complexity of Latin comedy and the allegory of the 'Morality' plays into a new design, suffused with a gentle and dream-like romanticism. With his eye upon the Queen and his audience of courtiers, he gave his mythologies a contemporary and topical reference. His greatest achievement lay in the wit of his dialogue. If his plots were artificial then so was his audience.

While Lyly works consistently in one manner, a number of his contemporaries attempt a variety of moods. Robert Greene (1560–92), a man of all trades in Elizabethan literature, a poet, novelist and pamphleteer, wooed popular taste in imitations of Marlowe. He discovered his dramatic identity in his comedies, *Friar Bacon and Friar Bungay* (about 1589) and *James IV* (about 1591). He contrived to make a plot in which characters drawn from different social groups and actions with varying degrees of credibility were drawn into unity by an atmosphere of romance. In *Friar Bacon*, magicians mingle with courtiers and kings, and a Prince of Wales woos Margaret, the dairymaid of Fressingfield, and in *James IV* the kings of England and Scotland live in the same play as Oberon, king of the Fairies. Though the road may be a long one it is leading towards *A Midsummer Night's Dream*. Among the other dramatists of the time George Peele (c. 1557–97) is a figure more difficult to define. His *Arraignment of Paris*, probably his earliest work, is a mythological play, acted before the Queen, and designed in every way for a courtly audience. His *David and Bethsabe* is an interesting link with the old religious drama. He begins with a biblical theme, but he develops it for

Robert Greene, poet, novelist and pamphleteer

the sake of the narrative itself, and for the opportunities of employing his own fanciful verse. His best-remembered play – and, among others, Milton remembered it in *Comus* – is *The Old Wives' Tale*, where a charming romantic opening is allowed to lead into a dramatic satire.

By the nineties of the sixteenth century the theatre in England was fully established, but complicated conditions governed the activities of the dramatists. In London the situation, stated simply, was that the Court favoured the drama, but the civic authorities, partly from Puritan scruples and partly for social reasons, found it an unmitigated nuisance. Those who produced plays, wishing to perform not only to the Court but to the public, evaded the civic authorities by conducting their performances outside the city walls. At first the plays were performed in inn yards, but already in 1576 a theatre had been constructed in Shoreditch, outside the city boundary. Within the city, the one playhouse in the sixteenth century was Blackfriars, where at first only the child actors performed. The actor had to face many obstacles, for by law his profession was not recognized and he could be treated as a rogue and a vagabond. As a device to overcome the difficulty the players wore the livery of retainers of some lord or high official. The privilege kept them free from the law, though it left them economically dependent on the practice of their own art. So in the Elizabethan period the companies of players are known as the Queen's men, the Lord Admiral's men or the Lord Chamberlain's men, according to the great name that gave them legal status.

The public theatre of the sixteenth century differed in many important ways from the modern theatre. In the earlier period it was open to the sky, and without artificial lighting, so that the plays had to be performed by daylight. The stage was a raised platform, with a recess at the back supported by pillars and roofed. On the top of this roofed recess was a turret, from which a trumpeter could announce the beginning of a play and from which a flag would indicate that a play was in progress. There was no curtain, and the main platform could be surrounded on three sides by the audience. A few privileged persons were allowed on the stage itself. Hamlet, in Elizabethan times, did not peer out from his lighted picture-frame stage into a dark auditorium, but stood in the light of day, on the raised platform, and delivered his soliloquies surrounded by his auditors. A consequence of this open intimacy of the platform was that scenery, apart from a few essential properties, was impossible. The poet with his words had to supply the atmosphere in which the play was to live. Elaborate and expensive costumes gave colour to the comparatively empty background of the scene. At the rear of his main stage was a structure, with a door at each side, from which actors could enter, and also a curtained recess, in which an action could be 'discovered'. The auditorium was oval-shaped, and the ordinary spectators stood in this space, except for the portion occupied by the

The interior of the Swan playhouse in 1596. The platform stage was open, thus making scenery impossible, apart from a few essential properties

raised platform of the stage. Around the theatre were galleries, in which spectators could sit, and one of these galleries passed over the back of the stage. On occasion it could be employed in the action for the upper wall of a castle, or for Juliet's balcony. Part of one of the lower galleries at the side of the stage was occupied by musicians, who so often contributed with their art to Elizabethan drama. In the seventeenth century the enclosed theatre, on the model of Blackfriars, developed in importance. These 'private' theatres were lit by artificial lighting, and more elaborate stage devices were encouraged within them. In Charles I's reign, mainly under the influence of that great architect, Inigo Jones, courtly masques were popular, in which every emphasis was given to décor and stage machinery. The influence of those courtly entertainments was reflected in the increasing attention to scenic device in the 'private' theatre of the seventeenth century.

The interior of the Red Bull playhouse, with one of Shakespeare's most popular characters, Sir John Falstaff. The Elizabethan audiences liked Falstaff so much that Shakespeare wrote a special comedy for him, *The Merry Wives of Windsor*

Chapter 7

Shakespeare

To THE public theatre of the sixteenth century came William Shakespeare (1564–1616) as actor, playwright and shareholder in theatrical undertakings. Of his life it is enough to say that, to any unprejudiced view, it is clear that the Stratford man wrote the plays and that he had a wider reading and more opportunities for mingling with the great than is sometimes realized. After the obscure years he came to London, possibly in 1584, and worked as an actor and an apprentice playwright. In the years that followed, until the Globe was burnt down on 29 June 1613 during the first performance of *Henry VIII*, the theatre dominated his life. Of his personality, it can be affirmed that he had, in an absolute form, the intuition for gathering every 'unconsidered trifle' and every weighty matter that could profit his art, with, in addition, the concentration which is a necessary attribute of genius. Of his art in its relationship to ideas, it cannot be disputed, despite the divisions made in his plays by categorizing historians, that he held to a consistent outlook. In human conduct, he was everywhere possessed by the conception of loyalty and disloyalty, and their consequences in human life. In the exercise of the passions, which often entranced with their delights, he contemplated the strange conflict of reason and emotion, and the disorder that arose when reason was obliterated. He allowed his characters a freedom to live their own lives to the uttermost confines of good and evil, but he was ever conscious that they existed in a moral world, functioning under a divine Providence. While this consistency is maintained, his art permits of an almost infinite variety of mood and, as he progresses, the vision deepens.

He wrote always for the contemporary theatre, manipulating the Elizabethan stage with great resource and invention. The speeches in which Hamlet addresses the players show that he felt the restriction of the actor's ability to interpret and of the audience's intelligence in appreciation.

Knowing the limitations of the actors' art he still admired them ('they are the abstract and brief chronicles of the time'), and he faced his contemporary audience, answered its needs and contrived a drama which the Court could appreciate and the public enjoy, despite the competition of the bear-gardens. He was able to satisfy the desire for dramatic pleasure at a number of different levels of appreciation, sometimes even incorporating them in a single play. *Hamlet* or *Othello* can give pleasure to those who wish melodrama only, but beyond this there is the subtle presentation of character and a language unequalled in its sources of suggestion. To satisfy his audience was his primary purpose, but this was not enough, for he had to satisfy himself. It is clear from *Hamlet* and *Lear* that he wrote out the play fully as his own genius directed, knowing that deletion would be imperative when his script reached the theatre. With his skill in theatrical invention, he combined a genius for applying poetic language to drama. In the early comedies it seems, sometimes, that language intoxicated him. This is particularly true in his early and ingenious comedy of *Love's Labour's Lost* where he speaks of

> *Taffeta phrases, silken terms precise,*
> *Three-piled hyperboles, spruce affectation,*
> *Figures pedantical* (V.2)

Gradually he disciplined words increasingly to dramatic purpose. He had a range of imagery which was more comprehensive than in any other poet, and remains a proof of the universality of his interest. He was not unaware of the power which worked within him.

Unfortunately, the conditions of his period did not permit of the regular and authorized publication of his plays. Some of them were published in his lifetime with one play in each volume. These 'Quartos', as they are called (because they are printed on a quarto size page), were sometimes unauthorized and corrupt copies, though the circumstances of the publication of the second Quarto of *Hamlet* show that Shakespeare, when he had the chance, was not indifferent to the fate of his work. After his death, two of his fellow players, John Heminges and Henry Condell, gathered his works together in the 'Folio' edition of 1623. Modern scholarship has come increasingly to respect the way they accomplished this difficult task. Indeed, they could be described as the two most important men in Shakespeare's world. What they did was unusual. Ben Jonson, who was a scholar, had made an edition of his works in 1616 and had been teased by another playwright, Heywood, for doing so:

> *Pray tell me Ben, where does the mystery lurk,*
> *What others call a play you call a work.*

But Heminges and Condell had the courage to proceed, partly to preserve the rights of their Company but mainly from affection and admiration for their old companion. There are thirty-six plays in the

Martin Droeshout's engraving of Shakespeare as it appears in the first 'Folio' edition of his plays. This picture, drawn seven years after Shakespeare's death, is one of the few likenesses of him to have survived

Folio and if anyone wishes to say that any one of them is not by Shakespeare, let him prove it. Without the Folio editors we should have no record of eighteen plays including in tragedy *Macbeth, Coriolanus, Antony and Cleopatra*, in comedy *Twelfth Night, As You Like It,* and the late romances *The Winter's Tale* and *Cymbeline*.

His earliest work was in the plays on English history. He wrote, possibly with collaboration, three plays on the reign of Henry VI. They were the beginning of his epical treatment of English history, from the reign of Richard II to the reign of Richard III. No other group of his plays illustrates his range so completely as the whole sequence of the historical plays, though they were not planned as a unit. In the earliest of them he shows some dependence on contemporary models: *Henry VI, Parts 1, 2* and *3,* have much of the episodical method of the older chronicle plays, though with an added firmness in characterization, shown especially in the common people of the Jack Cade scenes. In *Richard II* and *Richard III,* Shakespeare adapts the history play to tragedy, following Marlowe's example. In the two parts of *Henry IV* he has liberated himself from any contemporary example, and evolved a drama which, while presenting history, allows for the comic scenes of Falstaff and his company.

A well-defined balance of character, especially between Hotspur and Prince Hal, gives a dramatic design to the historical material, while the human relations of Prince Hal and his father Henry IV bring an intimacy into the larger, public movement of events. Nor is Falstaff a mere comic excrescence. He is given some of the most profound speeches in the play. His speech on 'honour' is in absolute contrast to all the values that Hotspur esteemed, to his high-sounding rhetoric and the machinations of those who control great events, and are responsible for war and all its consequences.

Henry V, with its pageantry of national achievement, is no less original in design, and Shakespeare's skill is seen by his elimination of Falstaff at the very opening, so that he shall not delay with his great bulk the action which is to follow. Throughout the history plays, Shakespeare had Raphael Holinshed's *Chronicles*, and other sources, to give him the record of events, but the interpretation was his own. He presented consistently the conception that only by loyalty could the State survive, and that this virtue must be supremely the attribute of kingship. Without loyalty, out of which order and rule develop, Chaos will raise its ugly head, and once Chaos is come, no one will be safe, not even the father from the hand of his son, or the son from the hand of his father, as Shakespeare shows in a symbolical scene in *Henry VI, Part 3*. In *Henry V* he allows himself to escape the major theme in the exuberance of patriotic allegiance and of conquering success.

In the *Henry IV* plays, through Falstaff, Shakespeare matured his conception of comedy, but he had written comedies before he came to Falstaff. *Love's Labour's Lost*, possibly the earliest, is a miraculous invention in which he gives the semblance of courtly life and graceful manners. How keenly he studied words can be seen here in his satire on all the contemporary affectations in style and vocabulary. In *The Two Gentlemen of Verona* he made his first experiment in romantic comedy, and, possibly dissatisfied with his attempt, he tried the Plautian play of comic situation in *The Comedy of Errors*, with the assistance of twin brothers and twin servants. The play has ample entertainment, though this derives from a mechanism of mistaken identity rather than from human values, and in *The Taming of the Shrew* he returns to humanity, or half returns, for the wooing of Katharina is comic animalism, which the Elizabethan audience enjoyed without sentimental scruples. All these early experiments combine to give *A Midsummer Night's Dream* its magic. No play in Shakespeare is so original, so ingenious, or so perfectly designed. The romantic element is now played out light-heartedly through the lovers, but romance is gently rebuked by Reason operating through Bottom and his ass's head. The romantic action is enriched by the faery elements on one side, and by the rustics on the other, while the verse gives that atmosphere which Shakespeare can construct distinctively for each dramatic action.

He did not return to write any play similar to the *Dream*, for in that kind he had reached perfection. The play seems to have deepened his own conception of romantic comedy, and in *Much Ado About Nothing*, *As You Like It* and *Twelfth Night* he brought to the romantic stories, not only a subtle stage-craft, but excellent and well-devised characters. Of

Left: George Clifford, Earl of Cumberland, the Queen's Champion at the Accession day tilts in 1595, by Nicholas Hilliard, and (above) Queen Elizabeth dancing the volta with Robert Dudley, Earl of Leicester. Many of Shakespeare's early comedies were modelled on courtly life

these *As You Like It*, with its light-heartedness played out on a background of very gentle melancholy – Rosalind and Touchstone against Jaques and the Forest of Arden – has been deservedly one of the main favourites of the English stage. In incidentals the play is careless, or perhaps one should write carefree, but there is an admirable control of atmosphere and of the central intention. *Much Ado* showed that the romantic story was always in danger of becoming too serious, though this is saved by the good wit of Benedick and Beatrice and by the very witlessness of Dogberry. All that the romantic comedy could yield is gathered into the beauty of *Twelfth Night*, where amid the graces of the sentiment and laughter, Malvolio emerges, one of the most finished characters in the plays of this period. Romantic comedy existed in its own world, and once it faced the challenge of reality some of its values seemed brittle, even false. Often the characters struggle towards realism, while their master restrains them, so that they shall dance the pretty paces he has designed. Thus in *The Merchant of Venice* Shylock steps out of that fairy world of Bassanio and the caskets and the wooing of Portia and Jessica, to rise in tragic stature as the tormented Jew. Shylock's most moving speech is expressed in a plain prose, completely unadorned:

> Hath not a Jew eyes? hath not a Jew hands, organs, dimensions, senses, affections, passions? fed with the same food, hurt with the same weapons, subject to the same diseases, healed by the same means, warmed and cooled by the same winter and summer, as a Christian is? (III.1)

Yet ultimately in *The Merchant of Venice* it is the wash of coloured and romantic words that triumph, as in Lorenzo's speech to Jessica in the fifth act:

> *Look how the floor of heaven*
> *Is thick inlaid with patines of bright gold:*
> *There's not the smallest orb which thou beholdst*
> *But in his motion like an angel sings,*
> *Still quiring to the young-eyed cherubins;*
> *Such harmony is in immortal souls;*
> *But whilst this muddy vesture of decay*
> *Doth grossly close it in, we cannot hear it.* (V.1)

This fantasy world of romantic comedy would obviously not satisfy Shakespeare's whole nature. He continued to employ its pattern in *All's Well that Ends Well* and in *Measure for Measure*, where the vision which he had to unburden was too profound for its moonshine delights. The contrast between the story and the vision gives these plays a strange atmosphere, so that they have been named 'the dark comedies'. In them Shakespeare seems for some reason to be clinging to romantic comedy when tragedy was his proper medium.

It may have been the same mood which led him to *Troilus and Cressida*, where he seems to be contemplating satirically the Grecian world which men had called heroic. His satire exposes the treachery of love, the deceit of honour and the uselessness of war, and in this play hope is unknown. It is among the more difficult of Shakespeare's plays and yet its theme and its thought have attracted modern audiences. Never did Shakespeare declare more clearly his faith that, if chaos replaces order, all will perish. This appears in the great, though complex speech of Ulysses, on 'degree', which opens with the following lines:

> *Degree being vizarded,*
> *The unworthiest shows as fairly in the mask.*
> *The heavens themselves, the planets and this centre*
> *Observe degree, priority and place,*
> *Insisture, course, proportion, season, form,*
> *Office and custom, in all line of order.* (I.3)

The great period of Shakespeare's tragedy is to be found in the plays which begin with *Hamlet*, and include *Othello*, *Macbeth*, *King Lear*, *Antony and Cleopatra* and *Coriolanus*. These were all composed in the first six years of the seventeenth century. It would, however, be false to consider Shakespeare's achievement in tragedy as confined to these great plays. Already in the English history plays he had found a form of tragedy, partly with Marlowe's aid, in *Richard II* and *Richard III*. He had turned from the romantic comedies to fashion the romantic tragedy of *Romeo and Juliet*. In *Julius Caesar* he had combined Roman history with the interpretation of Brutus's tragic character. Tragedy, then, belongs not exclusively to any single period of his work, but is with him in all stages of his career, except the last, in *Cymbeline*, *The Winter's Tale* and *The Tempest*. At the same time, in the period of the great tragedies, his vision seems deeper and his powers in verse and dramatic genius are at their highest. The great tragedies share some characteristics. Each portrays some noble figure, caught in a difficult situation, when some weakness or bias of his nature is exposed. Upon his action depends not only his own fate, but that of an entire nation. While attention is concentrated on this central action, Shakespeare portrays the whole world in which his hero moves. Each of the plays is so made that it can appeal to different audiences at different levels of intelligence. *Hamlet* is a story of murder, suicide, madness, to those who call for melodrama, but for others it is a most subtle analysis of character, and a play in which verse is used with great skill.

Hamlet, the earliest of the great tragedies, is the most self-conscious. The renaissance atmosphere of art, ostentation, learning and crime governs a play in which the central character is himself a renaissance scholar-prince, clever, melancholic, introspective. Like a character in life itself, Hamlet may not be capable of full interpretation, though it is clear that through him Shakespeare explored the whole problem of action and the reflective mind. Nowhere are the varying moods of the language more entrancing. There is much wit, as in Hamlet's talk with Polonius and the actors; there is the longest and most brilliant sentence

The Globe Theatre, from a seventeenth-century panorama of London; it was burned to the ground during a performance of Shakespeare's *Henry VIII*. Below: Richard Tarlton, Queen Elizabeth's favourite clown, who was also a writer of ballads and plays, a drummer, tumbler and qualified Master of Fencing

in all the plays ('This heavy-headed revel east and west': I.4) where Hamlet discusses drunkenness and also imbalance of temperament, a theme on which all the tragedies depend; there is, throughout, verse charged with imagery.

In *Othello* he showed that he could compose a much more closely designed play, where the theme is as compact as an argument. Never did his knowledge of the stage show itself more completely, for the much-praised Iago owes his existence only to his master's knowledge of what the stage can make credible. If that fine villain stepped out of the theatre, as so many critics encourage him to do, he would fall into the hands of the veriest Dogberry of a policeman. The verse served the action admirably in *Othello* and never more effectively than in the final scene when Othello kills himself.

The poetry so effective in *Othello* reaches a greater height of magnificence in *Macbeth*, though as a tragedy the play has been over-praised. No actor has made his reputation by playing Macbeth, a part difficult in the later acts to make interesting, and impossible to make convincing. *Lear,*

David Garrick in the storm scene from *King Lear*.

Blow winds, and crack your cheeks; rage, blow
You cataracts, and hurricanoes spout,
Till you have drench'd our steeples, drown'd the cocks
King Lear III.2

the 'epic' of the tragedies, is rugged, primitive and Wagnerian. It cannot be appreciated if it is thought of in terms of the modern stage. Once scenery and all the appurtenance of realism have gone, Lear may stand out in the storm scenes as the greatest figure in our literature, but the absence of the graces and variety of *Hamlet*, and the incredible opening, will leave it the most admired, rather than the best loved of the tragedies. It is a better play for the theorist than for the theatre. The language is more complex and formidable than anywhere else in Shakespeare. Even the mad language has a meaning, a secret meaning which could not at any period have been available to the audience in the theatre. In no other work did Shakespeare so indulge his own creative activity to its uttermost, independent of players or audience. Of course there is more than enough for all of them but so much kept in reserve.

Antony and Cleopatra stands apart, for in none of the other tragedies has love been given such a part in the plot, or woman such a place amid the *dramatis personae*. Critics have often condemned the play as being too diffuse. How many of these critics have ever seen it acted in its entirety? The two central characters, particularly Cleopatra, are among the best observed and most realistic in Shakespeare. It has not the complexity of language or motive of *Macbeth* or *Lear*. It has a return to the comparative simplicity of all the Roman plays where Shakespeare was guided as he was in *Julius Caesar* and *Coriolanus* by Sir Thomas North's translation of Plutarch's *Lives* under the title of *The Lives of the Noble Grecians and Romans*. In some of his most entrancing passages he is following closely the language of North's prose. So he does in the most famous passage in the play when Enobarbus describes Cleopatra's barge:

> The barge she sat in, like a burnish'd throne,
> Burn'd on the water: the poop was beaten gold;
> Purple the sails, and so perfumed that
> The winds were love-sick with them; the oars were silver,
> Which to the tune of flutes kept stroke, and made
> The water which they beat to follow faster,
> As amorous of their strokes. For their own person,
> It beggar'd all description: she did lie
> In her pavilion – cloth-of-gold tissue –
> O'er-picturing that Venus where we see
> The fancy outwork nature: on each side her
> Stood pretty dimpled boys, like smiling Cupids,
> With divers-colour'd fans, whose wind did seem
> To glow the delicate cheeks which they did cool,
>   And what they undid did. (II.2)

Coriolanus, in marked contrast, is a tragedy, political in theme and austere in treatment, with an almost classical economy in its closing scene.

What brought the tragic period in Shakespeare to a close no one can tell. Some change of vision, perhaps even a creative exhaustion, led him on to the changed atmosphere of the last romances, *Cymbeline*, *The Winter's Tale* and *The Tempest*. The elaborate and improbable romance of *Cymbeline* seems as if Shakespeare had resigned: the tumults and high passions are excluded and instead there is gentleness, and a story as elaborate as it is fantastic. The dead are only seemingly dead but this does not prevent Shakespeare writing two of his most moving lines when Arviragus carries in the body of Imogen, who is believed to be dead:

> *The bird is dead*
> *That we have made so much on.* (IV.2)

It also permits him to write the most beautiful lyric in all the plays, again over the seemingly dead body of Imogen:

> *Fear no more the heat o' the sun,*
> *Nor the furious winter's rages;*
> *Thou thy worldly task hast done,*
> *Home art gone and ta'en thy wages:*
> *Golden lads and girls all must,*
> *As chimney-sweepers, come to dust.* (IV.2)

In the early scenes of *The Winter's Tale* he can be seen handling again the 'Othello' theme, but the language breaks under the pressure of his vision. Suddenly he rejects it all, and enters into a pastoral world, beautiful and genial, where instead of tragedy there is reconciliation. It can be argued that this last mood was always present, and that it is only part of the Christian teaching of atonement and forgiveness. Even at the close of *Lear* there is an almost mystical recognition of pity and reconciliation. Yet in these last plays all is changed, for the reconciliation is made too easily. Through Lear's world there blew a storm, wild and uncontrollable, but the storm in *The Tempest* answers Prospero's every gesture. This last play has, however, like *A Midsummer Night's Dream*, a miraculous quality, for it seems compact of originality. The characters are half-allegorical, the theme full of suggestions, the action a unity, and all made beautiful, except for the evil of Caliban, and in him it would seem that Shakespeare, having exhausted humanity in his previous creation, went outside man, and made a monster all of his own devising. It may be surmised that the change of style in *The Winter's Tale* and *The Tempest* marked the adjustments he had to make from the open stage of the Globe to the closed stage with its complex contrivances. Though one is not on sure ground and it may be even a little sentimental, it is difficult to resist the temptation to think that in Prospero's speech after the Masque he is recognizing that the theatre is changing and making his own farewell:

These our actors,
As I foretold you, were all spirits and
Are melted into air, into thin air:
And, like the baseless fabric of this vision,
The cloud-capp'd towers, the gorgeous palaces,
The solemn temples, the great globe itself,
Yea, all which it inherit, shall dissolve
And, like this insubstantial pageant faded,
Leave not a rack behind. We are such stuff
As dreams are made on, and our little life
Is rounded with a sleep. (IV.1)

Prospero and Ariel, from the statue by Eric Gill
on Broadcasting House, London

Oceana as a Light Bearer, from one of Inigo Jones' designs for Ben Jonson's
Masque of Blackness, 1605

Chapter 8

English Drama from Shakespeare to Sheridan

THE GENIUS of Shakespeare should not allow the rest of the drama of his age to be obscured. Contemporary with him was Ben Jonson (1573–1637), a combative, powerful personality, in almost every way a contrast to him. Jonson was a classicist, a moralist and a reformer of the drama. He was the stepson of a bricklayer, and though he began his education at Westminster School, he had to be removed before his studies were completed to work in the family trade. This he left to become a soldier and he killed his men in single combat in the Flanders Wars. How he gained all his learning is a mystery but its extent was ultimately recognized by both the universities who gave him degrees by 'their favour not his study'. In the theatre he began as an actor, and so graduated into becoming a writer of plays.

In comedy he turned his back upon romance, and presented the London of his own day with a strenuous effort towards realism, and an attempt to contain the action within the 'unities' of time, place and theme. His ideal was that each play should have a single scene, and that its action should take place in a single day:

> *The laws of time, place, persons, he observeth,*
> *From no needful rule he swerveth.*

Nor was he content that his excellence should escape the attention of his audiences. In prefatory verses he will thunder out the virtues of his play, like some dowager presenting estimable but ungainly daughters. While Shakespeare is showing Belmont and the Forest of Arden, Jonson depicts the rogues of Bartholomew Fair and Thames Side. From his first successful play, *Every Man in his Humour* (1598), he showed a consistency of method, though with much development in skill. His characters were, as he described them, 'humours' characters: one element in their moral nature was displayed throughout the play and exposed for ridicule. He defined the nature of 'humours' in his Prelude to *Everyman Out of His Humour* (acted 1599, Quarto 1600):

> *when some one peculiar quality*
> *Doth so possess a man that it doth draw*
> *All his affects, his spirits and his powers*
> *In their confluctions all to run one way,*
> *This may be truly said to be a humour.*

The nearest approach to this method in Shakespeare is in Malvolio, but Jonson used this 'static' type of character with great success to emphasize the weakness and the moral diseases of human nature. His gallery of 'humours' is so extensive that he is in a way the Dickens of the seventeenth century, though without Dickens's sense of buoyant high spirits, or his sentimentality. The corruption of the new wealth, which commerce was giving to the middle classes, affected Jonson deeply enough for him to add bitterness to his comedy.

In four plays his original mind, working within its self-prescribed limitations, achieved outstanding success, and they have been seen on the English stage less often than they deserve: *Volpone*, *The Silent Woman*, *The Alchemist* and *Bartholomew Fair*. Of these, the most perfect in structure and delightful in its treatment is *The Alchemist*, the most brilliant realistic comedy in the whole Elizabethan theatre. Three rogues, Subtle, Face, and Doll, have taken possession of the house of Lovewit who has left London on account of the plague. They pretend that they have magical gifts and play on the greed of a number of rogues in an atmosphere more genial than in some of Jonson's other comedies. *Volpone*, a study of avarice on the heroic scale, has a Rembrandtesque grandeur in colouring, to which none of the other plays attains. So Volpone addresses his gold:

> *Open the shrine that I may see my saint.*
> *Hail the world's soul and mine.*

Bartholomew Fair is the most Dickensian of the plays, a confident picture of Elizabethan 'low' life. *The Silent Woman*, in lighter mood, approaches the comedy of manners which was to delight Restoration audiences. In tragedy, Ben Jonson was less successful. *Sejanus* and *Catiline* can claim the pedantic virtue of being an attempt to write Senecan drama in English; they have the spurious virtue that they attempt to keep to history. It is not enough; the verses will not move. As Tennyson said, they are like glue, and the characters will not come to life. In comedy Jonson's genius is found at its best, and his influence was considerable. The Restoration dramatists leaned strongly upon him. It is only to be regretted that from the eighteenth century the idolatry of Shakespeare has deprived Jonson of the place which should be his upon the English stage. Apart from his plays Jonson excelled in the production of courtly masques. In 1605 he prepared the *Masque of Blackness* for which Inigo Jones did the designs, and in which the Queen and her ladies appeared. In addition he made a notable contribution in non-dramatic verse, both in the lyric and the ode. He also wrote criticism, and though he made reference to Shakespeare's seemingly unlearned methods and rapid and unrevised writing, he spoke generously of his achievement on his death.

Jonson is at once the clearest personality and the most original of the dramatists of Shakespeare's age. He was also the most learned, unless that claim be challenged by George Chapman (1559–1634), who is more famous for his translation of Homer than for his dramas. Of his life little is known but he had a long and varied career both as a dramatist and a non-dramatic poet. He had early in his career a deep admiration for Homer ('Of all the books extant in all kinds, Homer is the first and last'). He began publication of the *Iliad* in 1598 and concluded it in 1611. There followed his translation of the *Odyssey* (1614–15). The two trans-lations were published together in a great folio volume in 1616. It was a copy of this that Keats read, and discovered that whatever its limitations it was in itself a poem. In drama his most distinctive achievement was in three historical tragedies: *Bussy D'Ambois*, *The Revenge of Bussy D'Ambois* and *The Tragedy of Biron*. He chose French history as his background, though mingling it freely with his own invention, and in the Bussy plays his scene is a contemporary one. In Bussy, he drew the proud character on Marlowe's model, allowing him a bold licence in speech and action as he asserts himself in the French Court.

While the drama of the early seventeenth century has certain common characteristics, it is not difficult to distinguish a number of distinctive types. The element of realism, which Jonson mastered, was pursued by a number of writers. Thomas Dekker (c. 1570–1632) combined it with a genial vein of romantic sentimentality. In *The Shoemaker's Holiday* he gives the happiest pictures of the workmen and apprentices of London, and in Simon Eyre, the shoemaker who became Lord Mayor, he glorifies the workers in whom he delights. Later, in the more profound play of *The Honest Whore*, he added pathos to his sentimentality, and employed his realism in an alert portrayal of character. While Dekker depicted the citizens, Thomas Heywood (c. 1573–1641), notably in *A Woman Killed with Kindness*, adapted tragedy to the sensibilities of the rising middle classes. The values contrast with the heroic standards of Shakespeare's *Othello*; for high tragedy, Heywood substituted sentiment and introspec-tive morality. Frankford allows an impecunious friend Wendoll to stay in his house, and Wendoll seduces his wife and is discovered. In Shakes-pearian tragedy Mrs Frankford would have been put to death. Frankford pities her, puts her to live in seclusion on one of his estates and there she repents and dies in his presence. While the middle classes and the citizens were thus being given fresh and individual treatment, the citizens were, however, not always presented favourably in the drama.

Those who wrote with their eye on the Court watched the manners of the City and the apprentices with a critical eye. Beaumont and Fletcher in *The Knight of the Burning Pestle* used their observation to make a merry game of the credulity of the citizens and of their delight in romantic stories.

John Fletcher (1579–1625) and Francis Beaumont (*c.* 1584–1616) wrote for some years in happy collaboration. As dramatists they have suffered because critics will compare their work with Shakespeare's. Three plays show them at their best: the tragi-comedy *Philaster* and two tragedies, *The Maid's Tragedy* and *A King and No King*. The world they depict is removed from the ordinary world which men know. Upon the background of an artificial courtly life they portray exaggerated passions, often corrupt and unnatural, high flown sentiments and honour coded into elaborate formularies. The plots which carry the burden of their devices are elaborate, but invented with great ingenuity, and admirably conducted. The verse, too, has a softness and grace which is pleasing, and in the scenes of strong emotion it rises in strength.

Beaumont and Fletcher failed to give tragedy the normality which Shakespeare retained. Nor were they alone in thus limiting its range. The first forty years of the seventeenth century produced a number of examples of tragedy conceived in some extravagant and unreal world, or developed with a disregard for the motives of good and evil, or, indeed, in defiance of the moral order of being. The most profound of these tragic writers is John Webster (*c.* 1580–1625), who is remembered for two plays, *The White Devil* and *The Duchess of Malfi*. Both plays depend on the 'revenge' theme, which was already popular when Shakespeare wrote *Hamlet*, and continued in favour throughout these decades. Webster succeeds in building a world around his plots, but it is the sinister world of Renaissance Italy, where cunning is the equivalent of good, and intrigue, contrived with the most ingenious devices, elevated into a fine art. At first sight his plays seem mere melodrama, where horror is exploited and violence displayed. It is true that he troubles little to construct his plots. He is content to concentrate on theatrically effective scenes, and is careless whether the scaffolding holding them together is clumsy or too obvious. Yet when these two plays are read, or seen in the theatre, it is soon apparent that they are more than melodrama. Behind this world of theatrical violence, Webster, with a poet's mind, sees life itself as pitiless, cruel and corrupt, and this elevates his violence into vision.

Cyril Tourneur (1575–1626) in *The Revenger's Tragedy* and *The Atheist's Tragedy* drew a world more abnormal than that of Webster. In *The Revenger's Tragedy* he depicts a Court governed by lechery and cruelty. So corrupt are the characters that they seem symbols of the vices rather than human figures. These unnatural puppets he moves with the precision of a master of some macabre ballet, and this certainty of theatrical intention gives an intensity to the whole action. Like Webster, he is a poet, and the verse, by its imagery, suggests a world where, beneath the light of the torches, one can see the sinister faces, the monstrous intrigues, the scenes of horror and the lurking figure of the Revenger.

While Webster and Tourneur can best be remembered for one type of play, there are some dramatists of this period who are versatile in a bewildering way. Many of them worked in collaboration, and it is difficult to assign any exact responsibility for authorship. Such problems occur in considering Thomas Middleton (*c.* 1570–1627), who wrote comedies, including the uproarious *A Chaste Maid in Cheapside*, and tragedies. Outstanding is *The Changeling*, a play in which he collaborated with William Rowley. This tragedy seems a compound of Shakespeare and Webster: its theme is romantic and its characters evil, but around the central figure of Beatrice, despite the fact that she has instigated a murder, the more human values of Shakespeare are retained. She is forced by her passion to place herself in the power of a vicious and merciless lover, De Flores, and her horror and loneliness, despite her crime, arouse pity in the audience.

Philip Massinger (1583–1640) shared much of the versatility of Middleton. Yet, so far as the history of the stage is concerned, his foremost success was a comedy, entitled *A New Way to Pay Old Debts*. Here, in Sir Giles Overreach, he portrays a miser who combines miserliness with cruelty and a love of power. Massinger shares Jonson's power of showing human nature as diseased, but in the severity of the satire Massinger exceeds Jonson.

A scene from Ben Jonson's *The Alchemist* with David Garrick as Abel Drugger

AN
ORDINANCE
OF BOTH HOVSES
OF
PARLIAMENT,

For the fuppreffing of Publike Stage-Playes throughout the Kingdome, during thefe Calamitous Times.

Hereas the diftreffed Eftate of Ireland, fteeped in her own Blood, and the diftra{{Cted}} Eftate of England, threatned with a Cloud of Blood, by a Civill Warre; call for all poffible meanes to appeafe and avert the Wrath of God appearing in thefe Iudgements: Amongft which, Fafting and Prayer having bin often tryed to be very effectuall, have bin lately, and are ftill enjoyned: And whereas publike Sports doe not well agree with publike Calamities, nor publike Stage-Playes with the Seafons of Humiliation, this being an Exercife of fad and pious Solemnity, and the other being Spectacles of Pleafure, too commonly expreffing lacivious Mirth and levitie: It is therfore thought fit, and Ordeined by the Lords and Commons in this Parliament Affembled, that while thefe fad Caufes and fet times of Humiliation doe continue, publike Stage-playes fhall ceafe, and bee forborne. Inftead of which, are recommended to the people of this Land, the profitable and feafonable Confiderations of Repentance, Reconciliation, and peace with God, which probably may produce outward peace and profperity, and bring againe Times of Joy and Gladneffe to thefe Nations.

Die Veneris, Septemb. *the* 2. 1642.

ORdered by the Lords and Commons Affembled in Parliament, that this Ordinance concerning Stage-Playes be forthwith Printed and Publifhed.

John Browne Cler. Parliament.

Septemb.3.   London printed for Iohn Wright.   1642.

The ordinance for the Suppression of the Theatres, passed by Parliament in September 1642. The theatres remained officially closed until the Restoration of Charles II in 1660, but entertainment had continued in 'private places'

In the years before the theatres were officially closed by the Puritans in 1642, there was little new development in the drama. Rather it would seem that the old themes were being played again, though with added excesses. Compared with Dekker or Shakespeare or Jonson, the drama of those later years is decadent. It insists upon unnatural passions, intricate crimes and devices of horror. It can be redeemed only when it is handled by a poet, and the remarkable feature of the whole drama of that period is the excellence of the poetry which was at its service. So did John Ford (1586–1639) in 'Tis Pity She's a Whore and The Broken Heart employ poetry to bring pathos and a tender feeling to plays whose themes dwell amid incest, horrors and perversities.

Similarly James Shirley (1596–1666), as he touched again many of the types of drama that had preceded him, brought verse to endow them with a brightness which they would not otherwise have possessed.

With the Civil Wars the greatest period in English drama came to a close. Nothing was the same again in England after that conflict, and the drama never again had the same brilliance, or the same contact with the whole of the national life. When this drama began with Marlowe, men were near enough to the Middle Ages to be touched by the living terrors of sin and death, and near enough to the Renaissance to feel its magnificence, and the new and perilous adventures which were indicated to the spirit of man. If magnificence were to survive, it had to dwell apart, removed from life. It had existed as a wraith in the masques of the Stuart Courts, for Charles I, whatever his weaknesses, had enjoyed and encouraged the arts. The masque was a dramatic artifice in which poet and stage designer met to make an entertainment with dances, music and elaborate scenic devices. The court was fortunate that for the words of the masque it could call on poets such as Jonson, Chapman and Carew, and for the design upon a great architect such as Inigo Jones. The scenic elaboration of the masque had its effect on legitimate drama, as can be seen in Shakespeare's Tempest. But in the seventeenth century the vision of the dramatist did not keep pace with the mechanical devices at his disposal. The national spirit in the drama had disintegrated, and, though much that is brilliant is to follow, the old way could never return.

When Charles II came back with the Restoration of 1660 the theatres were reopened. Actually the break between 1642 and 1660 was not complete, for entertainments of one kind or another had continued. The main link between the periods was Sir William Davenant (1606–68), son of a vintner of Oxford and some would say Shakespeare's godson. In the earlier Jacobean age he had seen active service, and Charles I had made him laureate in succession to Ben Jonson. As early as 1656 he was organizing entertainments in 'private places' but after May 1660 all subterfuge over performances became unnecessary. With the reopening of the theatres the older writers were not forgotten: Jonson's plays reappeared on the Restoration stage; Shakespeare was no less a favourite, though his plays were modernized to meet the fashions of the day. Spiritually the change was profound. The Restoration was not only the period of Charles's Court, but the age of Bunyan, of the Royal Society and the philosophy of Locke. Drama did not represent the whole of the age, for it became only an entertainment of the Court, and those that aped its fashions. It answered only to one side of men's needs. Samuel Pepys was a very regular playgoer, and much that Pepys saw upon the stage he practised himself outside, when opportunity arose; but Pepys, the founder of the Navy, could not have discovered in that theatre anything to answer the deeper and more creative part of his nature.

It was in comedy that the Restoration found its peculiar excellence. The comedies of that period were many and varied, but it was in the work of three writers, Etherege, Wycherley and Congreve, that the one distinctive type, the comedy of manners, was evolved. Sir George Etherege (1635–91), after earlier and less successful attempts, first discovered the formula in *The Man of Mode*. In a comedy absolved from all obligation to portray a moral world, and from which romantic elements were excluded, he gave a witty portrayal of elegant ladies and gentlemen of the day in their conversation and their amorous intrigues.

The more powerful mind of William Wycherley (1640–1716) penetrated deeper into the world which Etherege had displayed. He presents the same elegant, immoral scene, but he portrays it with mockery and satire. He has a more virile and boisterous nature than any other writer of the period, and a greater restlessness. With four plays he holds a permanent place on the English stage: in *Love in a Wood* (1671) and *The Gentleman Dancing-master* (1672) he is still experimenting, but *The Country Wife* (1672–3) and *The Plain Dealer* (1674) show him fully in possession of his powers. He had studied his world closely, and Jonson's mode had taught him to depict character in strong and vivid colours. He was also influenced by Molière. *The Plain Dealer*, for instance, owes much to Molière's *Le Misanthrope*, though his central character Manly, 'an unmannerly sea-dog', has not the delicacy of Molière's Alceste. The intrigue, the gaiety, the foibles, all these he conveyed, though one is conscious, amid the laughter, of his contempt. His satire is founded not on moral scruples, but on his cynical mockery of the human puppets who pursue their pleasures and find them so illusory.

William Congreve (1670–1729), the most elegant of the trio, drew back from the depths which Wycherley had exposed and returned to the surface gaiety of Etherege. At the same time he conducted his comedies with a brilliance of dialogue which Etherege had never achieved. He had made his reputation suddenly and easily at the age of twenty-five with *The Old Bachelor* (1693). Three comedies followed: *The Double Dealer* (1694), *Love for Love* (1695) and *The Way of the World* (1700). With these he wrote one tragedy, *The Mourning Bride* (1697), before at the age of thirty he turned his back upon the stage.

THE

Plain Dealer,

A

COMEDY,

As it is Acted

At the THEATRE ROYAL.

Written by Mr. WYCHERLEY.

———Ridiculum acri
Fortius & melius magnas plerumque secat res.
HORAT.

LONDON:

Printed for W. FEALES, at Rowe's Head, against St. Clement's Church in the Strand; R. WELLINGTON, at the Dolphin and Crown, and C. CORBETT, at Addison's Head, both without Temple-Bar; J. BRINDLEY, at the King's Arms in New Bond-street; A. BETTESWORTH, and F. CLAY, in Trust for B. WELLINGTON.

MDCCXXXV.

Arnold Vanhaecken delin   Giles King sculpsit

The frontispiece to the 1735 edition of William Wycherley's *The Plain Dealer*. Wycherley's comedies mocked and satirized the genial elegance of Restoration society

His greatness as a dramatist lies in the completeness of his vision. It is the vision of a very shallow world, but he has an exquisite accuracy in depicting its values. The triumph in his world is not of good over evil, but of the elegant over the inelegant, of the witty over the dull, of the graceful over the boorish. Sentiment is never allowed to intrude, nor morality, in an assembly where the right artifice in manners, fashion and conversation gives the only passage to success. This he portrays admirably in the spontaneous humour of that adroitly constructed comedy, *Love for Love*. With greater deliberation he achieved a more subtle effect in *The Way of the World*, where in Millamant he made one of the great comic figures of the English stage.

The brilliant indecencies of Restoration comedy did not pass without criticism. Jeremy Collier (1658–1726), in the *Short View of the Immorality and Profaneness of the English Stage*, brought the weight of the Church and middle-class society to bear against drama, in an elaborate and scholarly indictment. It cannot be said that any immediate improvement is apparent, though gradually, in the eighteenth century, middle-class morality has an increasing hold on drama. Before this calamity, Sir John Vanbrugh wrote *The Relapse* (1696), in which it would be difficult to find any concession to Collier, unless it is in the few touches of sentimentality. Vanbrugh was an astonishing personality, who apart from his successes in the theatre was the baroque architect who designed Castle Howard, his own Haymarket Theatre and Blenheim Palace. In 1706 George Farquhar produced *The Recruiting Officer* which extracted comedy from the processes of recruiting in a country town. This was followed in 1707 by *The Beaux' Stratagem*, which in a way is a link between the manners comedy and the broader world of the eighteenth-century novel.

Nothing in Restoration drama matches the comedy. The 'heroic drama' of that age is now remembered only in the text-books of literature. In this strange form the motives of love and honour were exaggerated to incredible lengths, and the characters were given grandiose and ranting speeches, which they declaimed in regular heroic couplets. The psychologist may find these plays interesting, for they suggest that an audience whose life was governed by cynicism found some relief in this dream-world picture of a fantastic conception of honour. The one notable thing about the heroic drama is that Dryden devoted his great talents to it. Of this kind his best play was his *Aurengzebe* (1675). Much of his prose, which began in 1668 with *An Essay of Dramatic Poesy*, was concerned with the heroic play, and it is to be regretted that such an admirable writer was restrained by such a poor subject. The heroic play was too bizarre a fashion to live long. Dryden in *All for Love*, re-telling the Shakespearian story of Antony and Cleopatra, had given up the rhyming absurdities of the heroic play for a closely presented action in blank verse. With even greater success, Thomas Otway returned to the Elizabethan manner in *The Orphan* (1680) and in *Venice Preserved* (1682). Dryden's contribution to the 'heroic drama' was among the least of his achievements. Elsewhere in this volume will be found an assessment of all he achieved as a non-dramatic poet and a critic. It may be recalled that apart from 'heroic dramas' he wrote comedies. They were not his most spontaneous productions but in them are embedded some of his most delightful lyrics.

The drama of the eighteenth century does not reach the same high level as the novel. One has to wait late in the century, for Goldsmith and Sheridan, to find writers who make any permanent contribution to the English stage, and even then there is nothing to equal *Tom Jones* or *Tristram Shandy*. Of a number of reasons which might be invented in explanation it is at least certain that the Licensing Act of 1737 restricted the freedom of expression by dramatists and drove a number of good men out of the theatre. Henry Fielding had been a dramatist before that date, and without Robert Walpole and the Licensing Act his more mature genius might have gone into the theatre instead of the novel. The theatre was hampered by the restrictions of censorship from 1737 until the abolition of theatre censorship in 1968. If the century can make no claim to dramatic supremacy, it posseses two names pre-eminent in our acting tradition. The art of the actor is pathetically ephemeral, and he is in danger of being forgotten as soon as the applause has died away after his last exit, but despite this the names of Garrick and Mrs Siddons have become a permanent part of the English tradition. In the same way in the early nineteenth century Edmund Kean as an actor is far greater than any dramatist of the period.

Outstanding in the early decades of the century is John Gay's *The Beggar's Opera* (1728). The permanent appeal of the lyrics of Macheath the highwayman, of Polly and of the whole of this 'Newgate pastoral', has remained to the present day, but it had an added piquancy to audiences who could detect within it a satire on Walpole. *The Beggar's Opera* was imitated by Gay and by others, but it has no parallel.

The genuine intrusion of middle-class values into the drama comes with George Lillo (1693–1739), whose *The London Merchant or The History of George Barnwell*, produced in 1731, depicts the life of an apprentice with all the seriousness which in the earlier drama had been restricted to those of rank.

A scene from Gay's *The Beggar's Opera*, by William Hogarth. Polly pleads for the Highwayman's life

Forgive us then, if we attempt to show
In artless strains, a tale of private woe,
A London 'Prentice ruin'd is our theme.

The play, with its moral emphasis and its melodramatic theme, made a wide and immediate appeal.

The depths of sentimentalism were reached by dramatists such as Hugh Kelly and Richard Cumberland. The curious can turn to such a play as Cumberland's *The West Indian* (1771) to find how every human issue can be obscured in the welter of emotion. From such depths the drama was rescued by Goldsmith and Sheridan. Oliver Goldsmith (1728–74) might have been one of the greatest figures of our literature, if he had only taken more pains. His early play *The Good-Natured Man* (1768) reads feebly now, though its intentions of mocking the excesses of false charity are obvious. *She Stoops to Conquer* (1773) has preserved its place on the stage, and particularly on the amateur stage, until the present day. In a way it is the great example of comedy of amateur genius in the language. It goes back to the atmosphere of Farquhar's *Beaux' Stratagem*, and brings back a breath of genuine humanity to a drama stifled with excessive emotions. Far more distinction attaches to the comedy of Richard Brinsley Sheridan (1751–1816), who in his extraordinary career was at one time Under-Secretary for Foreign Affairs and Secretary to the

The stage at the Theatre Royal, Drury Lane, on the opening night of Sheridan's *The School for Scandal*, 8 May 1777

Treasury. Unfortunately he was early distracted from his career as a dramatist, so that his fame depends on three comedies, *The Rivals* (1775), *The School for Scandal* (1777) and *The Critic* (1779). With Sheridan something of the brilliance of Restoration dialogue returned into comedy, though without the narrow and immoral Restoration world. Instead, a more genial and romantic atmosphere is created, as if some memories of Shakespeare were descending into eighteenth-century Bath. The characters are firmly presented, with clarity reminiscent of Jonson, though the atmosphere in Sheridan is gayer. Some concessions to sentimentalism he felt bound to make but the ironic spectator need not take them too seriously. There is no depth in Sheridan's world, no new interpretation of human nature. In this he is nearer to Wilde than to Jonson. *The Rivals* shows an ease and mastery which in a first play is almost incredible. Already in *The School for Scandal* he has improved on this brilliant beginning, both in the balance of the action and the technical perfection of the scenes. The main memory from his plays is of the verbal dexterity and the laughter which his well-planned scenes can create.

The first production of George Bernard Shaw's *Back to Methuselah*, at Birmingham in 1923

Chapter 9

English Drama from Sheridan

THE DRAMA of the early nineteenth century was on the whole deplorable. While poetry and fiction were drawing upon the genius of the romantics, the theatre was the home mainly of irregular spectacle, melodrama and farce. Even the revivals of the more creditable drama of earlier ages were presented with but little taste or understanding. Most of the romantic poets attempted drama, but with little success. The one outstanding exception was, surprisingly, Shelley's *The Cenci* (1819), though the theme of incest made the play impossible for the stage. A number of reasons have been assigned to this decay of drama. A simple external reason can be found in the monopoly held by the two houses, Covent Garden and Drury Lane, for the performance of serious drama. They had become too large for the subtle effects of the actor's art, and the managers had been led to numerous expedients to maintain solvency. The Act of 1843 for regulating the theatre removed the monopoly and allowed the smaller theatres to produce drama equally with the two patent houses. As a result, in the sixties, a number of new theatres were built in London.

The decline of the drama cannot be assigned to any single cause. The prosperous middle-class society had no genuine appreciation of drama as an art, and the actor, with a few notable exceptions, remained a member of a profession without honour. The home was the centre of early Victorian life, and in the home the novel was the universally favoured form of literature. Dickens, who had talents as an actor, would in another age have exercised them in the theatre. As it was he had to content himself with the concoction of amateur performances and recitals.

The danger in the nineteenth-century theatre was, above all, that it was unrelated to the life of the time. The changes in the structure of society had so modified the human personality itself that a new interpretation was essential. In England, in the nineteenth century, the most valiant attempt to bring the drama closer to life is found in the work of T. W. Robertson (1829–71). He had begun writing as early as 1845 but there was little to distinguish his work from that of his contemporaries

A drawing of Nora's Tarantella from Act Two of Ibsen's *The Doll's House.* Ibsen dealt with social problems, like the emancipation of women, with a sensitivity that was unknown on the English stage at the time

until he produced *David Garrick* (1864), based on one of his own novels. The play, which has elements of realism, was popular and is still occasionally revived. He was encouraged to give a fuller scope to his intentions and in 1867 he produced *Caste*, for which he is best remembered. When read today the play seems crude and vulgar, with sentimentality and melodrama corrupting the vision of comedy, but, on the stage, the whole comes to life, the characters live, the action seems real, and often very moving. First produced in 1867, *Caste* was a great advance, though when it is remembered that Ibsen wrote *Peer Gynt* the same year one is reminded of the danger of confusing talent with genius.

Much has been written of the influence of Ibsen on the English drama, but apart from G. B. Shaw it is difficult to find anyone deeply affected by the great Norwegian. His work towers over all that the English stage has produced in the modern period: with his poetic plays, *Brand* and *Peer Gynt*, we have nothing even to offer in comparison, while his social and psychological dramas from *The Doll's House, Ghosts* and *An Enemy of the People* to *When We Dead Awaken* are far more subtle in stagecraft, and profound in thought, than anything in the modern English theatre.

The descent from Ibsen to Henry Arthur Jones (1851–1929) and Sir A.W. Pinero (1855–1934) is steep. Both combined a keen estimate of what would constitute a commercial success with a desire to give their audience the deeper effects which they knew drama could achieve. It is true that Jones's most popular play was a melodrama, *The Silver King*, but he did attempt 'problem' themes in such plays as *Saints and Sinners* and *Mrs Dane's Defence*. Compared with Ibsen, these are the work of an amateur cobbler who has never mastered his tools. Pinero, generally a more attractive and able figure, was far more adroit in handling the mechanism of the stage, though, again, compared with Ibsen, he is a bungler. He attempts to deal with real situations, though most of them have an odd air of theatricality. His best-known play, and one of the most effective, is the once notorious *The Second Mrs Tanqueray* (1893), which treats of the marriage of 'a woman with a past'. The return of intelligence to the theatre can be seen more clearly in the comic operas of Gilbert and Sullivan. Their work seems to prepare the audience for the comedy of Oscar Wilde and G. B. Shaw. Wilde (1854–1900) had been ridiculed by Gilbert in *Patience*, but as a writer of comedy he shared with Gilbert a verbal wit which had been dead on the English stage since Sheridan. His imprisonment, in 1895, for homosexual practices, was a disaster to the theatre. In four comedies, *Lady Windermere's Fan* (1892), *A Woman of No Importance* (1893), *An Ideal Husband* (1895) and *The Importance of Being Earnest* (1895), he had shown not only his own brilliance but the rapidity with which he was progressing in his art. In addition the versatility of his talent was shown by *Salomé*, his play in French, published in 1894. His earliest comedies were enmeshed in melodrama, but from this he was working his way out to *The Importance of Being Earnest*, which is compact with a light, comic artifice in the very spirit of Congreve. There are few more superb passages of sheer comedy than when Lady Bracknell questions John Worthing to see if he is worthy of the hand of her daughter. She has discovered, approvingly, that he has a town house, a country estate, and ample investments. Things become a little more difficult when he confesses that he has lost both his parents. 'Both?' says Lady Bracknell. 'That seems like careless-ness!' Finally he has to confess that he was 'Found'.

> JACK: The late Mr Thomas Cardew, an old gentleman of a very charitable and kindly disposition, found me and gave me the name of Worthing, because he happened to have a first-class ticket for Worthing in his pocket at the time. Worthing is a place in Sussex.
> LADY BRACKNELL: Where did the charitable gentleman who had a first-class ticket for this seaside resort find you?
> JACK: [*gravely*] In a handbag.
> LADY BRACKNELL: A handbag?
> JACK: [*very seriously*] Yes, Lady Bracknell, I was in a handbag – a somewhat large, black leather handbag, with handles to it – an ordinary handbag in fact.
> LADY BRACKNELL: In what locality did this . . . Mr Thomas Cardew come across this ordinary handbag?
> JACK: In the cloak-room at Victoria Station. It was given to him in mistake for his own.
> LADY BRACKNELL: The cloak-room at Victoria Station?
> JACK: Yes. The Brighton line.
> LADY BRACKNELL: The line is immaterial.

The twentieth century showed a talent in the drama with which the nineteenth century could not compete. H. Granville-Barker and Vedrenne produced seasons of plays at the Court Theatre, which brought an enlightenment into production and a discipline into acting. Harley

Granville-Barker (1877–1946) was himself a dramatist, who explored contemporary problems with a brave and unyielding realism. That he had a romantic element appeared in the very early play, *The Marrying of Ann Leete* which he had completed as early as 1899, and again much later, and more obviously, in *Prunella*, where he collaborated with Laurence Housman. The distinctive quality comes through in the realistic tragedies. *The Voysey Inheritance* (1905) shows a young lawyer carrying on his father's frauds to save the family reputation. *Waste* (1907), which proved unacceptable to the Censor, deals with the death through an illegal operation of the mistress of a promising young politician. *The Madras House* (1909), the most successful of his plays, portrays the thwarted lives of women at the beginning of the century.

John Galsworthy (1867–1933), who was actually a better artist as a novelist than as a dramatist, also based his plays on social and contemporary problems. His success with audiences in the theatre began with *The Silver Box*, performed in 1906, the year of the publication of *The Man of Property*, the first of his Forsyte series. There followed *Strife* (1909) and *Justice* (1910) and his success continued in his later plays, including *Loyalties* (1922). He seems sometimes to have formulated his selected social problem rather blatantly and his characterization is simple, while the theme is pressed home with a heavy emphasis. Though his plays are well constructed, the mechanism tends to remain apparent. His sense of pity was controlled usually by his intelligence, but it was always in danger of becoming excessive. *The Forsyte Saga*, first through radio readings and later by television dramatization has given him a popularity unparalleled by any of his contemporaries and the National Theatre showed his *Strife* topically and successfully in 1979. St John Ervine in his earlier plays, notably in *Jane Clegg* (1911) and *John Ferguson* (1915), continued the realistic tradition with great sincerity and with less obvious intentions. Further, John Masefield, in *The Tragedy of Nan* (1908), gave a poetic quality to domestic realism which is reminiscent of seventeenth-century drama.

St John Ervine worked with Irish dramatists whose work was produced in the Abbey Theatre in Dublin. One of its originators was Lady Gregory, herself a dramatist. W. B. Yeats (1865–1939) brought his poetical gift to the service of the movement, and though he remained a lyrical writer rather than a dramatist, in *The Countess Cathleen* (1892) and *The Land of Heart's Desire* (1894) he evoked the mysticism and folk-lore of the Irish imagination. Greater as a dramatist was John Millington Synge (1871–1909), who had travelled widely on the Continent before he was encouraged by Yeats to seek in the Aran Islands the rhythms of a simple and unadulterated language for drama. In *The Playboy of the Western World* (1907) he gave a comic interpretation of Irish character, governed by a deep, even poetical, understanding. In tragedy, his short play, *Riders to the Sea*, in which a mother acknowledges the dark power of the fate that will destroy her last son, had a Greek quality, combined with a simplicity befitting its peasant setting. *Deirdre of the Sorrows*, the play upon which he was working at his death, shows what a loss was suffered when he died before he was forty. That the Irish drama did not die with Synge can be seen in the work of Sean O'Casey (1880–1964). His background was very different from Yeats's aristocratic associations. As a child, he lived in the sordidness of the Dublin slums; he knew Jim Larkin the labour agitator and he involved himself in the Irish Citizen Army. In 1923 *The Shadow of a Gunman* was produced in the Abbey Theatre at Dublin: it showed O'Casey's originality, comedy mixed with tragedy and a vocabulary where the language of the Dublin slums mingles with that of Shakespeare. *Juno and the Paycock* appeared in 1924. In 1926 *The Plough and the Stars* led to a riot at the Abbey, for O'Casey could see not only the tragedy of the Dublin tenements but the self-seeking of those who exploited rebellions. When in 1928 the Abbey Theatre rejected his *The Silver Tassie*, which had an uneven brilliance, he settled in England. There followed intermittent successes, outstandingly *Red Roses for Me* (1946), but the exile did not write as convincingly as the Dubliner.

English drama was not confined to the social realism of Granville-

Sarah Allgood as Juno Boyle in the first production in London of Sean O'Casey's *Juno and the Paycock*. This kind of realism was inimical to the sentimental fantasy of the playwright J. M. Barrie, who created a legend with his play *Peter Pan*. Right: Barrie, shown with characters from his play, by Arthur Rackham

Barker and Galsworthy. The fashion is to despise Sir James Barrie (1860–1937), but it is dangerous to dismiss one who invented a mythology in a play of permanent popularity. This Barrie did in *Peter Pan* (1904). His sentimental phantasy becomes less acceptable when extended to ordinary life, but this need not disguise the craftsmanship of plays such as *The Admirable Crichton* (1902) and *Dear Brutus* (1917). Somerset Maugham, already successful as a short-story writer and novelist, captured the stage in 1919 with two sophisticated comedies, *Caesar's Wife* and *Home and Beauty*, where cynicism and commentary mingled. Many comedies followed, among them *The Circle* (1921), the most finished and mature, which has a Restoration style, and *Our Betters* (1923), showing how heartless and degenerate was the world he portrayed.

All this must take second place to the achievement of George Bernard Shaw (1856–1950). His career was the longest in English dramatic history; beginning with *Widowers' Houses* in 1892 it continued to 1939 with *In Good King Charles's Golden Days*, while ten years later in 1949, when he was ninety-three, *Buoyant Billions* was performed at the Malvern Festival, so closely connected with his name and work. Shaw first entered the theatre as a dramatic critic, and the volumes of *Our Theatre in the Nineties* show his brilliant commentary. He alone had understood the greatness of Ibsen, and he was determined that his own plays should also be a vehicle for ideas. His temperament had nothing of Ibsen's grimness. If he saw, with unusual clarity, the ills of the world, he possessed an inalienable Irish capacity for jest and a verbal wit equal to that of Congreve or Wilde. The combination of wide social enthusiasms with a gift for comedy was, to say the least, unusual, and it is thus that Shaw's plays have a quality all their own.

William Archer has described Shaw, as a young man, sitting in the British Museum Reading Room, with Marx's *Das Kapital* and the score of *Tristan und Isolde* set out before him. The picture is not an unfair image of his work. If he had Socialism, the Fabian Society, sex, ethics, religion as themes crowding up for admission into his plays, he had also a genuine artistic gift for form. He was impatient of clumsy workmanship, though for him mechanical perfection is not enough: to compare his comedies with those of Jones or Pinero is to realize at once his advance in construction, and in the management of his characters. His originality had tended to obscure these more ordinary virtues, but his own essays show how closely he had studied every detail of theatrical workmanship. In the early plays the originality lay largely in the conception of character. He would take a conventional stage type, reverse it, and then prove that the reversal was the truth. Thus, in *Arms and the Man*, for the romantic stage soldier he substitutes the mercenary, who knows fear and hunger; in *Mrs Warren's Profession* he replaces the romantic courtesan with the woman who is conducting the profitable, but unpleasant, trade of prostitution.

This reversal of the ordinary conception of character has remained the most consistent feature of his satirical comedy, and he has employed it in plays from *Caesar and Cleopatra* to *St Joan*. It gave his drama a vague classical quality, akin to the 'humours' characterization of Jonson.

He had, from the first, accepted a burden in his dramas, beyond the presentation of plot and character. He had signed a contract with himself, and with the spirit of Ibsen, that each play should present a problem and discuss it thoroughly. Character, thus, never comes first in his plays, and, among the early comedies, in *Candida* (1895) alone, where he follows Ibsen in championing woman's freedom, does he show a character who is memorable apart from the sentiments she has to convey. Aristotle gave plot an importance in drama before characterization, and so does Shaw, but for a different reason. His fable must be so chosen that it will allow him to discuss the theme he has set himself. Some critics suggest that his plays have no plot. If so, he was cleverer even than he was reported to be. Actually, the conception of plot varies from one play to another. Sometimes he approaches the ordinary story plot, as in *The Devil's Disciple* or in *St Joan*, but occasionally he reduces the story to a minimum as in *Getting Married*. Probably the most acceptable plays of the middle period were those in which he discovered a balance between the two methods, as in *Major Barbara*, *The Shewing-Up of Blanco Posnet* or *John*

Sybil Thorndike in the title role of the first production of Shaw's *St Joan*, in 1924

Bull's Other Island. Though he used his plays for discussion, he accompanied them with prefaces in which he explored the themes more fully. In some instances, as, for example, *Androcles and the Lion*, with its prefatory essay on Christianity, the major burden of the discussion has been left to the preface. On the whole, the later plays of the post-war period, *Heartbreak House* (1920), *The Apple Cart* (1929), *Too True to Be Good* (1932), *The Millionairess* (1936) and *Geneva* (1938), showed an increase of discussion, with very great skill in using a pattern of plot to keep the talk in sound dramatic order. Of these plays *Heartbreak House* has had the most continuing success on the stage. It marked Shaw's return to the theatre after the First World War. It is his portrait, influenced by Chekhov's *The Cherry Orchard*, of how England drifted into the First World War.

It is difficult to gain any just perspective in estimating a great and, for many, still a contemporary figure. Whether Shaw survives or not is a matter for posterity. Despite great changes in taste in the theatre his plays still hold the stage. The brilliant philosophical comedy of *Man and Superman* has already lost something of its first dazzling freshness, and the same is true of *Back to Methuselah*. Neither has the same survival value as *Pygmalion*, in which Shaw gives a human and modern variation of the old fairy-tale theme, of the poor little girl who is transformed into a lady. It would be interesting to know whether he would have agreed for *Pygmalion* to be transformed into the 'musical' of *My Fair Lady*: he would certainly have been interested in the fortune which under his will this production brought to the Royal Academy of Dramatic Art, to the British Museum and to the National Gallery at Dublin.

The thirties were marked by an enterprising development in verse drama, which succeeded in the theatre. As early as 1924 T. S. Eliot (1888–1965) drafted a play about Sweeney, and the fragments were united in *Sweeney Agonistes* (1932). From *Prufrock* to *The Waste Land* his verse had dramatic intuitions, but after *Sweeney Agonistes* he was interested in the theatre and this became a preoccupation for over thirty years. For a pageant play, *The Rock* (1934), he composed only a scene and choruses, but audiences attracted him and he was fortunate in finding a well-integrated theme for *Murder in the Cathedral* (1935). In the theatre he faced the problem of immediate intelligibility. On this occasion, his audience was integrated, for the play was performed in the Chapter House of Canterbury Cathedral. It remains the most popular of his dramatic works and, while repeating motives of his non-dramatic verse, it was intelligible to audiences who would find his non-dramatic verse difficult. To write a successful play in verse on the Christian theme of the death of Thomas Becket was an achievement; Eliot was tempted towards the drama, almost as Tennyson was tempted towards the long poem and the *Idylls*.

Of his later plays the first, *The Family Reunion* (1939), owed something to the story of Orestes pursued by the Furies, though Eliot transformed the values with the Christian concept of redemption, repeating some of the motives of his poem, 'Burnt Norton'. There followed a gap of ten years after which he made a deliberate attempt to capture the audiences in the commercial theatre: *The Cocktail Party* (1949), *The Confidential Clerk* (1954) and *The Elder Statesman* (1959). Much was abandoned. For instance, *The Cocktail Party* no longer employed the chorus, apart from one chant; the verse was simplified and its rhythms so disguised that sometimes they seemed near to prose. He attempted to expose the spiritual vacuity and defeatism of post-war society and showed how the Christian life was to be lived either by ordinary people in a routine life or by saints in martyrdom. Despite its gloom the play had a dramatic adroitness that carried contemporary audiences. If *The Cocktail Party* was superficially a comedy of manners, *The Confidential Clerk* went back to the old theme of mistaken identity, while *The Elder Statesman* had many elements of melodrama. This was a lively intrusion into the commercial theatre, but only in *Murder in the Cathedral* is there a play that will be regularly enjoyed by ordinary theatregoers.

Eliot was not alone in this revival of verse drama. W. H. Auden, collaborating with Christopher Isherwood, had followed *The Dog Beneath the Skin* (1935) with *The Ascent of F6* (1936) and *On the Frontier* (1938). These plays were performed mainly to special audiences. They confirmed the ideas and the political agility of Auden's non-dramatic verse, but they made no major impact. *The Ascent of F6* alone had a strong central theme, describing how an expedition was sent to conquer F6, a mountain previously unclimbed. As verse experiments these plays were exciting, for they attempted to release drama from the idle themes of the commercial theatre.

Christopher Fry (b. 1907) achieved success with verse drama in plays which captured London audiences. Performed at various times, they were published as *The Boy with a Cart* (1939), *A Phoenix Too Frequent* (1946), *The Lady's Not for Burning* (1949), *Venus Observed* (1950) and *A Sleep of Prisoners* (1951). At the height of his popularity he was compared with Elizabethan dramatists for brilliance of imagery and felicity of language. He had an individual style, and the verse, with coruscating gestures, gaiety and daring, seemed a welcome contrast to the dull prose of realistic drama. On reflection it became clear that his verbal exuberance was not accompanied by dramatic depth. *The Lady's Not for Burning*, his most popular play, showed Fry's talent in verse and dramatic adroitness. Only those who saw these plays against the thinness of the ordinary dramatic production of the commercial theatre can realize the degree of delight they gave on first appearance.

Among the dramatists of the thirties, who survived to obtain audiences in the post-war period, was the Scot, 'James Bridie' (1885–1959). He had considerable range, using in *Tobias and the Angel* a miracle play theme, while in *The Anatomist* he provided a more realistic setting on a Scottish background with the body-snatching activities of Burke and Hare. In *The Sleeping Clergyman* (1933), one of his most elaborate plays, he dealt with three generations, while *Mr Bolfry*, a play that had much popularity, showed the devil arriving in the Western Highlands dressed as a Minister of the Church of Scotland. In these and other plays he displayed high competence as a dramatist, though perhaps never reaching the degree of originality which was hoped of him.

J. B. Priestley's (b. 1894) contribution to drama, like his contribution to the novel, is likely to be underestimated because of his facility and popularity. Some of his dramatic work, as in *Time and the Conways* and *I Have Been Here Before*, showed his interest in the time theories of Dunne and Ouspensky. In addition he wrote plays of social commentary including *Johnson Over Jordan* (1939), *They Came to a City* (1943), *The Linden Tree* and *An Inspector Calls* (1947). Priestley had identified himself with the movement towards improved social conditions, as demonstrated later in the Welfare State, and discovered a lively method of conveying his themes dramatically. His production was prolific and his plays found wide acceptance, and some of them have a gift of comedy and observation which give an element of permanence to Priestley's contribution.

Little that was effective in drama came from the theme of the First World War, though R. C. Sherriff, until then unknown, had a major success with *Journey's End* (1928), a trench warfare play with an all-male

R. C. Sherriff's play *Journey's End,* produced ten years after the end of the First World War, recalled trench warfare with a successful mixture of realism and sentiment

cast. Clemence Dane in *A Bill of Divorcement* (1921) dealt with war's aftermath and the problem of the law and insanity. Charles Morgan's plays brought to the drama his long study of the theatre as a dramatic critic, and in three plays: *The Flashing Stream* (1938), *The River Line* (1952) and *The Burning Glass* (1953), he displayed himself as an intellectual in the theatre.

It might be urged that the thirties and the forties were a period rather of great actors than of great dramatists. On the stage were John Gielgud, Laurence Olivier, Ralph Richardson, Donald Wolfit and Robert Donat, and, with the end of the war, they gave performances of distinction, mainly in Shakespearian plays. During the war the State had found funds for the arts through C.E.M.A. (Council for the Encouragement of Music and the Arts) and this had been established with a Royal Charter in 1946 as The Arts Council of Great Britain. It supplied resources to the Old Vic Company and others and this led to fine productions of plays from the classical repertory of the English theatre. At the end of the war the theatre at Stratford was developed under the direction of Sir Barry Jackson. As a result, there were almost continuous performances both in Stratford and in London. There was little, though, during these years, of new dramatic work to stretch any of these actors, and it cannot be asserted that the English stage matched the best of what was being produced on the Continent or in America.

It is difficult to know which of the popular writers to include. A most successful entertainer was Noel Coward (1899–1973), who in comedy, *Blithe Spirit* (1941), approached Wilde in verbal felicity. In *Cavalcade*

Noel Coward as Nicky Lancaster in his play *The Vortex*

(1934) he captured contemporary audiences with a national panorama. In his later years, after his knighthood, public esteem obliterated the controversy associated with some parts of his career. A little of the comedy may survive, but ultimately he may be remembered for a few lyrics. Terence Rattigan (b. 1911) began in farce and once extended himself unsuccessfully to deal with Alexander the Great. He found acceptance with *The Browning Version* (1948) and *The Deep Blue Sea* (1952). In *Separate Tables* (1954) Rattigan portrayed a study of lonely and defeated characters in the setting of a contemporary boarding house. The most popular entertainer of all was Agatha Christie (1891–1976) whose play *The Mousetrap* has, in 1979, held the stage for twenty-seven continuous years.

The theatre had suffered with the war and in 1940 Hitler contrived to do what even the Puritans had failed to achieve by closing the London theatres. Only the little Windmill Theatre with a programme of non-stop variety remained open. By 1941, particularly after Germany's attack on the Soviet Union, London had some relief and managements began to consider new plays, but the break in tradition had been formidable. By 1942 London theatre productions were approaching normal, but the public venturing out in the black-out preferred revivals to new plays.

The major theatrical adventure of the post-war years was the establishment of a company at the Royal Court Theatre, which was Vedrenne's old theatre where Shaw had made his early successes. Here the London Theatre Group under George Devine's courageous direction found new English authors and also produced plays in translation. Another independent and lively direction came from Joan Littlewood's Theatre Workshop, which functioned at the Theatre Royal, Stratford in East London.

To the Royal Court Theatre in 1956 came John Osborne's (b. 1929) *Look Back in Anger*, which caught the imagination of a generation. He broke into the theatre with what seemed an authentic picture of a post-war society. Here was a turning point in the modern English theatre. In Jimmy Porter, the angry, almost hysterical, often self-pitying young man who finds society cruel and unjust, and his own world a chaos, many of Osborne's contemporaries seemed to find an image of their own lives. Porter is not merely an orphan of the upheaval of war, he is, or at least sees himself as, a victim of the change in English society. He has been to University, but, without the will or the resources has discovered no profession and is living sordidly with a friend on the proceeds of a sweet-stall. He is married to Alison, whose family belongs to the old Anglo-Indian tradition which has now come to an end. He rages at Alison as if he were to make her the image against which his despair is to be expressed. Yet he is compulsively attached to her and she to him, and in an ending not without sentimentality, they are left together. The world from which the play emerged was fresh to the English stage, the

John Osborne's *Look Back in Anger* with Alan Dobie (left), Jocelyn Britton and
Michael Bryant. This authentic portrayal of post-war England represented a turning
point in the modern English theatre

dialogue brilliant and contemporary, the action dramatically effective.
The mind behind it all was violent, yet poignant and arresting. The
dramatic skill was confirmed by *The Entertainer* (1957) which, showing
Archie Rice, a shabby, flamboyant, self-deceiving character of the decay
of the English music-hall, seemed by some strange symbolism to image
a decay in England itself. Osborne had the good fortune that Laurence
Olivier gave a brilliant interpretation of Archie Rice. Osborne had
written in 1954 *Epitaph for George Dillon*, which was produced at the
Royal Court Theatre in 1957. This was a brilliant play on a realistic
contemporary theme, once again set in the shabbiest lower-middle-class
setting. The dialogue captured all the rhythms, deficiencies and abrupt-
ness of conversation with great dramatic effectiveness. Osborne gave an
image of the sheer dreariness of this type of life and the complete
absence of power of his characters to escape from it. At its centre was

George Dillon himself, rebellious, faithless, who once sought to be an artist and once had a vision of something better than the sordid scene in which now he played a parasitic part. *Luther*, first produced in 1961, showed John Osborne operating in sixteenth-century Germany instead of mid-twentieth-century England and instead of Jimmy Porter and Archie Rice there was the historic but much individualized figure of Martin Luther. Some of the main values remained, but there was a broadened view and the obsessive class hatred was less apparent. In *Luther* Osborne portrayed a sense of physical and spiritual uncertainty, of self-torment, of debasement, the challenge to imperial authority, with an underhand admiration for it, and at the end the break-down into sentiment. Osborne is still an exciting writer, capable of new developments. In *Inadmissible Evidence* (1964) he studied a sex-absorbed solicitor defending himself in a semi-symbolical court, and there is again a freshness of approach in *A Patriot for Me* (1965), a quasi-historical study of a homosexual Austrian officer.

In approaching contemporary work, criticism has to be hesitant. In

A scene from the first production of *Waiting for Godot* by Samuel Beckett. The story of two tramps who wait, with a mixture of hope and despair, for someone who never comes was regarded by some as a profound illumination of a contemporary dilemma

the long tradition of English literature much has been sorted out by the taste of successive generations. Who can say what the end of the century will think of current elements in the theatre? All that can be recorded is that liveliness is there. It arises from a generation facing life in the post-atomic age, disillusioned, at once alert and quick, addicted to sordid scenes and periods of despair. It appeared in Samuel Beckett's (b. 1906) *Waiting for Godot* (1956), by some regarded as a profound illumination of the contemporary dilemma. Beckett, who also achieved success in the novel and the short story, showed his sustaining qualities as a dramatist with *End Game* (1957), *Krapp's Last Tape* (1959) and other plays. Such was his distinction that he was awarded the Nobel Prize for Literature. Tom Stoppard (b. 1932) gained a major reputation for wit and original-ity, beginning with *Rosencrantz and Guildenstern are Dead* (1967) and followed with much success by *Jumpers* (1972) and *Travesties* (1974). More puzzling and yet at times more rewarding, is Harold Pinter (b. 1930) whose reputation began with *The Caretaker* (1950) and con-tinues to *Betrayal* (1979). With an almost sinister quietness, he explores the problems of communication and seeks to reward the audience with answers that are partly concealed.

THE
COVNTESSE
OF ·PEMBROKES
ARCADIA,

WRITTEN BY SIR PHILIPPE
SIDNEI.

SOIT·QVI·MAL·Y·PENSE

HONI

QVO FATA VOCANT

LONDON
Printed for William Ponsonbie.
Anno Domini, 1590.

The title page from Sir Philip Sidney's *Arcadia,* written for his sister, the Countess
of Pembroke. This complex romance of chivalric adventure remained a popular
work until the eighteenth century when the prose narrative developed into the
modern novel

Chapter 10

The English Novel
to Defoe

THE STORY is the most widely distributed form of literature. Epic, ballad, anecdote, romance, they are all stories. At the same time, the novel as we know it today is a late growth and a special form of story-telling: some would place its origins in the eighteenth century with Richardson's *Pamela*. Certainly it cannot, in England, be traced back earlier than the sixteenth century, with Sir Philip Sidney's *Arcadia*, and most modern readers would feel that this work fulfilled few of the requirements of a novel. It is necessary, then, to distinguish the novel from story-telling. The novel is a prose work, while most of the early story-telling was in verse. Chaucer's *Troilus and Criseyde* has many of the features a modern reader would expect in a novel, except that Chaucer writes in verse. Verse returns into popularity from time to time as a method of story-telling. Scott and Byron in their verse romances had the last popular success of this kind; but Scott showed that prose gave possibilities of width and background to the story with which verse cannot compete. Width and background are two ways in which the novelist distinguishes his art from that of the story-teller. He is not only telling a story, but portraying something through the story. Along with the story, the novel gives a portrait of character, or of social background or, in more modern work, records a stream of consciousness. Whatever ambition governs the novelist, he will do well to remember that he began as a story-teller, and this origin he can never altogether escape. Thus the novel can be described as a narrative in prose, based on a story, in which the author may portray character and the life of an age, and analyse sentiments and passions, and the reactions of men and women to their environment. This he may do with a setting either of his own times or of the past. Further, beginning with a setting in ordinary life he may use the novel for fantasy or some portrayal of the supernatural.

Though the novel is a great art, it is also an art which admits of much mediocre talent. The history of the novel is difficult to describe, because the number of novels is so great. Stated generally, the history of the novel shows an increase in complexity and a growing dissatisfaction with the story merely as a story. The different types of novel cannot be easily defined, for they are so many. Probably the most valuable distinction is between the novel which deals with the writer's own age and the novel which uses a historical setting. The former is often realistic, and the latter frequently incorporates adventure of the spectacular kind. This realistic and contemporary novel is slower in its growth historically than the romance, but once it develops it has a great hold on the public imagination. In itself, it has many divisions, almost as many as Polonius's divisions of drama in *Hamlet*: comic in *Pickwick Papers*; sociological in Charles Reade's *Never Too Late to Mend*; philosophical in Meredith's *Diana of the Crossways*.

The other convenient division of the novel is according to form, and here the complexity is no less great. The novelist may tell a story in a straightforward manner, narrating events in their chronological order. Few novelists have been satisfied with this, though some writers, such as Anthony Trollope, seem to gain by ordering the narrative in as simple a way as possible. With some novelists, the form of the narrative holds the attention first, as in Sterne's *Tristram Shandy*, and Sterne is a precursor of the modern novelists who have experimented with form, notably Dorothy Richardson, James Joyce, Virginia Woolf and particularly, though in a diluted way, Anthony Powell in his series of brilliant novels, *A Dance to the Music of Time*. The experiment need not be so extreme as in these writers, nor so deliberate. Thomas Love Peacock and Aldous Huxley have both, in separate but allied ways, departed from plain narrative to make the novel a vehicle for ideas and conversation. In the eighteenth century Samuel Richardson discovered, by accident, that the best way in which he could give his analysis of sentiment in the novel was by letters. One returns here to the realization that the novel is a mixed form. When the novelist uses dialogue and reduces description to a minimum he approaches drama. Jane Austen's *Pride and Prejudice* contains all the essential dialogue for a play on that theme, and so does Meredith's *The Egoist*. At the other extreme, the novel draws towards the essay and the discourse, in such reflective works as Walter Pater's *Marius the Epicurean*.

In the pages that follow, the history of the English novel has been traced through the works which seem to reveal these aspects of its development. The beginning can be made with Sir Philip Sidney (1554–86) at Wilton, the beautiful house of his sister, the Countess of Pembroke, writing *The Countess of Pembroke's Arcadia*, for the purpose of amusing his friends. This is a complex romance, of shipwrecked princes, beautiful princesses, chivalric adventures, with a pastoral setting, an ideal world, the daydream of a courtier. It remained popular until the eighteenth century, and when Richardson, the bourgeois printer, named his serving-maid heroine, he called her 'Pamela', in memory of a character in Sidney's story. A very different work came at the same time from that brilliant young Cambridge man John Lyly (1554–1606), who would be better remembered also as a writer of comedies had not Shakespeare followed him so closely. His *Euphues* (1578) and his *Euphues and his England* reduce story to a minimum, but they are brilliant in the discussion of manners, sentiment and moral reflection. Some of his matter he borrowed from Castiglione's *The Courtier*, an Italian guide-book to gentlemanly behaviour. Lyly dedicated his work to the ladies of England, a prophetic anticipation of the large number of women readers the novel was to possess. A third group of Elizabethan writers, who lived much lower down the social scale, wrote for money, though, as their lives suggest, the payments must have been small, despite all their efforts to follow popular taste. Robert Greene (*c.* 1560–92), dramatist, pamphleteer, poet and bohemian, composed a number of pieces in which he merely popularized the effects of Sidney and Lyly. These included *Pandosto* (1585) which Shakespeare used for *The Winter's Tale*. He also developed a manner of his own in describing the 'low' life of Elizabethan London, the thieves, rogues, drabs, their tricks and their victims. Thomas Lodge (1558–1625) also tried fiction both ways, with a story in Sidney's manner, entitled *Rosalynde* (1590), and with realistic pamphlets. More entertaining is Thomas Deloney (1543–1600) who describes the work of craftsmen, in narratives that are simple, anachronistic, but grounded in realism. In *Jack of Newbury* he shows the life of the weavers and in *The Gentle Craft* he tells the whole story of the shoemakers with some vivid and seemingly authentic scenes.With these Thomas Dekker, who was also a dramatist, portrayed contemporary life in a number of tracts, of which the most successful is the *Guls Horn-Booke* (1609), in which the 'low' life of London is paraded.

Realistic though these writers were they had little form in their narratives, but some progress in this direction is made by Thomas Nashe (1567–1601). In *Jack Wilton* he constructed a chronicle of adventures, many of which he had encountered in his own stormy career. His rogue hero begins his career in the army of Henry VIII and in his travels meet a number of living people. Here is the nearest approach to the realistic novel which the sixteenth century has produced.

It is strange and unaccountable that these beginnings of fiction in the Elizabethan age do not develop, as might be expected, in the seventeenth century. The religious controversies, the social dissensions and ultimately the Civil Wars, left a trial of innumerable pamphlets, and some have thought that the energies so absorbed left no leisure for prose fiction.

The second half of the seventeenth century did however produce developments. If the novel itself made little progress, we do begin to hear the voice of the private citizen describing his own life. Samuel Pepys and John Evelyn, in their diaries, are recording the type of material which novelists were one day to use. The attitude to life, which led them and others to note the everyday detail of existence, is developing the atmosphere which will one day make fiction so acceptable.

The greatest fiction writer of the seventeenth century, and one of the great figures in our literature, who would have himself disclaimed all title to being a novelist, was John Bunyan (1628–88). Son of a Bedfordshire tradesman, he was a soldier in the Republican Army, a preacher, a mystic and a prisoner for twelve years for refusing to submit at the Restoration. His earliest work is his moving spiritual autobiography, *Grace Abounding* (1666). The first part of *The Pilgrim's Progress*, written during one of his terms of imprisonment, was published in 1678 and a second part followed in 1684. Equally effective, though less well known, were *The Life and Death of Mr Badman* (1680), the counterpart to the story of the good pilgrim, and the spacious and magnificent *Holy War* (1682).

In *The Pilgrim's Progress* he determined to recount the vision of life allegorically, as the narrative of a journey. Allegory may be anything from a dull mechanism to a great and lively work of the imagination. Bunyan was endowed with a gift for detail and anecdote, for the description of scenery and the invention of conversation. This he combined with his allegory, so that his narrative, despite all its spiritual meanings, is a realistic story, contemporary and authentic. Some have tried to seek sources for his work but the wisest course is to accept his own verdict that it was the result of inspiration. The union of this realism with his spiritual experience can be seen by the exactness with which he describes in *Grace Abounding* the incidents which led to his conversion. A moving work, of great psychological interest, it portrays, on the basis of his own experience, the way to faith from the first conviction of sin through all the struggles and setbacks.

John Bunyan's dream in prison. He was imprisoned on two occasions for preaching as a Dissenter

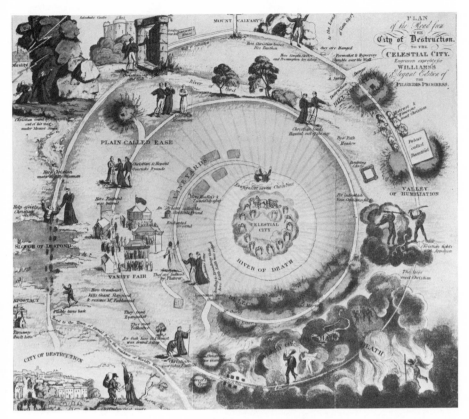

A plan of the road from the City of Destruction to the Celestial City, from Bunyan's
The Pilgrim's Progress

With all these earlier developments of the novel, it is left to the
eighteenth century to consolidate fiction as a form of literature, and from
that time onwards there has been no cessation in novel-writing. A
beginning is made with an enthralling and mysterious figure, Daniel
Defoe (1660–1731), to whom the English public, with all its taste for
biography, has never taken kindly. Educated in a Dissenting College
at Stoke Newington, Defoe, apart from being an inexhaustible writer,
was a Government agent, both for the Whigs and the Tories; some
suspect at the same time. He was a speculator, an inventor, a bankrupt,
a traveller and a journalist. Once he endured the pillory and he was on
several occasions imprisoned. Though his moral nature was not strong,
he kept reserved, very compactly, in one corner of his mind, the Puritan
values in which he was educated. Novel-writing was only one of his
activities, and he came to it late in life and rich in experience. Outstanding among his earlier productions is *The Review* (1704–13), which marks
the turning-point in the history of our journalism and periodical literature. Apart from the short narrative of the *Apparition of Mrs Veal* (1706),

The Bill of Mortality for the week ending 19 September 1665. In this week over seven thousand people died of the plague in the parishes of the City of London. Daniel Defoe used these records sixty years later when he wrote his *Journal of the Plague Year*

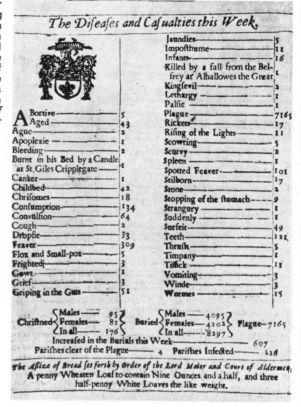

The Diseases and Casualties this Week.

Disease	Count	Disease	Count
Abortive	5	Jaundies	5
Aged	43	Impofthume	11
Ague	2	Infants	16
Apoplexie	1	Killed by a fall from the Belfrey at Alhallowes the Great	1
Bleeding	2	Kingfevil	2
Burnt in his Bed by a Candle at St. Giles Cripplegate	1	Lethargy	1
Canker	1	Palfie	1
Childbed	42	Plague	7165
Chrifomes	18	Rickets	17
Confumption	134	Rifing of the Lights	11
Convulfion	64	Scowring	5
Cough	2	Scurvy	2
Dropfie	33	Spleen	1
Feaver	309	Spotted Feaver	101
Flox and Small-pox	5	Stilborn	17
Frighted	3	Stone	2
Gowt	1	Stopping of the ftomach	9
Grief	3	Strangury	1
Griping in the Guts	51	Suddenly	1
		Surfeit	49
		Teeth	121
		Thrufh	5
		Timpany	1
		Tiffick	11
		Vomiting	3
		Winde	3
		Wormes	15

Chriftned — Males 95, Females 81, In all 176
Buried — Males 4095, Females 4202, In all 8297, Plague—7165
Increafed in the Burials this Week — 607
Parifhes clear of the Plague — 4   Parifhes Infected — 126

The Affize of Bread fet forth by Order of the Lord Maior and Court of Aldermen, A penny Wheaten Loaf to contain Nine Ounces and a half, and three half-penny White Loaves the like weight.

which reads like a work of imagination, but which Defoe wrote from the results of his researches, his first work of fiction is *Robinson Crusoe* (1719). Published when Defoe was sixty, its success encouraged him, and there followed, in rapid succession, a series of volumes among which are *Captain Singleton* (1720), *Moll Flanders* (1722), *Colonel Jacque* (1722), *A Journal of the Plague Year* (1722) and *Roxana* (1724). Defoe's outlook on the novel is best illustrated through *A Journal of the Plague Year*, which was once considered as a work of the imagination constructed from cleverly invented incidents. Actually, apart from a slender fictional centre, it depended on memories of the Plague which were still circulating in Defoe's childhood, and on his own research among documents. Further, the subject was topical when he wrote, for there was a threatened recurrence of the scourge. He regards the novel, not as a work of the imagination, but as a 'true relation', and even when the element of fact decreases, he maintains the close realism of pseudo-fact. The combination of these qualities has given *Robinson Crusoe* its immediate and continuous appeal. The story had its basis in fact, in the adventures of Alexander Selkirk, the sailor who lived alone for years on the island of Juan Fernandez, and this initial circumstance is supported by Defoe's

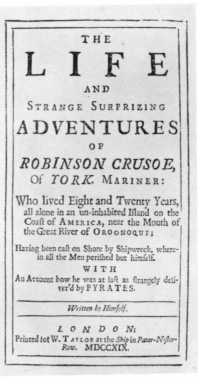

The frontispiece to the first edition of Defoe's 'Autobiography' of *Robinson Crusoe*

wide reading in works of travel and by his own multifarious experience. The skill of the novel lies in its detail, in the semblance of the authentic. Form, in its subtler sense, does not affect Defoe: his novels run on until, like an alarm clock, they run down; but while movement is there the attention is held. He has some interest in mental states, but Defoe reveals less of the mind of Crusoe than one would expect, and it would be interesting to see how Henry James would have re-told the story. The dullest part of the work lies in the moral and religious reflections, and here Defoe was making use of that part of his mind which retained unadulterated Puritan values. He also knew that his audience would like it. The success of *Robinson Crusoe* obscures the lively merit of the moral, but picaresque, novels which follow. *Captain Singleton*, with piracy and Africa as its background, is a vivid tale, and the 'female rogues', Moll Flanders and more elegant Roxana, are among the most lively of his creations.

Lovelace discovers Clarissa. Mr Lovelace's intentions are not as honourable as Clarissa had hoped. From the 1785 edition of Richardson's *Clarissa Harlowe*

Chapter 11

The English Novel from Richardson to Sir Walter Scott

DEFOE HAD no contemporary, no immediate successor, and the next development in the novel, and possibly the most important in its whole history in England, comes by accident. Samuel Richardson (1689–1761), the son of a joiner, came to London and was apprenticed as a printer. He remained a printer throughout his life and followed the path of the virtuous and successful apprentice, even to marrying his master's daughter. He was asked to prepare a series of model letters for those who could not write for themselves. Richardson told maid-servants how to negotiate a proposal of marriage, apprentices how to apply for situations and even sons how to plead their father's forgiveness. This humble task taught Richardson that he had at his fingers' ends the art of expressing himself in letters, and in the years that followed he published three long works, on which his reputation rests, *Pamela* (1740–1), *Clarissa Harlowe* (1747–8) and *Sir Charles Grandison* (1753–4).

In each instance, the central story is a simple one. Pamela was a virtuous servant, who resisted the attempts at seduction by the son of her late mistress and, as a reward, gained from him a proposal of marriage, which she gleefully accepted. Clarissa, again, was virtuous but a lady. Tormented by the pressure of her family, who urged on her a detestable suitor, she fled from home to the protection of the attractive Mr Lovelace, who, once he had her in his power, declared his attentions in a manner which even her virtuous upbringing could not mistake. Nor was he content with declarations. For when these failed, he forced himself upon her and, as an indirect consequence of his actions, she died. Sir Charles Grandison was a model gentleman, who rescued one lady, and was betrothed to another, a situation which he controlled with incredible delicacy, to the apparent satisfaction of all parties.

From the outset, the themes of Richardson's novels have been attacked on account of their self-satisfied and calculating middle-class morality. Pamela is accused of having made virtue pay dividends by marriage, and even Clarissa is alleged only to have reserved payment for another world, making a long-term investment with eternity, while Sir Charles, despite his aristocratic glamour, is a prig. But his mastery exists in the absolute integrity of the picture of sentiment and of pathos. Richardson was an artist and a Puritan and, while the Puritan invents the stories, the artist is in almost absolute control of the detail. Criticism has often been too content to mock at the stories without recognizing the great master who controls their slow and deliberate unravelling. Nowhere in English criticism has Richardson had complete recognition of the greatness of his art. Yet his work was immediately popular and, particularly in *Clarissa Harlowe*, he gained an audience that was European: Rousseau was indebted to him for his treatment of sentiment, as was Goethe in *Werther*.

Richardson has suffered from the appearance of a contemporary who disliked his work, and who took an early opportunity of satirizing it. Henry Fielding (1707–54) was of an aristocratic family, educated at Eton and Leyden, a reader with a wide and genuine taste for the classics, and a dramatist, until Sir Robert Walpole's Licensing Act of 1737 drove his plays from the stage. He was a journalist, a lawyer and a Justice of the Peace serving at Bow Street. Ill-health drove him to Lisbon where he died and is buried.

In 1742 he published *Joseph Andrews*, to ridicule Richardson's *Pamela*.

He contrived this satire by reversing the situation in Richardson's novel. Instead of the virtuous serving-maid, Fielding presents Joseph, the chaste servant, whom Lady Booby so tempts from the path of virtue that he has to run away. At this moment in the story, Fielding became so engrossed in his own narrative, and the exercise of his own comic gift, that Richardson is almost forgotten. There follows a series of adventures on the road, where Joseph is accompanied by Parson Adams, a clerical Don Quixote. The comedy is admirably contrived, with the Hogarthian figure of a pig-keeping parson as one of its main delights. Fielding's purpose in this first novel is nowhere a simple or direct one. Apart from the motive of satire, he is attracted, in a learned way, by the contrasts between the novel, with its picture of humble, contemporary life, and the classical epic. With this in mind he calls his novel 'a comic epic in prose', and it leads him, with encouragement from Cervantes, to introduce a burlesque element into the style and frequently into the incident. It was the motive of satire which completely dominated his second narrative, *The History of Jonathan Wild the Great* (1743), in which he took the life of a thief and receiver, who had been hanged at Tyburn, as a theme for demonstrating the small division between a great rogue and a great soldier, or a great politician, such as Sir Robert Walpole.

Left: An illustration to Richardson's *Pamela*, by Highmore. Pamela is married, and her virtue is rewarded.
Right: Tom Jones discovers his tutor, the upstanding Philosopher Square, lurking behind a curtain in Molly Seagrim's bedroom. From an illustration to Fielding's *Tom Jones*

'The Arrest' from *The Rake's Progress* by William Hogarth. Both Hogarth and Fielding revealed the intricate relationships of good and evil and of tragedy and comedy in eighteenth-century society

Underlying the humours of *Joseph Andrews* there lay a view of life, seldom disclosed openly, but of obvious importance to Fielding himself. It could be discovered in the difference between the calculating moral code of Richardson, and the generous and warm-hearted approach to life which Fielding admired. When Joseph lay naked on the roadside, all the members of a passing coach, good Richardsonians, would neglect him from some motive of prudence or modesty, all except a coach-boy, afterwards deported for robbing a hen-roost, who threw him his coat with an oath. The contemplation of the more intricate relations of good and evil, and the anomaly that generous impulses frequently exist in those whom society condemns, grew in Fielding with such emotional intensity that they gave a depth to his major novel *Tom Jones* (1749). Nothing in his work compares with this great novel, so carefully planned and executed that though the main theme follows Tom Jones's life from childhood onwards, the reader is kept in suspense until the close as to the final resolution of the action. For the modern reader the heavy pseudo-epic apparatus of commentary can be tiresome. The story itself is elaborate, with most diverse social elements. But, if one is prepared to deal with all this lightly and to hold on to the main theme, *Tom Jones* is a profound portrait of what Fielding considered to be a full man.

Fielding's last novel, *Amelia* (1751), is less successful. He idealizes the main woman character, and this leads to an excess of pathos, which deprives the novel of the balance which *Tom Jones* possesses. Yet, with Fielding, the novel had come of age. He had established it in one of its most notable forms, middle-class realism. He had endowed it with a conception of form, and made it an art not unworthy of comparison with the pictorial art of Hogarth. In Tom Jones he had drawn one of the great human characters of our literature. Background alone was lacking, and was to remain absent until Scott gave it lavishly in his fictions. Above all, he had less reticence than Richardson, and less than any of the novelists who succeeded him in the nineteenth century.

Tobias Smollett (1721–71) was Fielding's contemporary, though he is not of equal stature. Born in Scotland, he studied medicine and served on a warship as a ship's surgeon. If he brought to the novel nothing that was new in form, he was able to introduce a new background, in accounts of the sea in the livid days of the old Navy. Irascible and insensitive, he had an apparent enjoyment of the rough naval life, of its cruelty and the wild practical joking. To this he added, in a rather incongruous way, a superficial element of sentiment. In his first novel, *Roderick Random* (1748), which was greeted with success, he portrays the life of his rogue-hero until his marriage with the loyal, beautiful and incredible Narcissa. The picture of the reckless and ferocious sea life in this novel is his most solid claim to be remembered. *Peregrine Pickle* (1751) is again the novel of a rogue who follows a depraved life until he marries the virtuous Emilia. More attractive than this 'hero' are some of the minor characters such as Commodore Trunnion and Boatswain Pipes. The background is still vividly drawn and includes a picture of the cruelties of pre-Revolutionary France. The rest of his work is less impressive; although in *Humphrey Clinker* (1771), modifying Richardson's epistolary manner, he writes in a more humorous and equable manner than in his earlier novels. Smollett's violent and boisterous stories were widely enjoyed, and in popular estimation he lived long enough to influence Dickens.

Of the eighteenth-century novelists the strangest and the most variously judged is Laurence Sterne (1713–68). The great-grandson of a bishop and the son of a soldier, he was educated almost in the barrackroom, but found his way to Cambridge, was ordained, and obtained a living in Yorkshire. But though he read theology and published sermons, he had also studied the works of his 'dear Rabelais and dearer Cervantes'. Even in the eighteenth century, when there were many odd clergymen, Sterne has a high claim to be the oddest. His *Life and Opinions of Tristram Shandy, Gent* (1759–67) is a novel without predecessors, the product of an original mind, and immediately popular. Judged by ordinary storytelling standards *Tristram Shandy* is preposterous. The reader has to wait until the third book before the hero is born, and even then his future life remains undefined. The narrative consists of episodes, conversations, perpetual digressions, excursions in learning, with unfinished sentences, dashes, blank pages, fantastic syntax, caprices in humour, bawdy and sentiment. In the midst of all this there are characters clearly identifiable: Tristram's father, Corporal Trim, Doctor Slop and My Uncle Toby, the veteran of Marlborough's campaigns and the clearest source of the sentimental in the novel. At first sight it all seems a perversion, a wanton destruction of form, but to judge thus would be to judge superficially. Sterne is asserting, however indirectly, that the orderly narrative of events, with their time and space realism, have little relation to the disorder of the human mind, where sequence is not logical but capricious. In Sterne sentiment often seems excessive to the object to which it is attached, and Sterne himself uses the term in the title of his *Sentimental Journey* (1761), where he portrays a journey through France with a quieter mood than is present in *Tristram Shandy* and with less display of learning.

After the work of these four masters, the stream of fiction broadens continually, until it reaches the flood with which no single intelligence can contend. Even in the late eighteenth century the developments are too diverse to be easily described. Some works stand alone. Samuel Johnson's *Rasselas* (1759), though nominally an Abyssinian narrative, employs the story only for the philosophical argument, which is a trenchant attack upon eighteenth-century optimism; it parallels in intention, though not in outward form, the almost contemporary *Candide* of Voltaire. Nor does Oliver Goldsmith's *The Vicar of Wakefield* (1766) belong to any one school. Despite all its coincidences and improbabilities this has remained a popular and individual work.

The most direct English successor to Richardson was Fanny Burney (1752–1840), daughter of Charles Burney, the musician, who in her youth was petted and praised by Johnson. She lived to be a lady-in-waiting to Queen Charlotte and to marry a French émigré, General d'Arblay. *Evelina*, her first and best novel, which took the town by storm in 1778, describes, with admirable illustrative incidents, the entry of a country girl into the gaieties and adventures of London. It can still be read with amusement, though the praises of Johnson, Burke and Reynolds now seem strangely excessive.

The sentimentalism which Sterne began remained popular, and gained its most lachrymose exposition in Henry Mackenzie's *The Man of Feeling* (1771), in which the hero is for ever weeping under the stress of some pathetic scene or emotional excitement. If Rousseau is to be discovered as one of the influences on Mackenzie, he was clearly the foremost teacher of Thomas Day, whose incredible life is worth reading, and whose *Sandford and Merton* (1783–9) is still remembered, if only by name.

Amid these later eighteenth-century developments, one is notable for the dubious path down which it invited readers and authors to tread. The novel of 'terror', or the 'Gothic' novel, leads into that underworld of fiction which continues into the tales of horror and crime so popular today. Whatever may be its value by any artistic standard, the 'terror' tale attracted strong minds, and its influence worked upwards into the higher regions of art, affecting the compositions of Scott and the Brontës, and the poetry of Shelley.

The origin of this type of fiction can be ascribed to Horace Walpole's (1717–97) *The Castle of Otranto* (1765). Horace, son of Sir Robert Walpole, knew much of the great world which his father so long dominated. But his mind, brilliant without deep convictions, was wearied by the intrigue and perpetual search for power that surrounded him. Fortified by a number of sinecures, he indulged himself in antiquarianism and a numerous acquaintance, which included Gray, the poet. Of his life he has left a record in a voluminous correspondence, one of the most varied and entertaining collections of letters in the language. He sought release in allowing the imagination to contemplate, in solitude, the relics of medieval art to be found in the ruins of abbeys and castles, often existing within a gentleman's own estate. The same longing for the

Horace Walpole was so obsessed by the Gothic that he built a medieval castle at Strawberry Hill, where he wrote *The Castle of Otranto* (left), a mysterious tale full of supernatural intrusions and secret terrors

An illustration from Mary Shelley's *Frankenstein,* one of the most famous horror stories of all time. 'A flash of lightning illuminated the object'

antique world led to the revival of a taste for ballads and chivalry, for the whole wonder and mystery which successive generations have found in the Middle Ages. Walpole carried out the medieval cult more completely than most of his contemporaries, and at Strawberry Hill he constructed a Gothic house, where he could dream himself back into the days of chivalry and monastic life without any practical obligation to either discipline. From these medieval daydreams *The Castle of Otranto* resulted: set in medieval Italy, the story includes a gigantic helmet that can strike dead its victims, tyrants, supernatural intrusions, mysterious and secret terrors. It is as if all the poetry and character had been removed from Shakespeare's *Macbeth*, only to leave the raw mechanism of melodrama and the supernatural. No one could have foreseen how long would be the catalogue of his imitators. William Beckford (1759–1844) was another gentleman of fashion and wealth, who had built himself a Gothic edifice, Fonthill Abbey, and who had written a romance of mystery. As Fonthill was more extravagant than Strawberry Hill, so is *Vathek* (1786) a more bizarre composition than *The Castle of Otranto*. Walpole, though he day-dreamed, had a sound sense of the material world, but Beckford seemed actually to live in a territory of fantasy. *Vathek* is an Oriental story of a caliph who pursues his complex cruelties and intricate passions, aided by his mother and supported by an evil genius.

Of the later practitioners of the 'terror' tale the most able and popular was Mrs Ann Radcliffe (1764–1823), of whose five novels the best known are *The Mysteries of Udolpho* (1794) and *The Italian* (1797). She accepted the mechanism of the 'terror' tale, but combined it with sentiment. In this way she brought the 'terror' tale into contact with the interest in nature present in eighteenth-century poetry. *The Mysteries of Udolpho* gives the formula of her work in its most unadulterated form: an innocent and sensitive girl in the hands of a powerful and sadistic villain named Montoni, who owns a grim and isolated castle, where mystery and horror stalk in the lonely corridors and haunted chambers. It is true that before the end of her story Mrs Radcliffe delights in presenting a rational explanation of her horrors.

Though Mrs Radcliffe was pre-eminent in her success, many other writers practised this popular manner. Matthew Gregory ('Monk') Lewis (1775–1818), who had read Goethe and the German romanticists, employed all the worst of his reading in *The Monk* (1795). He used a modification of the Faust theme for such a portrayal of sensuality that contemporary taste was offended, though the book was very popular. It brought him fame all over Europe and the friendship of Scott, Byron and the Prince Regent. Far more honest as an artist was Charles Robert Maturin (1782–1824), whose *Melmoth the Wanderer* (1820) had a wide influence in France. One of the most competent of the 'terror' tales was *Frankenstein* (1817), written by Mrs Shelley with a hint from Byron and Shelley. It describes the invention by Frankenstein of a mechanical monster, with human powers but of a terrifying aspect.

The nineteenth century was to produce works of fiction of far greater significance than the 'terror' tales. Seldom has the novel been conceived with such deliberate and successful art as in the novels of Jane Austen (1775–1817). Her brother served at the Nile and Trafalgar, but her own life was spent in a narrow world at Steventon, Bath, Chawton and Winchester, where she died and is buried. From the first she seems to have realized the limits of the scene which she could portray, and nothing can tempt her outside. For the past she had no curiosity, and the events which stirred the Europe of her day left no impression on her pages. In the same manner she detached herself from the weaknesses of her predecessors. As her French admirer, Louis Cazamian, has written: 'All Jane Austen's work is transfused with the spirit of classicism in its highest form, in its most essential quality: a safe, orderly harmony among the powers of the mind, a harmony where of necessity the intellect is paramount.' To the 'terror' tale she presented the assault direct in *Northanger Abbey* (not published until 1818), and she combined with her satire of the 'Gothic' school a deeply studied picture of imaginary horror working in the human mind. The moral outlook of Richardson left her unimpressed, and her art is the more detached for its absence. Sentimentalism found her equally unmoved. Her observation, with whatever difference of scale, has the 'negative capability' of Shakespeare. More than anyone since Fielding, she regarded the novel as a form of art which required a close and exacting discipline. The resulting narratives are so inevitable in their movement, so precise in their realism, that they give the impression of ease, but the facility is a gift to the reader, exacted from the fundamental brainwork of the author. Her integrity as an artist is shown by the fact that she had continued to write and to revise novels even when her work seemed unlikely to find acceptance from publishers. *Pride and Prejudice* (1813), which shows her early manner, probably remains her most popular work. The characters are all familiarly known to a wide circle of readers: Mrs Bennet, the match-making mother, Collins, the sycophantic clergyman, the imperious 'great Lady' Catherine de Bourgh and Elizabeth, the gay, clever young woman whose Prejudice is matched with the Pride of Darcy, the aristocrat who conceals a goodness of heart beneath a haughty manner and an almost Brahministic

Right: Mr Collins and Lizzie from Jane Austen's *Pride and Prejudice*. 'Almost as soon as I entered the house I singled you out as the companion of my future life'
Below: Day dresses; 1800

power of detecting class distinctions. Much of the novel is in dialogue and its opening has a brilliant immediacy:

> It is a truth universally acknowledged, that a single man in possession of a good fortune must be in want of a wife.
>
> However little known the feelings or views of such a man may be on his first entering the neighbourhood, this truth is so well fixed in the minds of the surrounding families, that he is considered as the rightful property of some one or other of their daughters.
>
> 'My dear Mr Bennet,' said his lady to him one day, 'have you heard that Netherfield Park is let at last?'
>
> Mr Bennet replied that he had not.
>
> 'But it is,' returned she; 'for Mrs Long has just been here, and she told me all about it.'
>
> Mr Bennet made no answer.
>
> 'Do not you want to know who has taken it?' cried his wife impatiently.
>
> '*You* want to tell me, and I have no objection to hearing it.'
>
> This was invitation enough.
>
> 'Why, my dear, you must know. Mrs Long says that Netherfield is taken by a young man of large fortune from the north of England; that he came down on Monday in a chaise and four to see the place, and was so much delighted with it, that he agreed with Mr Morris immediately; that he is to take possession before Michaelmas, and some of his servants are to be in the house by the end of next week.'

The narrow circle which her novels were to portray is here defined, the aristocracy and such classes beneath as may, in varying degrees, have some claim upon their intimacy and patronage. In the first place her art exacts that the novel shall have a classical precision of structure. This central design is manipulated through incidents exactly defined in their realism, and all regulated for their function in the narrative as a whole. Added to this is the gift of phrase, humorous, illuminating, economical, through which all is related, so that each incident can be enjoyed in itself, apart from the added pleasure of realizing its true proportion and place in the growing structure of the theme. She had, further, a gift of dialogue, which fails her only in the longer speeches. Background and description she eliminates, except where the balls and parties, the formal calls and visits are necessary for the narrative. *Sense and Sensibility* (1811), her other early volume, again presents two contrasted characters, and there is the same skill in the structure of the plot, though possibly the contemporary flavour of this novel makes it less universal in its appeal.

Three other novels followed, and the critics of Jane Austen have disputed their merit in comparison with her earlier work. *Mansfield Park* was published in 1814, *Emma* in 1816 and *Persuasion* followed in 1818. Without entering into controversy, it can be asserted that these later novels lack the continuous comedy, and the semblance of spontaneity, which *Pride and Prejudice* possesses. In compensation, they have a more complex portrayal of character, a more subtle irony, a deeper, possibly a warmer-hearted attitude to the players on her scene. Jane Austen respected the novel as a great art. In *Northanger Abbey* (1818) she had satirized the 'terror' novel, and in her own work she substituted her cleverly worked realism and comedy. Her letters show how conscious she was of what she was doing, and of her own limitations: 'I must keep to my own style and go on in my own way: and though I may never succeed again in that, I am convinced that I should totally fail in any other.' The complete control of her world gives her work a Shakespearian quality, though the world she controlled was smaller.

Seldom has a single age been presented with two artists of such different range and outlook as Jane Austen and Sir Walter Scott (1771–1832). Never was a writer more generous than Scott to good work among his contemporaries nor a critic more catholic in his taste. He praised Jane Austen, and distinguished her art from his own 'bow-wow' manner. He was born in Edinburgh, the son of a lawyer, and though he employed himself in the same profession, he had early an enthusiasm for literature and for the antiquities of Scotland. A series of 'raids' into the Highlands stored his mind with legend, which was to be invaluable to him later as a novelist, and his researches led him to publish *The Minstrelsy of the Scottish Border* (1802–3). From being a collector of poetry he became himself a poet. A series of verse romances, beginning with *The Lay of the Last Minstrel* (1805), rewarded him so well financially that he saw in literature a way of paying for the growing expenditure which the satisfaction of his expensive tastes incurred. Of an upright domestic morality, he was free from the entanglements which have encumbered some writers of his imaginative intensity. His weakness lay elsewhere and arose, in part, from the very generosity of his nature. He wished to be a 'laird', to associate with the aristocracy on terms of equality, and to be the master of his own broad acres.

In satisfaction of this desire he acquired Abbotsford as his home, and even before he was a novelist he was entangled in publishing ventures to raise funds to meet his perpetual plans of increasing his mansion and his mania for buying land. Throughout his career as a novelist, this pressure for rapid and successful production pursued him, until he was overtaken by the tragedy of his commitments when in 1826 his publishers were involved in bankruptcy. It is idle to speculate what sort of an artist he would have been had he not possessed this passion for lavish expenditure. To remove it would be to deny him a part of his nature. It is more profitable to record that his *Journal*, written in the period of the collapse, is the most moving of all his works.

Until the later years, this rapidity of production left little trace on his composition. If he wrote with a minimum of revision, he still wrote well, and his mind was so crowded with stories, characters and incidents, that invention came without apparent effort. His energy was phenomenal, and some have suspected that certain of the novels must have been written in his earlier years, and hoarded until he had committed himself to his secret and anonymous profession. His performance is the more remarkable when it is remembered that he combined authorship with a number of legal and official duties, while to his guests at Abbotsford he seemed the gentleman of leisure, ready to while away the vacant hour in sport and entertainment. The solution, partial though it must be, lies in the fact that his journeys to the Highlands had stored his memory with the background, and much of the material, from which the best in his fiction was to develop. These had been invaluable years of preparation, though Scott was probably unconscious at the time of the use to which he would apply them.

Scott, though he had some antecedents, including Maria Edgeworth's picture of Irish life in *Castle Rackrent* (1800), may be said to have invented the historical novel. Instead of the contemporary scene, and the detailed study of middle-class life, he steps back into the past, frequently using well-known characters, and constructing a narrative which is at once an adventure and a pageant of an earlier world. Where Fielding and Jane Austen had been content with characters and their immediate surroundings, Scott invented a background for his scene, with landscape and nature descriptions, and all the picturesque details of past ages. Though the central theme often introduces the leading personalities, the most secure element lies in his pictures of ordinary people, particularly the Scottish peasants whom he knew so well, and in whose portrayal his notable gift for comedy had free exercise. In variety of scene and in the wealth of characters he equals Shakespeare, and yet when their art is compared much is found missing in Scott. The continual impoverishment of English speech, in the frank description of the passions and the crudities of life, deprives his style of the range which Shakespeare possessed. Nor did he penetrate into the hidden places of his characters' minds. Their conduct and emotions are governed by simple motives. If he is rich in comedy, he approaches tragedy seldom, and with unequal success, nor did his happy nature know the agony of a tormented or thwarted soul. His history, too, is pageantry without a deeper understanding of the institutions which have affected men's lives. It is significant that in his treatment of the Middle Ages the Church, the dominant institution, escapes consideration. For mystery he had a great gift sparingly used, but the metaphysical and the mystical leave him untouched.

While it is convenient to use the label 'historical novelist' for Scott, the term, without examination, is misleading. His earliest novel, *Waverley* (1814), dealt with the Jacobite rising of 1745, and though in one sense historical, he was able to formulate the background from the memories of living people whom he had met in the Highlands. This Scottish element, with Jacobitism, the last medieval movement in Europe as its main theme, is the most secure element in his whole work, and he recurs to it frequently: in *Guy Mannering* (1815), *The Antiquary* (1816) *Old Mortality* (1816), *The Heart of Midlothian* (1818) and *Rob Roy* (1818).

An illustration from Sir Walter Scott's *Ivanhoe*. 'One step nearer and I plunge myself from the precipice!'

In these novels it is difficult to dissociate memory from imagination. These both serve his creative purpose equally, and the central narrative is supported by the strong humanity and the frequently comic portrayal of lowly Scottish types. When Scott departed from the Scotland which he knew so well into the Middle Ages, he lost much of his power. *Ivanhoe* (1819) and *The Talisman* (1825), a history of the Crusades, were among the most popular of his novels, but they are superficial and theatrical compared with the certainty and depth of the Scottish novels. The same is true, though less obviously, when he crosses the Border to narrate the fortunes of Elizabeth and James I in *Kenilworth* (1821) and *The Fortunes of Nigel* (1822).

Once he had exhausted the popular appeal of a period, he hurried to seek another. Among these novelties a certain pride of place must be given to *Quentin Durward* (1823), which deals with the France of Louis XI, for in that novel he captured the attention of Europe. Never was his narrative more vivid, and in Louis he portrays a character more subtle than is usual with him. In this novel, though he has gone to France, he has taken his Scottish archers with him. More than once he returned from these wanderings, geographical and temporal, to employ Scotland as his scene. *Saint Ronan's Well* (1824), where he experiments with the novel of manners, is interesting without being completely successful, but *Redgauntlet* (1824), in which he bids farewell to the Jacobite theme, shows how Scotland was supremely his subject. In his work as a novelist he has given a wider enjoyment than any writer, with the possible exception of Dickens. Since his day the knowledge of the past has increased, but the inaccuracies in his portraits are still unlikely to trouble anyone who is not a specialist. In the nineteenth century the novel as a form developed in depth and structure, and as a consequence Scott's reputation suffered. His followers in the historical novel are innumerable, and include Bulwer Lytton, Dickens, Thackeray, Reade and George Eliot. Nor was his influence confined to England alone, for from France and Russia, and across the Atlantic to America, Scott was admired.

One novelist in this age stands apart from his contemporaries. Thoms Love Peacock (1785–1866) was a friend of Shelley, but a satirist of romanticism. He invented a novel which could contain irony, conversation and a mockery of romantic excesses. His characters exist as shadows only, but shadows with entertaining voices. His plots are only excuses for the voices to be heard exchanging the talk which Peacock has invented for them. Peacock himself had a wide learning, both classical and medieval, and in *Maid Marian* (1822) and the *Misfortunes of Elphin* (1829) he shows that he understands the attractions of romance. Few who have read his novels come away without entertainment, and *Headlong Hall* (1816), *Nightmare Abbey* (1818), *Crotchet Castle* (1831), encouraged writers as different as George Meredith and Aldous Huxley to try new ways in fiction.

A detail from 'Newgate: Committed for Trial' by Frank Holt

Chapter 12

The English Novel from Dickens

IN THE nineteenth-century novel Charles Dickens (1812–70) is pre-eminent. He is the greatest novelist that England has yet produced. After his preliminary *Sketches by Boz* (1836), he published *Pickwick Papers* (1836–7), the supreme comic novel in the language. The comedy is never superimposed, for it is an effortless expression of a comic view of life. Dickens seems to see things differently in an amusing and exaggerated way, and in his early work with much exuberance he plunges from one adventure to another, without any thought of plot or design. He is hampered by his age, which demands sentiment and reticence, but in the space that is allowed he scampers as if he knew no restraint. Had he the encouragement of a less squeamish audience he might have been Shakespearian. Dickens enjoyed life, but hated the social system into which he had been born. There are many indications that he was half-way towards being a revolutionary, and in many of the later novels he was to attack the corruptions of his time. Yet his age exacted its penalty in demanding that his novels, if they were to be popular, should keep to the conventions of middle-class society in morality and in vocabulary. Never was he less embarrassed by restrictions than in the exuberance of *Pickwick Papers*. In *Oliver Twist*, which followed in 1837–8, pathos is beginning to intrude on humour, and Dickens, appalled by the cruelty of his time, is feeling that he must convey a message through fiction to his hard-hearted generation. Yet some modern social historians assert that he disguised the depths to which the lower classes had been brutal-ized. His invention is still abundant, as he tells the story of the virtuous pauper boy who has to submit to perils and temptations. The strength lies less in the pathos than in the 'low' scenes, in the humour and satire of which the figure of Mr Bumble is the centre. With *Nicholas Nickleby* (1838–9) plot grows in importance, and Dickens shows his talent for the melodramatic. He draws his characters with the same firm lines as Ben Jonson had done in the seventeenth century. Satire is abundant in the Yorkshire school scenes, while much that is best lies in the humour of the theatre of Vincent Crummles and his company. *The Old Curiosity Shop* (1840–41) showed pathos transcendent over humour, especially in the death of little Nell: one feels that the only ritual known to Dickens's middle-class audience was the pageantry of funerals. *Barnaby Rudge* (1841), with its picture of the Gordon Riots, is Dickens's first attempt in the historical novel, and here plot, which had counted for nothing in *Pickwick Papers*, becomes increasingly important. Before *Martin Chuzzlewit* (1844) he made his American journey and the American scenes in this novel gave offence. Yet all of Dickens is here: Pecksniff and his daughters, Sarah Gamp, Tom Pinch, the gentle, kindly Dickensian figure Mark Tapley, vigorous and virtuous, a great variety of character and incident all well-managed. Between 1843 and 1848 he wrote his *Christmas Books*, including *A Christmas Carol*. This, the most popular perhaps of all his works, shows his belief in human kindliness worked almost to mysticism. *Dombey and Son* in 1848 displayed by its increased control of pathos how much his art had developed since *The Old Curiosity Shop*. In *David Copperfield* (1850) he brought the first phase of his novel-writing to an end in a work with a strong autobiographical element, and with such firm characterization as Micawber and Uriah Heep. 'Of all my books,' Dickens wrote, 'I like this the best.'

Bleak House (1853) is the most conscious and deeply planned novel in Dickens's whole work, and clearly his art has moved far from the spontaneous gaiety of *Pickwick Papers*. It was followed by *Hard Times* (1854), a novel dedicated to Carlyle. While in all his work Dickens is attacking the social conditions of his time, here he gives this theme a special emphasis. He satirizes in Coketown and Mr Gradgrind the whole *laissez-faire* system of the Manchester school and suggests that its en-

'The Ragged School', a cartoon by George Cruikshank. Dickens was appalled by the living conditions of the poor in his time and worked hard in the cause of social and educational reform

lightened self-interest is unenlightened cruelty. A social bias again governs *Little Dorrit* (1857), in which Dickens attacks the Circumlocution Office and the methods of bureaucracy: the picture of prison life, which was a comic motif in *Pickwick Papers*, is now a serious theme in the portrayal of the debtors' prison in the Marshalsea. With *A Tale of Two Cities* (1859) he returned to the historical novel and, inspired by Carlyle, laid his theme in the French Revolution. None of his works shows more clearly how wide and unexpected were the resources of his genius. He completed two other novels, *Great Expectations* (1861) and *Our Mutual Friend* (1864–5), before his premature death in 1870, and he left unfinished the manuscript of *The Mystery of Edwin Drood*.

Dickens had driven himself to death. From 1858 to 1868 he had given dramatic readings of his novels in England and America. They were profitable, and, despite the weariness of the journeys, he delighted in the applause. An audience to Dickens was like a potent wine, and, to make sure of the potency, he had to please the audience. This was true, not only of his dramatic readings, but of the novels themselves. Shakespeare satisfied his audience, with no sacrifice of vision, but Dickens knew more than he revealed. His own nature was involved in a high emotion-alism which prevented him from reaching the sense of tragedy of a Dostoyevsky, or that full vision of life which makes Tolstoy supreme among the novelists of the world. Short of this he had everything. Lik-all great artists he viewed the world as if it was an entirely fresh experie ence seen for the first time, and he had an extraordinary range of language, from comic invention to great eloquence. He invented character and situation with a range that had been unequalled since Shakespeare. So deeply did he affect his audiences that the view of life behind his novels has entered into the English tradition. Reason and theory he distrusted, but compassion and cheerfulness of heart he ele-vated into the supreme virtues. He knew in his more reflective moments that cheerfulness alone will not destroy the Coketowns of the world. This reflection he kept mainly to himself, and his intense emotionalism helped him to obscure it. When Dickens died in 1870 something had gone out of English life that was irreplaceable, a bright light that had shone upon the drab commercialism of the century, calling men back to laughter and kindliness, and the disruption of the cruelties in which they were entangling themselves.

William Makepeace Thackeray (1811–63) and Dickens were such near contemporaries that it is natural that their work should often have been compared, although they have little in common. In education and social status they were widely separated. Dickens had little regular education: his father was often in prison for debt and he himself started to earn his living in a blacking factory. Thackeray, born in Calcutta, the son of an East India Company official, had the benefits of Charterhouse and Cambridge. Dickens when he was poor knew the meaning of poverty,

'Rebecca's farewell', one of Thackeray's illustrations to *Vanity Fair*.
'I hate the whole house ... I hope I may never set eyes on it again'

but for Thackeray to be poor merely meant that for the time he relied on credit. Dickens was excitable, while Thackeray was lethargic and had to drive himself to composition. Throughout his whole life Thackeray was a journalist. Up to 1854 he was a regular contributor to *Punch*, and later he was editor of *The Cornhill*. As a novelist he began late with *Vanity Fair* (1847–8) when he was thirty-six. Ten years later he was working at his last considerable novel. *The Virginians* (1857–9). For one brilliant decade the bright yellow shilling numbers in which his novels were published became a feature of English life. In those years he had published *Pendennis* (1848–50), *Henry Esmond* (1852) and *The Newcomes* (1853–5). In 1863 he died. He was only fifty-two, and life seemed to have much to offer him. Only a year before he had built himself a mansion in Kensington. His tastes were extravagant and his income had to keep pace with them. Not for him the little house at £40 a year with 'a snuffy little Scotch maid to open the door' which seemed to suit Tom Carlyle. Like Dickens he drove himself to give appearances in lectures in London and in America. He flogged his income up to £10,000 a year and this, and his methods of living, brought him down.

Vanity Fair showed him at his best, in a clear-sighted realism, a deep detestation of insincerity, and a broad and powerful development of narrative. His characterization and, indeed, all his effects are more subtle than in Dickens. He is less concerned to present a moral solution than to evoke an image of life as he has seen it. This gives the true mark of greatness to his portrait of Becky Sharp. She is an adventurous and a deceitful woman, but Thackeray so presents her that the audience can never retain an attitude of detached judgement. As an artist he showed no consistent development from this first brilliant work. *Pendennis* and *The Newcomes* are too involved in digressions to have the strength of design which *Vanity Fair* possesses. The skill remains in individual scenes and characters. In the portrayal of sentiment he is more delicate than Dickens, and in Colonel Newcome he makes the final portrait of what an English gentleman should like to be. The defect in structure in these novels is corrected in *Henry Esmond*, in which Thackeray wrote a historical novel on the eighteenth century, a period of which his lectures on *The English Humourists* and *The Four Georges* show him a master. He reconstructed in *Esmond* the atmosphere of the age of Queen Anne, through a plot carefully devised and with a theme difficult to control.

Though nothing in the early nineteenth century approaches Dickens and Thackeray, the novel in that period showed great variety. Fiction had become the dominant form in literature, and the problem of recording even its main types becomes difficult.

Some novelists tried a number of different forms, as if they were attempting to adjust themselves to all the changes of public taste. Bulwer Lytton (1803–73) is an outstanding example of this versatility. Following Scott he produced a number of historical novels, of which *The Last Days of Pompeii* (1834) is the best known and *Rienzi* (1835) possibly the most competent. He made a popular union of the novel of crime and the novel of social protest in *Paul Clifford* (1830) and in *Eugene Aram* (1832), which had the added interest that it was based on recent events. In *Zanoni* (1842) he made his own contribution to the novel of terror. Later, when the more realistic novel had re-established itself, he wrote *The Caxtons* (1849) and *My Novel* (1853). Bulwer Lytton's diversity has often led criticism to dismiss him too cursorily, as if he were merely a facile imitator. He has ingenuity and skill, and often a capacity for invention. His earliest novel, *Pelham* (1828), with its portrait of the Byronic rebel and dandy, is one of his most consistent works, while towards the close of his long career he wrote *The Coming Race* (1871), in which he anticipated the Utopian novels of Samuel Butler and H. G. Wells. There is a similar variety in the work of Charles Kingsley (1819–75), whose work varied from the propaganda novels of *Yeast* (1848) and *Alton Locke* (1850), advocating Christian Socialism, to historical romances such as *Hypatia* (1853) and *Westward Ho!* (1855), and the fantasy of *The Water Babies*. Variety the century did not lack, and much of the work cannot be easily defined: A. W. Kinglake (1809–91), in a work which is not properly fiction but has an imaginative quality, bringing it close to the novelist's art, used the East for his travel book *Eothen* (1844); Sir Richard Burton translated *The Arabian Nights* (1885–8); and George Borrow wrote of his wanderings and adventures, and of gypsy-lore, in *Lavengro* (1851), *The Romany Rye* (1857) and *Wild Wales* (1862). The observation and alert vagrancy of Borrow recur again later in the century in Richard Jefferies (1848–87) in volumes such as *After London* (1885), and in W. H. Hudson (1841–1922) in his descriptions of South America and of rural England. Hudson commanded a lucid and moving prose. His autobiography *Far Away and Long Ago* (1918), describing his early life in the Argentine, is possibly his greatest achievement. It is rivalled by his descriptions of humble, rural life on the Wiltshire downs in *A Shepherd's Life* (1910). *Green Mansions* (1904), which describes 'Rima', the semi-human embodiment of the forest, was made widely familiar by Epstein's once notorious statue.

The social attack through the novel, which Dickens had exploited, was carried on with documentary exactness by Charles Reade (1814–84), as in his exposure of the prison system in his melodramatic narrative, *It is Never Too Late to Mend* (1856). Reade is sometimes compared to Zola, but this seems unfair to Zola, for though Reade had patience in the accumulation of facts, his exaggerated violence and pathos are only too often apparent. He was happier in his excursion into the historical novel in *The Cloister and the Hearth* (1861), where he portrays a lively and detailed, though largely illusory, picture of the Middle Ages. A more powerful quality attaches to the novels of Benjamin Disraeli (1804–81), whose reputation as the most vital figure in the politics of the century has obscured him as a writer of fiction. His most effective work is to be found in the three novels which are an exposition of his political idealism: *Coningsby* (1844), *Sybil* (1845) and *Tancred* (1847). Here he advocated the 'Young England' policy of a Tory Democracy, and his belief in a new conception of nationality. To re-read those novels is to find that neither in their themes nor in their politics are they as outworn as might be anticipated. In a very different way Mrs Gaskell (1810–65) exposed the cruelty of the industrial system as she had seen it in Manchester in *Mary Barton* (1848) and *North and South* (1855). She had a talent for combining social criticism and melodrama, though her skill is not confined to these novels of social protest, for in *Cranford* (1853) she showed gentleness and humour in a picture of provincial life. When Victorian readers wished to turn from politics or the social evils of their times, they had in Wilkie Collins (1824–89) a writer who could arouse mystery and terror in a far more subtle way than Horace Walpole or Mrs Radcliffe. In *The Woman in White* (1860) and *The Moonstone* (1868), he showed a poetical, almost a mystical quality in combination with the power for constructing an elaborate and well-defined mystery plot.

In originality none of these writers could compare with Charlotte and Emily Brontë. Nor must the talent of their sister, Anne (1820–49), be altogether ignored, for *Agnes Grey* and *The Tenant of Wildfell Hall* are still readable. There is no story more inexplicable in our literature than the way these three sisters, living in the isolated village of Haworth, in Yorkshire, and with little encouragement from their domineering father, came to write novels which have been read with pleasure by

Haworth Moor, Yorkshire.

> *For the moors, for the moors where the short grass*
> *Like velvet beneath us should lie!*
> *For the moors, for the moors where each high pass*
> *Rose sunny against the clear sky!*
>
> Emily Brontë

successive generations of readers to this day. The lives of the sisters have often been recounted, but never more vividly than by Mrs Gaskell. Emily Brontë (1818–48) in her single novel *Wuthering Heights* (1847) created somehow out of her own imagination a stark, passionate world, reminiscent at times of the storm scenes in *King Lear*. In other hands the story might be mere melodrama, but so might *Othello* if told in a different way. As Emily Brontë narrates it, this story has a wild and cruel reality, and is original beyond any other novel in the century. How her mind came to conceive such a world can never be known, but behind her apparent loneliness there must have been a mysterious, ever-quickening inner activity, as her poems show. The talent of Charlotte Brontë (1816–55) was more diffuse but was maintained through a number of novels: *Jane Eyre* (1847), *Shirley* (1849), *Villette* (1853) and *The Professor* (1857). She combined scenes from her own life, in Yorkshire and in the school at Brussels, with the far richer and more romantic experiences which she had imagined. Thus her work is grounded in realism, but goes beyond into a wish-fulfilment. She had the courage to explore human life with greater fidelity than was common in her age, though the reticence of her period prevents her from following her themes to their logical conclusion. *Jane Eyre* shows the elements that make up her conception of life. Jane was a governess, and part of the actuality of Charlotte's own life. But Jane, unlike Charlotte, goes to the house of Mr Rochester, with whom she is in love. In part he is her fantasy of what the male as an instrument of sexual passion might be, and in part he is

Montoni of Mrs Radcliffe's *Mysteries of Udolpho* or a Byron transferred to a middle-class setting. The air of mystery which can be felt by the reader in every fibre of his being is created in Rochester's house. This was Charlotte Brontë's power, the creation of an atmosphere of terror without departing from a middle-class setting.

While the Brontës remained continuously secure in their reputation, George Eliot's (Mary Ann Evans, 1819–80) for a time suffered something of a collapse. From the thirties of the twentieth century onwards her reputation, not only in critical circles but with the general reader, has continuously advanced. American scholarship has seen to the publication of her letters and of her biography, so increasing sympathy with her personality and enhancing respect for the range of her mental capacity. Of all the women novelists of the nineteenth century, she was the most learned and, in her creative achievement, the most adult. Before she wrote fiction she had translated Strauss's *Leben Jesu*, and acted as assistant editor of the *Westminster Review*. She nearly married Herbert Spencer, the philosopher, only he found her too 'morbidly intellectual'. Spencer introduced her to G. H. Lewes, a writer of great competence. Lewes's distinction has had to wait for mid-twentieth-century criticism to gain adequate appraisal. He was learned in philosophy and in the biological sciences, but as far as George Eliot was concerned he was the great stimulant of her genius. Her personal problem was that though she could live with him she could not marry him. Lewes encouraged her to divert her attention from philosophy to fiction. Her

Dinah Morris, from George Eliot's *Adam Bede,* preaching on Hay Slope Green; a painting commissioned by Queen Victoria from E. H. Corbould.

... Dinah walked rather quickly, and in advance of her companions, towards the cart under the maple tree. ... The stranger was struck with surprise as he saw her approach and mount the cart – surprise, not so much at the feminine delicacy of her appearance, as at the total absence of self-consciousness in her demeanour

early *Scenes of Clerical Life*, on its periodical publication in 1857, had an immediate success. She followed these short narratives with a long novel, *Adam Bede* (1859), and her reputation was made. On the background of English rural life which she knew so well she created a far stronger theme than the Victorian novel previously permitted. In Hetty Sorrel she showed a young girl, seduced and led to child murder, and her imagination plays sympathetically around this lively and pathetic figure. While in Hetty she allowed a free play to her intuitions, her intellect controlled the 'good' characters in the novel, Dinah and Adam Bede. The problem for George Eliot as a novelist was whether her intuitions or her intellect would ultimately gain control. In the end her intellect won, and that was the hour of her crisis as an artist. In *Adam Bede* she was still tolerably free, and in description and character she showed not only intimacy and understanding but a power of humour. *The Mill on the Floss* (1860) showed her dilemma even more clearly. This was a Wordsworth story told in prose as a novel. In part, it is the life of a brother and sister, presented with great sensitivity: the girl passionate, dimly mystical, introspective, reacting against the blunter and more boisterous values of the boy. All this George Eliot knew intuitively, but her intellect had constructed a plan for the novel which hardens this natural study into a melodramatic close. The different elements in her mind found a balance in the shorter narrative of *Silas Marner* (1861), where all is admirably ordered to one design. The turning-point of her career was her attempt in *Romola* (1863) to write a historical novel of the Italian Renaissance. All that learning could offer in preparation for the novel George Eliot possessed, but the spirit of that period of strangely conflicting values is absent, and Romola herself appears as some graceful nineteenth-century Pre-Raphaelite who has wandered by mistake into Renaissance Italy. *Felix Holt* (1866), a novel of Radicalism of the Reform Bill period, with its over-elaborate plot, showed the penalties she was paying for the loss of her early spontaneity. But the end was not yet, for in *Middlemarch* (1871–2) she co-ordinated her powers to construct one of the great novels of the century. Intellect had come to terms with genius, and they both worked together, unless one is to admit that there was some uneasiness in her own subconscious mind. She had returned from the past to contemporary times, and gathered into sympathetic portraiture the lives of a number of families and studied their reactions. Her intellect was sufficiently employed in the difficult problem of structure not to impede her imagination. She had achieved the nearest approach in English to Balzac.

Her contemporary, Anthony Trollope (1815–82), was dominated by no such ambitious desire. In his delightful *Autobiography* (1883) he discussed novel-writing as if it were as simple as cobbling. This modest attitude to his own art disguised for some decades after his death a true appreciation of his talent. His early life had been a struggle but he made

The cover of an early edition of Trollope's *The Warden*, a picture of clerical life. Right: Henry James with John Bright, orator and statesman (left) and the painter Sir John Everett Millais (right). James longed for the imagined elegance of the Old World, and made up for not finding it in reality by putting it into his books

his way to prosperity by his double career as a civil servant in the Post Office and as a novelist. His pictures of clerical life, which began with *The Warden* (1855) and continued in *Barchester Towers* (1857), have gained increasing appreciation in the twentieth century. Trollope's production was continuous and included *The Three Clerks* (1858), *Framley Parsonage* (1861) and *The Eustace Diamonds* (1873). He has been increasingly admired for his political novels, particularly by historians. He had an easy and unpretentious gift for narrative, a fertile imagination, a style that seems to carry the reader on effortlessly and a happy imagination for creating character and incident. He is a male Jane Austen, cruder and more expansive, but equally secure in his knowledge of what he can do, and with the same clear determination not to transgress into worlds which he does not understand. More original to the nineteenth century in structure and intention were Trollope's contemporaries George Meredith and Thomas Hardy. The reputation of George Meredith (1828–1909) has declined sadly and in the mid-century there is very little sign of a revival, but surely it must come. That his novels are difficult must be admitted, but there was no more sensitive mind among the novel-writers of his century. Intellectually his main weakness was a share of the pride which he condemned in his characters, and it may be admitted that he made the first chapters of his novels intentionally difficult, so that they might be signposts to the dull-witted to follow him no farther. Unfortunately, he has been neglected not by the dull-witted

alone. For Meredith, the novel was far more than mere story-telling. Through his conception of comedy he wished to show up the dangers that beset the human spirit in its struggle to abandon the brutishness from which it had arisen. The body, the mind and, above all, the heart betrayed men from the normality which constituted the ideal way of life. The heart was treacherous because of the excessive and insincere feelings which sentimentalism tempted it to affect. This teaching Meredith expounded in a series of incidents created to explore the 'finer' shades of sentiment. He is a nineteenth-century Richardson, with a much finer intelligence than Richardson possessed. Following this philosophical purpose, Meredith, in three of his novels, *Richard Feverel*, *Evan Harrington* and *Harry Richmond*, analyses the most formative years in a young man's development, and the different types of exploration provided by these three studies show how varied was his art. The study of sentimentalism led him later to give women characters a central position in his theme, and again the variety is maintained in such contrasting studies as *Rhoda Fleming* (1865), *Vittoria* (1867) and *Diana of the Crossways* (1885). At his best his work had the brilliance of a Restoration comedy, and this is suggested above all by *The Egoist* (1879). He had learned from his father-in-law, T. L. Peacock, how to use entertaining dialogue in the novel, but he is seldom content with brilliance alone. He is for ever dissecting the frailty and deceit of the human spirit. He seems at times to make life too complex, and as he progresses in his work the complexity increases until, in *One of Our Conquerors* (1891), the reader may well feel that the effort demanded of him has not been fully rewarded.

Meredith's subtlety in the novel is paralleled in the work of Henry James (1843–1916), who, born in New York and educated in America (his brother was the distinguished philosopher, William James), settled in Europe in 1875, and was naturalized in 1915. His early novels, such as *Daisy Miller* (1879), portray the contact of Americans with European life. There followed a series of studies of English life itself, in *The Tragic Muse* (1890) and a number of other novels. As his work progressed, so did the intricacy of his style increase. He seemed to seek for every fine nuance of feeling, and he discriminated, with microscopic clarity, moods and changes that had not been before apparent. This mature stage can be discovered in *The Wings of the Dove* (1902), *The Ambassadors* (1903) and particularly in *The Golden Bowl* (1904). Henry James belongs only in part to English literature. His view of Europe was possible only to one with his American background. He had longed for the imagined elegance of the Old World, its tradition, its courtesies and its ritual. When he discovered that in reality they did not exist, he invented them, until his world is a Bostonian's platonic idea of what aristocratic life in Europe should be. With this idealization he combined a reticence in vocabulary, which arose not so much from any moral scruple but from a detestation of the vulgar and the physical. Sometimes in his work one longs for the spirit of Chaucer or Rabelais, or even for the blunt, clear *argot* of the street. He seems even to have hesitancy and faint-heartedness in the whispered suggestions of his elaborate and insinuating sentences. Yet he had enlarged the conception of the novel itself by his subtle discriminations in sentiment, and by the presentation of human relationships. Here were the ruling classes of the old pre-war Europe, idealized, apotheosized, by one who had loved their culture so passionately that he could not see that life itself was far more cruel than his view would suggest. His strength as an artist lay in the consistency of this invented world, which was so faithfully recorded that often one could believe that it was not invented at all but only an elegant reality that one had missed. In the sixties and onwards his works have had a remarkable revival, sustained by television performances of his novels. In this devious way he has had a posthumous success as a dramatist, an achievement he so longed for in his lifetime and with such humiliation failed to achieve.

If Henry James saw England as a stranger, Thomas Hardy (1840–1928) saw it as an Englishman born in Dorchester, and living for the greater part of his life in the Wessex which he portrayed. It is an interesting comment on the variety of the novelist's art that though Thomas Hardy and Henry James are contemporaries their worlds never meet. In 1871 Hardy published his first novel, *Desperate Remedies*, and from that year until the appearance of *Jude the Obscure* in 1895 he produced novels regularly, of which the most memorable by common consent are *The Return of the Native* (1878), *The Trumpet Major* (1880), *The Mayor of Casterbridge* (1886), *The Woodlanders* (1887) and *Tess of the D'Urbervilles* (1891). An architect by profession, he gave to his novels a design that was architectural, employing each circumstance in the narrative to one

Thomas Hardy with his second wife, Florence and his dog, Wessex. Hardy revolted against the optimism of nineteenth-century materialism, and most of his books describe the working of malign Fate

accumulated effect. The final impression was one of a malign Fate functioning in men's lives, corrupting their possibilities of happiness, and beckoning them towards tragedy. While this intuition about life did not harden into a philosophy, it was so persistent that it had every aspect of a doctrine. His intellect contributed to it in revolting against the optimism of nineteenth-century materialism, and in refusing the consolations of the Christian faith. While he saw life thus as cruel and purposeless, he does not remain a detached spectator. He has pity for the puppets of Destiny, and it is a compassion that extends from man to the earth-worms, and the diseased leaves of the trees. Such a conception gave his novels a high seriousness which few of his contemporaries possessed. It was as if a scene of Greek tragedy were being played out among his Wessex rustics. An early criticism of his work lay in this very incongruity, that his rustic characters should have the high passions, the noble and tragic proportions, which he gave them.

No theory can in itself make a novelist, and Hardy's novels, whether they are great or not, have appealed to successive generations of readers. He possessed varied gifts. First, he had supremely the gift of anecdote, the power of inventing lively incidents through which his story could move. He had patience in displaying through the incident the gradual interplay of his characters. His knowledge of country life made vivid the details in his stories, coloured and attractive in themselves, apart from their importance in the secure structure of his theme. Nor would he allow himself to be confined by the reticence which had limited the art of so many of his contemporaries. *Tess* and *Adam Bede* deal in part with the same theme, and to read them together is to see how far Hardy had progressed towards freedom of expression. In *Tess* and in *Jude the Obscure* he brought the novel in England near to the dignity of high tragedy. Nature, which to Wordsworth and the romantics had seemed stimulating and benign, appeared to Hardy as cruel and relentless. At the same time his kindliest characters are those who have lived away from the towns in a quiet rural life, refusing to challenge the wrathful spirits which play such havoc with life. His quality as a novelist has led to the most varied assessments. At first he was condemned as a 'second-rate romantic', and in the year of his death he was elevated into one of the greatest figures of English literature. The first view is ill-informed and the second may well be excessive, but the sincerity and courage and the successful patience of his art leave him a major figure in English fiction.

Both Meredith and Hardy had been influenced by the teaching of Darwin and the biological scientists, and this influence is found in an even more open way in Samuel Butler (1835–1902). In a century that was little given to satire he revived in *The Way of All Flesh* (1903) something of the spirit of Swift. This novel, which was largely autobiographical, showed an education in a clerical household, and in a bitter

An illustration to the first edition (1872) of Samuel Butler's *Erewhon*

and comic manner destroyed the compromise with which Victorian society sheltered itself. In an even closer approach to Swift's manner Butler atacked contemporary values in two satires, *Erewhon* (1872) and *Erewhon Revisited* (1901). Intellectually he was a rebel, and while this drove him at times into eccentricity, it allowed him to challenge the values of contemporary society. Butler saw that the worship of the machine made man its slave and that the machine as master would challenge and destroy civilization. He explores the treatment of disease, crime and education, exposing shallow inconsistencies and dubious values. He does not approach as closely as Swift to despair, for one is aware ever of a certain zest and enjoyment in life. He has also a quiet, wan optimism. If reason were allowed to function, he believes that life might be tolerable and kindly. Much that Butler wrote reads today like prophecy. His contribution was rather to ideas than to the form of fiction, though the opening of *Erewhon* shows how naturally and vividly he could write.

Between 1870 and 1880 there appeared new values both in the fiction produced and in its audience. There was an increase in the number of people who could read, and many of them were without tradition and opposed to the long three-volume novels which had previously been popular. Publishers did not at once become aware of this change, but gradually they found that shorter and cheaper volumes were more profitable. Robert Louis Stevenson (1850–94) was one of the earliest writers to make publishers aware of these changes. He had published without much success, in a boys' periodical, a romance entitled *Treasure Island*. When an enterprising publisher reissued this in volume form in 1883, it was immediately popular with the new adult public. With the short novel came the short story, to which Edgar Allan Poe had already given such vogue in America. Stevenson again made an important contribution, with the *New Arabian Nights* (1882). There followed a number of romances and mystery stories including *Kidnapped* (1886), *The Black Arrow* (1888), *The Master of Ballantrae* (1889) and *The Wrong Box* (1889). In *Dr Jekyll and Mr Hyde* (1886) he departed from his usual manner to write a modern allegory of the good and evil in the human personality. At his death he was working on an unfinished novel, *Weir of Hermiston*, which some have thought his best work. Stevenson in all that he wrote, in his essays, his letters, and his novels, remained an artist. He was in style self-conscious; sometimes one is led to think that the style was too good for the work. Stevenson is leading the novel back towards story-telling and to romance. It could be led to worse places, but one is conscious of the difference between him and the great masters of the art.

Stevenson is so consistent an artist that it is difficult at first to realize the phenomenon that had produced his success. The new reading public wanted a fiction that was easy, and not too long. The type of demand had always been present, but with the increase in the reading public the clamour for it increased. From this time onwards one can detect two types of novelists: those who deliberately or naturally adapt themselves to the great public, and those who follow their art into more difficult places and are often denied popular esteem. Thus the history of the great successes from 1870 is not necessarily the basis of the history of English fiction in that period. The following is a list of some writers who in their day have been oustandingly successful: 'Ouida', Rider Haggard, Conan Doyle, Mrs Humphry Ward, Hall Caine, Marie Corelli, Grant Allen and Edgar Wallace. All of their work was simple enough for the great audience to understand, though their approach to fiction as an art varied. Most of them could tell a story, and this is particularly true of such writers as Conan Doyle in the Sherlock Holmes stories, or even Edgar Wallace, who, had he taken more pains, might have written work that mattered. Rider Haggard again misses only by a little the opportunity of being something more than a writer of successful romances. He is obviously so much more competent than Grant Allen, whose *The Woman Who Did* was in 1895 not only topical, but daring. It was again a topical element that swept Mrs Humphry Ward's *Robert Elsmere* into every drawing-room in England. Her popularity was due not to the new, uneducated audience, but to the fact that in her discussions of the Christian faith she seized upon a theme uppermost in the mind of her time. Sometimes popularity may disguise an author's genuine merit. So P.G. Wodehouse's reception by a vast audience has obscured the fact that he is not only a writer of most brilliant idiomatic English but that he has added to our vocabulary. It is dangerous to judge any writer solely in the terms of the reception that he receives. At the same time, from the 1880s onwards the production of a large amount of very competent fiction written solely with the eye on the audience complicates any account of the novel in modern times.

With these writers one approaches a modern phenomenon that makes difficult the path of a critic. Conan Doyle has been known to several generations of English readers at all levels of education and critical intelligence, and his stories have been much enjoyed. His detective, Sherlock Holmes, and his dull, honest companion Dr Watson are, in England at least, household names. Yet if literature is to be considered as a great art, vital and important in our modern civilization, what place, apart from casual entertainment, is to be given to this type of writing? Does one touch here for the first time on the problem that modern man has more leisure, needs more entertainment, and if he turns to literature at all, is not likely to turn to the literature of which the critic will approve? Yet however solemnly Conan Doyle is judged it must be remembered that he was a story-teller of great talent, as is shown by *The Exploits of Brigadier Gerard*.

The problem can be seen in the reception given to two writers, both of great merit, George Gissing and Rudyard Kipling. George Gissing (1857–1903) has never been a popular writer and is never likely to be. Yet no one in English fiction faced the disease of his century with such a frank realism. In *Workers in the Dawn* (1880), *Demos* (1886), *The Nether World* (1889) and *New Grub Street* (1891), he portrayed the corruptions of society and refused to his audience the promise of an easy solution. It may be that his sense of helplessness has made him unpopular with the English, who prefer an element of comedy in their tragedy, and accept the grim pages of a Dickens only if they are accompanied by sufficient material for laughter. A kindlier atmosphere plays around *The Private Papers of Henry Ryecroft* (1903), and possibly this has made that genial volume the most popular of his works. Gissing's poverty and his unfortunate marriages to some degree frustrated his genius. He had imaginative interests which were not fully developed, as is shown in the impressions of Italy in *By the Ionian Sea* (1901) and in the post-humously published *Veranilda*, a novel of sixth-century Italy.

Rudyard Kipling (1856–1936), on the other hand, gained great popularity because his art naturally expressed much that a wide audience in England wished to hear. His work appeared at a time when England was becoming increasingly conscious of her Imperial position, and Kipling, born in India and working there for a time as a journalist in his early twenties, was able to give the colour and the strangeness of the greatest country which Englishmen in their adventures overseas had encountered. Like Stevenson he was a master of both the short story and the short novel, and this brevity, again, helped to attach him easily to the taste of his day. As T. S. Eliot has commented in a selection of Kipling's poems, he was a master equally in verse and prose.

Beginning with *Plain Tales from the Hills* (1888), he continued with volumes of short stories and with novels that included *The Light that Failed* (1891) and *Kim* (1901). Though the Indian scene was the source of

Rudyard Kipling at Paardeberg, South Africa, in 1907, the year he was awarded the Nobel Prize for literature. Part of Kipling's success as a writer was due to the fact that his art naturally expressed much that a wide audience in England wished to hear

his first popularity, he also wrote an original story of school life, *Stalky and Co.* (1899). His audience was further increased by his well-known animal stories of *The Jungle Books* (1894 and 1895) which describe how the child, Mowgli, was brought up by wolves and taught by them and the black panther, Bagheera, the law of the jungle. To these he added, again in a different mood, the Sussex fairy-world theme of *Puck of Pook's Hill* (1906). In India he had all the advantage of a new background, and his own style, quick and pungent, captured its strange sights and colours. He saw the East, romantically it is true, as part of the White Man's Burden, but his conviction was sufficiently strong to give force to his presentation. Nor were his Englishmen in India all alike; he could play maliciously with the social life of Simla, while he presented, with approval, the soldiers, and all who did a day's work efficiently. This delight in efficiency gave him pleasure in the mechanical aspects of his age, and often his imagery is derived from mechanism. His style was as simple in form as that of the Bible, but he had a lively imagination which threw in the vivid but unexpected word to enliven the sentence. So certain was he in his narrative that each sentence seems to be inevitable and nothing is wasted. Seldom does he attempt to present subtle characters, but in a few firm strokes places his people into the narratives which he could work so well. He had seen India as a child, and as a young journalist, and it is this child's vision that, when fully in control, gives his descriptions of Indian life a quality to which no other English writer attained. It appears in an unadulterated form in *Kim*, the most memorable of the novels, which remains a part of the small residue of imaginative literature that England's contact with India has produced.

Kipling was the voice of Imperialism triumphant, and though not often remembered his Imperialism was affected far more by South Africa and his admiration for Rhodes than by India. It was his South African experience that led to his poem *Recessional*, where he declared in no uncertain voice that he knew the dangers into which England might be led. Self-criticism, and even self-condemnation, appeared in the novel of the early twentieth century to an extent which Kipling would not have approved. With such a mood did John Galsworthy (1867–1933) begin his career as a novelist with *The Island Pharisees* (1904). Later, in a series of volumes beginning with *The Man of Property* (1906), he portrayed the life of the contemporary upper-middle classes. Published as *The Forsyte Saga* this volume, and its sequels, had great popularity in England and in other countries. After his death his reputation suddenly declined, but has been spectacularly revived by radio and television. At his best he had a gift similar to that of Anthony Trollope of making a whole class in society come to life. But he departs from Trollope in attempting through his portraiture to assess the values of his age. In *The Forsyte Saga* this is defined as the struggle of Beauty against the Idea of Property or Possession. Irene is Beauty and Soames

Forsyte, her husband, is Possession, exacting even forcibly his marital rights.

While Galsworthy portrayed the upper-middle classes, Arnold Bennett (1867–1931) showed the life of the 'Five Towns', the 'Potteries' of Staffordshire, and those who went out from them. Too often he succumbed to the temptations which a commercial world offers to the successful. In *The Card* (1911) he described a character 'wheedling' his way to the showy elegance of the capital. Bennett was a literary 'Card', but he was often an artist, and *The Old Wives' Tale* (1908) is as satisfactory a novel as any in the period. He had studied French models, particularly Maupassant, and his firm portrayal of two sisters of contrasting personality has a complete integrity. This solid realism was later underestimated, particularly when Virginia Woolf, in defending her impressionist manner, made Bennett her main adversary in *Mr Bennett and Mrs Brown* (1924). This attack might be true of his ponderous trilogy *Clayhanger* (1910), *Hilda Lessways* (1911) and *These Twain* (1916), but he returned to a more mature manner in a study of a miser, *Riceyman Steps* (1923).

Across the whole field of twentieth-century fiction are scattered the innumerable publications of H. G. Wells (1866–1946). From the time he jumped the counter of the draper's stores, where he was apprenticed, until his death, Wells wrote novels, essays, histories, outlines and programmes for world regeneration. In *The Time Machine* (1895) he invented a new form of scientific romance, possessing an apparent authenticity and lively detail. In quick succession appeared *The Invisible*

H. G. Wells playing 'Little Wars' from an *Illustrated London News* of 1913. In his early work, Wells invented a new form of scientific romance, possessing an apparent authenticity and lively detail

Man (1897), *The War of the Worlds* (1898), *When the Sleeper Wakes* (1899) and *The First Men in the Moon* (1901). In the romances which followed, *The Food of the Gods* (1904) and *In the Days of the Comet* (1906), ideas begin to intrude. Wells was already a Socialist and wished to bring the precision of science into human life. In *A Modern Utopia* (1905) he portrayed a vision of a reasonable world. Fortunately, added to this interest in ideas, he had a Dickensian gift for comedy, which he exploited in *The Wheels of Chance* (1896), *Love and Mr Lewisham* (1900), *Kipps* (1905) and *The History of Mr Polly* (1910). There followed novels of contemporary problems: *Ann Veronica* (1909), his portrait of the emancipated woman, and *The New Machiavelli* (1911), based on con-temporary political movements and figures. In *Tono Bungay* (1909) he mastered this new form in exposing the evils of commercial publicity. During the First World War he recorded his reactions in *Mr Britling Sees it Through* (1916) and later developed his hopes for reorganization in an interpretation of the past of the world in *The Outline of History* (1920). No one can understand the early twentieth century, in its hopes and its disillusionments, without studying Wells. He was no facile optimist. His last work was *Mind at the End of its Tether*. The cynics said it was the ageing Wells at the end of his tether, but the pessimistic theme that the earth was a temporary phenomenon, and that the human race was determined to destroy itself, appears ever intermittently in his work. In the later periods, the creative instinct was overwhelmed by the didactic, but he did tell mankind that without some sort of world government it had no chance of survival. It is encouraging that in the last decades of the twentieth century he is increasingly remembered.

Apart from the social novelists, fiction in the early twentieth century showed great variety. By common consent one of the most original was Jozef Korzeniowski, a Polish captain in the English merchant marine, and a naturalized British citizen known as Joseph Conrad (1857–1924). With a wide experience of the sea, of Asia and the Americas and the ports of the world, he wrote, in an English that was elaborate and strangely rhythmical, a series of novels beginning with *Almayer's Folly* (1895). In his own day much of his popularity was based on his early novels of the sea and of strange places. Outstanding were *The Nigger of the Narcissus* (1898), *Youth* (1902) and *Lord Jim* (1900), the story of a young Englishman who in a moment of panic deserts his sinking ship, but ultimately retrieves his honour by his death. These coloured, roman-tic novels won him his reputation and it is through them that he retains many of his readers. Yet to a selected element in a younger generation, led by an able chapter in F. R. Leavis's *The Great Tradition*, it was the complex novels of the middle and later period that established Conrad's major claims as a novelist: *Nostromo* (1904), *The Secret Agent* (1907), *Under Western Eyes* (1911), *Chance* (1914) and many others. The basis for Conrad's fiction is the adventure story, but told with a complex evoca-

A storm in the Adriatic.

The sea, as if agitated by an internal commotion, leaped in peaked mounds that jostled each other, slopping heavily against her [the ship's] sides; and a low moaning sound, the infinite plaint of the storm's fury, came from beyond the limits of the menacing calm

Joseph Conrad, *Typhoon*

tion of mood and a constant psychological interest. It is as if the work of R. L. Stevenson had been rewritten by Henry James. He is self-conscious in his art, and the self-consciousness intrudes. Like Flaubert he seeks for perfection, and sometimes the reader may watch him making his slow progress to his ideal. Often he writes of violence and danger, but not of these only, for, like some of the 'impressionist' painters, he seeks to capture elusive moods, using a rich and coloured vocabulary, almost as if he employed words as pigments. While he depicts the surface reactions of life, he endeavours, as do some of the Russian novelists, to portray the more mysterious moods of consciousness. In the later novels the moral dilemma of the characters is explored with a brilliance of detail. He has a greater integrity as an artist than many of his age, and one forgets that he is a foreigner writing English as one follows the strange and complex beauty of his prose.

By his very origins Joseph Conrad helped to give a cosmopolitan variety to the novel, and much of the enterprise in twentieth-century fiction has come from an interest in foreign models. George Moore (1852–1933) profited by years in France with a study of Zola, Maupassant and the Goncourts. His work is difficult to judge, for he has been surrounded by admirers who feel that any gesture of criticism is a mixture of heresy and vulgarity. He was self-consciously an artist but also a *poseur*, and his prose though often beautiful is seldom free from affectation. Irish by birth but Parisian by education, he dramatized his conception of himself as an artist, and possibly his best work is to be found not in the novels but in a series of autobiographical narratives, including *Confessions of a Young Man* (1888) and *Hail and Farewell: Ave* (1911), *Salve* (1912), *Vale* (1914). His talent was varied and included the bold naturalism of *Esther Waters* (1894), the graceful prose of *The Brook Kerith* (1916), a religious novel, and *Héloise and Abelard* (1921).

The variety of able works in this period is bewildering. Ford Madox Ford (1873–1939), the editor of the *English Review*, in *Parade's End*, a series of novels on the character of Tietjens – *Some Do Not* (1924), *No More Parades* (1925), *A Man Could Stand Up* (1926) and in 1928 *Last Post* – established a reputation more in the United States than in England for an elaborate study of personal relations, worked out with a deliberate and adult artistry. The brilliant though wayward talent of Wyndham Lewis (1882–1957) amounted at times to genius, but the uncertainty of his moods gave *Tarr* (1918), *The Apes of God* (1930) and *The Childermass* (1928) less popularity than they deserved. In other moods there was Robert Graves (b. 1895), a most diversified man of letters, who brought a new image to the historical novel with *I Claudius* (1934), *Claudius the God* (1934), *Wife to Mr Milton* (1943).

In the modern period fiction is derived from both English and American sources. This had been true since the days of Henry James, but increasingly so after the First World War. If one looks at the most notable fiction arising from that war, two volumes were written by Americans: Ernest Hemingway's *A Farewell to Arms* (1929) and William Faulkner's *Soldiers' Pay* (1926). It could be urged that, in modern times, literature in the English language should be criticized as one theme. Space does not permit the attempt here, but, apart from their greatness and their appeal, writers such as Hemingway and Faulkner and, in drama, Eugene O'Neill, have deeply influenced English writers, so that in many ways the story is unintelligible unless American literature is added. Thus no novel of the Spanish Civil War has a wider reputation than Hemingway's *For Whom the Bell Tolls* (1940).

From the twenties to the fifties there had been a high level of performance in the novel, yet its importance in society as a whole was declining. This was already true in the days of radio, but the effect was increased by television. Further, the conditions of modern life have told against reading. The Second World War with confinement to shelters and homes encouraged fiction reading, as Trollope's rediscovered popularity showed Possibly fiction reading can develop under modern conditions only as a minority activity. It can never be a central feature of society as it was in the Victorian age. Up to the beginning of the First World War the professional classes, and even Prime Ministers, had ample leisure. If political leaders no longer wrote books as did Gladstone and Disraeli, they read widely, and much of their reading was in the novel. The dominance of radio and the television screen has already been indicated. It introduced certain writers to an audience of millions. Trollope, Galsworthy, Kipling, Maugham, Wells and even Henry James, all found vast radio and television audiences. The decline in the large audience for the novel is reflected in the decay of the circulating libraries of which the chief was Mudie's in London, now long destroyed. It looked rather like a shabby and secular cathedral, and that, in a way, was what it was.

The middle-class public came there to seek, every week, on borrowing terms, its assignment of new fiction, conscious that Mr Mudie had blessed the works and said, in the manner of his Creator, that they were good. Mudie's emporium in New Oxford Street in London has, as was mentioned above, long disappeared, but when Boots the chemists closed their circulating libraries in 1965 the era of the fiction-lending library was at an end. On writers, the tradition had been restrictive: the audience and the libraries demanded a literature that was intelligent, discreet, but lacking in depth, and devoid of the outspoken, particularly in sexual themes. Hugh Walpole, whose work is mentioned later, is the most typical, if not the most brilliant, of these practitioners. He had taste and discernment. He collected pictures. He was himself painted by Augustus John and Sickert, and his head was sculptured by Epstein. He was aware of a literature of a depth and intensity different from his own. He was a friend of Conrad, and he joined in the campaign to defend D. H. Lawrence, but in his own writing he was one of Mudie's men. These novelists who belonged to the trade of fiction made fortunes, and were even national figures. Even as late as 1931, when Arnold Bennett was dying, straw was placed in the road, outside his London flat, to deaden the noise.

It is difficult to summarize the work of these decades when so much fiction was produced. Popularity sometimes affects critics in estimating a writer, and W. Somerset Maugham (1874–1965) has thus suffered conspicuously. His early novels, which included *Liza of Lambeth* (1897) and the autobiographical *Of Human Bondage* (1915), were realistic studies of London life, but in later novels he used China and Malaya as a background in *The Trembling of a Leaf* (1921) and *The Painted Veil* (1925). These, a number of other novels, volumes of short stories and his plays, gave him a very large audience despite the neglect of the critics. Early studies in Maupassant influenced his economy in narrative and helped him to exclude sentimentality and to deal with sexual relations with an unabashed frankness. He conveyed no message, as did many of his contemporaries, and when life appeared in unpleasant patterns he recorded them without apology. His realism had elements of cynicism, but his prose can have the unaffected strength of Swift. *The Razor's Edge*, which had a great success in 1944, is his nearest approach to a philosophical novel.

A more original writer to whom popularity did not come easily was E. M. Forster (1879–1970). He began with stories which had myth and fantasy and were later reprinted as *The Celestial Omnibus* (1911) and *The Eternal Moment* (1928). His first novel was *Where Angels Fear to Tread* (1905), followed in 1908 by *A Room with a View*, first drafted in 1903. He had found something emotionally incomplete in English life, particularly in the life of an English schoolboy, and here he explores the contrast of more passionate Italian life. *The Longest Journey* (1907), brilliant but uneven, again emphasized the inner, personal life. These themes were developed with maturity in *Howards End* (1910), an admirable picture of English middle-class life before the First World War and an exploration of its complexities. Again the emphasis was on the inner, emotional life. Forster travelled widely and residence in Egypt produced not only an unusual guidebook to Alexandria (1922), but *Pharos and Pharillon*. Wider recognition came from his Indian visits and the publication of *A Passage to India* (1924). His novel was based on much knowledge and a genuine affection for Indian people. It was a corrective to Kipling, for with a realism, subtly evoked, Forster showed not the romance of the East, but actual people and the difficulty they have in mutual understanding. The atmosphere, though clearly presented, is contrived with a minimum of detail. Its weakness lies in its injustice to the Englishman who worked in India. In his later years Forster achieved great authority in the literary world, and, apart from his novels, was known for his lectures, *Aspects of the Novel* (1927), and his essays, *Abinger Harvest* (1936). It is possible that as the twentieth century proceeds both the authority and the reputation will diminish. Forster was a homosexual, in an age when this was still a criminal offence. The fact that he could not speak out affected his art and it was only after his death that *Maurice*, his tepid homosexual novel could be published: he had completed it by 1914. *A Passage to India* is to be valued, for England's contact with India produced little such imaginative work. L. H. Myers (1881–1944) wrote out of his invention and reading the impressive historical trilogy *The Root and the Flower* (1935), which many Indians have admired. Kipling and Forster, though in different moods, employed contemporary scenes and their own experience. Later some writers were to express a nostalgic view of India, markedly Paul Scott (1920–77) who completed a quintet of novels, ending with a touching story, *Staying On*. The governing mood of *A Passage to India* is satirical, and the same spirit was to be found in a number of writers of the time, including the ironical mysticism of T. F. Powys's *Mr Weston's Good Wine* (1927).

Among original writers a high place is now given by common consent to D. H. Lawrence (1885–1930), the son of a miner in a village near Nottingham, whose tormented life is well recorded in his *Letters*. His background was different from that of any novelist of his time. He knew the miners, their wives, the cramped houses, the huddled life, the cruelties and debasements, and the smell of the slag heaps. But he knew, too, the country near by, and sometimes he ached for its fresh smells, its signs of growth, the sounds of birds and the footprints of a fox in the snow. If the background was different, so was his inner experience. Modern civilization thwarted his spirit and he could find no consolation, as Wells had done, in making blue-prints for a new world. The disease was one which admitted no intellectual cure, for the modern world seemed to

Lining up at the Company's store to get supplies. D. H. Lawrence, the son of a
Nottinghamshire miner, knew the cruelties and hardships of the miner's life

Lawrence to have corrupted man's emotional life. Even passion had become some niggling by-product of the intelligence. To discover again a free flow of the passionate life became for him almost a mystical ideal, for there was fulfilment and there was power. His early novels, of which the most successful was *Sons and Lovers* (1913), had only hinted at these later developments. He had been content in this, the most normal of his works, with a vivid, realistic picture of the Nottingham life which he knew. Gradually his own philosophy asserted itself in his fiction, in *The Rainbow* (1915), *Women in Love* (1921) and *Aaron's Rod* (1922). The European war, in which for medical reasons he had been a non-combatant, increased his sense of isolation, as he showed in *Kangaroo* (1923), the most revealing if not the most satisfactory of his works. This detachment from civilized life now became mixed with a certain irritability accompanied by a sense of surrender of the intellect to more elemental and irrational elements, and, as he shows in *The Plumed Serpent* (1926), he sought among more primitive people in Mexico for the more natural life which Europe could not give. In its emphasis on the physical, his work had aroused criticism in some quarters, and some of his novels had been banned. As if in revenge, he published in *Lady Chatterley's Lover* (1928) a franker description of the physical relations of two lovers than had yet appeared in English fiction. Its publication in England in an unexpurgated form long after Lawrence's death led in 1960 to an unsuccessful prosecution for obscenity. As a result, this novel had a far larger circulation than any of his other works, and won a licence for free expression for younger novelists of which Lawrence himself might not have fully approved.

Though he wrote with great care he added little to the form of the novel, though his own philosophy led to a much bolder description of sexual life than his predecessors had given. There are elements in his work which may be condemned. He rejected tradition, partly because he had never known it, and instead of struggling to remake civilization, he turned upon it a loathing that culminated in despair. The intellect, one of the major instruments allowed to man if he is to seek the reasonable life, he despised. So much may be said on the adverse side of the balance, and it must be admitted that in these directions his influence has been pernicious. But it is difficult to judge in a cold and calculating way one who suffered so much, and one who had such originality of vision and sheer genius. Nor even in the most detached summary can the estimate be left in this negative condition. His plea, taken in its simplest form, that civilization had degraded man's sexual life, was a pertinent one. At one period his belief in the passions seems almost to become mystical, as if he were regaining something of Blake's vision. But his sense of isolation thwarted him, and at length almost degraded his genius. To style, in the ordinary definition of the word, he was indifferent. He seems to hack his meaning out of the words, as his fore-bears had hacked coal from the pits. But the effects are original. He invented a language in which sexual experience can be described, and he had a rare eye for every movement in nature, as if there, without knowing it, he found the sole consolation for his spirit. Nowhere did he write more movingly than in his letters. It is difficult to see that any writer in English fiction in the twentieth century has achieved as much as Lawrence.

The boldness of expression which D. H. Lawrence had brought to the novel was found also in his younger contemporary, Aldous Huxley (1884–1963). No finer intelligence has applied itself to fiction in this century, and though for a time he submitted to Lawrence's influence he could not have had a more different background. In him the great influences of Victorian art and science met: on his father's side he was descended from Thomas Huxley, who had been Charles Darwin's champion in the discussions on evolution, and on his mother's side from Matthew Arnold. His education was not that of a Nottingham mining village, but of Eton and Balliol. Heredity with Huxley seems to have counted more than formal education, for he brought to the novel the knowledge and analysis of a scientist, and the curiosity in form of an artist. His early novels were comic and satiric narratives, prefiguring the disillusionment of young Englishmen in the years after the First World War. In *Crome Yellow* (1921) and *Antic Hay* (1923) he revelled in the comic exposure of life's deceit. Gradually the cynicism gave place to more serious inquiry and both elements met in *Those Barren Leaves* (1925). He was not seeking any easy solution of his dilemma, for like Lawrence he was tormented by the strange phenomenon of man, the animal with a mind. Unlike Lawrence, he did not regard sexual experience with pleasure, and certainly not as a medium of illumination; though the theme fascinated him, it filled him with disgust, as he watched the petty lecheries of his characters, unable to detach himself, yet tortured by his preoccupation. Like Swift, he was angered at the jest that makes life thus, but, unlike Swift, he was aware that this strange beast, man, had also created symphonies, painted pictures and had moments of vision. All this led to the most brilliant and original of his novels, *Point Counter Point* (1928). In the brittle illusion of a well-ordered mechanical world, he found no consolation, and he satirized such beliefs in *Brave New World* (1932). From 1933 the changed political scene in Europe gave to his thought a greater urgency and seriousness. The beast, which he had already discovered in man, now seemed ready to destroy the graces which had offered to the civilized world a minor compensation. In *Eyeless in Gaza* (1936) he expounded his deepened vision but he had reached an impatience with fiction as a medium. So in *Ends and Means* (1937) he set out his ideas without the embarrassment of a story. In *Time Must Have a Stop* (1945) and *Ape and Essence* (1949) he returned to fiction without adding much to the earlier novels. From 1938 he had lived in California and as his sight deteriorated he became more interested in mysticism, and a quieter tone pervaded his last novel *The Island* (1962).

James Joyce (1882–1941) and D. H. Lawrence were the most original novelists of the century, though in the sixties Joyce's popularity did not keep pace with that of Lawrence. Joyce, like Shaw and Yeats, was Irish. Unlike them, he did not reside in England. Much of his life was spent on the Continent, but spiritually he never left Dublin. His early short stories, *Dubliners*, were brief impressionistic studies, as clear-cut as those of Maupassant. His individual art began to show itself in *A Portrait of the Artist as a Young Man* (1916) and appeared fully formed in *Ulysses* (1922). After seventeen years this was followed by *Finnegans Wake* (1939). Joyce attempted to make a fiction that would image the whole of life, conscious and subconscious, without any concessions to the ordinary conventions of speech. He would break up the ordinary structure of the language until it could image these fluctuating impressions. More philosophically, he came to feel that time and space are artificial, that all is related and that art should be a symbol of that relationship. His work has become notorious, because in this pursuit he described, particularly in the close of *Ulysses*, these inner contemplations of his characters when they concentrate on their own sexual life. To judge him from these passages alone is to miss his seriousness as an artist. He had Dublin and the Catholic Church as his background, and from them both he revolted, as can be seen in *A Portrait of the Artist*. Both were highly organized unities, and to leave them, particularly to leave the Church, was emotionally to enter into chaos. Psychologically Joyce is for ever attempting to re-seek unity in a world that is disorganized. The greater his attempt to define the Unity, the more do the broken fragments fall in minute pieces through his hands. Compared

Dublin after the First World War. Even though James Joyce spent most of his life on the Continent, his writing is full of descriptions of Dublin, like this one from *Ulysses*:

> Cityful passing away, other cityful coming, passing away too:
> other coming on, passing on. Houses, lines of houses, streets,
> miles of pavements, piledup bricks, stones. Changing hands

with *Finnegans Wake*, the outline of *Ulysses* is simple. Instead of the wanderings of Homer's Ulysses over the geographical world, Joyce shows the mental wanderings of a character in Dublin for the space of twenty-four hours. He retains sometimes the ordinary grammatical structure in the sentences, and the sequences of thought, once one has caught his devices for suggesting the free association in the mind, are not difficult to follow. By the side of *Finnegans Wake* the earlier novel seems a primer, for in this immense work Joyce had written a collection of words, some derived from languages other than English, and many apparently invented, whose significance no single reader can ever hope to gain. His genius is, however, a sincere one and his boldness in invention has influenced a number of younger writers who have followed him at a modest distance.

Nothing in the novel in the twentieth century can fully compare with Joyce. To read him and Virginia Woolf together is to realize all that, out of upper-middle-class timidity, she was led to exclude. His expression might have been a more ample one if he had not been hounded by censorship. Talent there has been in amplitude in the twentieth-century novel, but genius seldom. In Joyce there was a fierce and absolute genius that is difficult to follow.

Virginia Woolf (left) with
the composer and
suffragette, Ethel Smyth

While the novel in Lawrence and Huxley depended mainly on ideas, a group of writers in the present century have employed it to explore the inner aspects of the human personality. Some of them have been encouraged by the study of the subconscious to penetrate beneath the surface reactions in life. They believed that the novelist who portrays a mind as if it conducted its thought in well-ordered sentences is giving only an artificial impression. This portrayal of the inner life has often entered into the novel, but in the present age it has been explored more profoundly, and with the aid of the psychological sciences, which have shown how disordered is our hidden mental existence. One of the earliest novelists of this type in England was Dorothy Richardson, whose *Pointed Roofs* (1915) was the first instalment of a series of novels in which the consciousness of a single character was exposed. Her work has not received the recognition accorded to Virginia Woolf (1882–1941), who began in the same year as Dorothy Richardson with *The Voyage Out* (1915) and who developed her art in a number of novels which include *Night and Day* (1919), *Jacob's Room* (1922), *Mrs Dalloway* (1925), *To the Lighthouse* (1927), *Orlando* (1928), *The Waves* (1931), *The Years* (1937) and *Between the Acts* (1941), which she left at her death not fully revised. Her method was usually to accept a plot which had a simple outline, but to exploit it with an impressionism which seized upon every detail, however minute, and to order these details not in a rational arrangement but as they stream through the mind of one of her characters. The novel was thus one variation on the interior soliloquy, though diffuseness was avoided by the retention of the central and well-ordered theme. Armed with an acute intelligence and sensibility, she suffused every evanescent mood with a romantic quality that added to the buoyancy of the narration. In addition, she possessed wit, as can be seen in *Orlando*, and a tenderness without sentimentality aided in evoking these previously unapprehended human relations. The characters which she thus captured in the undress of their mental life were such as shared her intelligence and her decencies. Even if she appeared to have exposed all, there was still much to disclose. This can be seen once her work is compared with that of James Joyce. In 1953 appeared extracts from her autobiography, showing she had a profound revelation of an artist's relation to the work created. Her life has been sympathetically portrayed by Quentin Bell, but it would be difficult to say that interest in her work as a novelist is being fully maintained, although the publication of her voluminous diaries and letters are giving a fresh interest to her personality.

Though Virginia Woolf may be one of the most original women writers of fiction in the twentieth century, other women have made a major contribution. Senior amongst them was Rose Macaulay (1881–1957). Her early talent was satiric, as in *Orphan Island* (1924), but her more ambitious work came later; the historical novel *They Were Defeated* (1932) and a brilliant last novel, with lighter movements, *The Towers of Trebizond* (1956). She lacked the aggressively original and distinctive talent of Ivy Compton-Burnett (1892–1969), who wrote *Dolores* as early as 1911, but invented a manner entirely her own with *Brothers and Sisters* (1929) and a series of subsequent novels. All these narratives are set in the period 1885–1901, chosen to give a background where family life was dominant, and when in large country houses life could be isolated, violent and eccentric; Greek tragedy given a Victorian setting. There is an atmosphere often associated with Ireland. The novels are almost entirely in dialogue, with much wit and aphoristic phrasing that have led some, mistakenly, to compare her with Jane Austen. Her world is far more sinister: *Brothers and Sisters* (1929) has incest; in *Men and Wives* (1931) a child kills his mother; in *Manservant and Maidservant* (1947), apart from other crimes, there is a contemplated parricide. Frequent ingredients are a tyrannical figure at the centre, much conspiracy within families and a flourishing of the wicked. She has had a coterie of most intelligent admirers, who select as among her best work: *Men and Wives* (1931), *More Women Than Men* (1933), *A House and Its Head* (1935), *Daughters and Sons* (1937), *A Family and a Fortune* (1939) and *Manservant and Maidservant* (1947). Her talent gives a surface of elegance with evil lurking underneath. Her genius has an element of the satanic, but one could wish that comedy had a larger place, for with the single phrase she could create brilliance: 'To know all is to forgive all, and that would spoil everything'; or 'Pride may go before a fall. But it may also continue after'. Her long career continued with an unusual evenness in achievement. Among the more recent novels were *The Mighty and Their Fall* (1961) and *A God and His Gifts* (1963).

Katherine Mansfield (1888–1923), a New Zealander, was the wife of Middleton Murry, critic, biographer and commentator on D. H. Lawrence. She had a vogue in her own day for her short stories: *In a German Pension* (1911), *Prelude* (1918), *Bliss* (1920) and *The Garden Party*

(1922), but her reputation has not endured. She concentrated on the individual emotion, and on sensibility, but the comparisons made to Chekhov now seem excessive. Her posthumously published *Journal* was a brave attempt at self-analysis in a much involved personality. Rosamond Lehmann (b. 1904), who also derived from a romantic tradition, wrote sparingly but with brilliance. Her early work, *Dusty Answer* (1927), seemed to have been influenced by Meredith. Her later novels show sensibility with a wider awareness of life than some of her contemporaries. *A Note in Music* appeared in 1934, but she may be best remembered for *The Ballad and the Source* (1944), which contrasted a young girl's impression of an older woman with the actuality of that woman's life. Rebecca West (b. 1892), a critic and observer of discretion, had an imagination more immediately in contact with current circumstance. Her novels included *The Return of the Soldier* (1918), *The Judge* (1922) and *Harriet Hume* (1929). To the novel of the elucidation of personal sentiment and human relations Elizabeth Bowen made a distinguished contribution beginning with *The Hotel* (1927) and followed by a number of novels including *To the North* (1932), *The House in Paris* (1935), *The Death of the Heart* (1938), *The Heat of the Day* (1949) and *The World of Love* (1955). Typical and most effective is *The Death of the Heart*, which explored with subtlety the emotions of an adolescent girl placed in a complicated and insecure human situation. The scene is contemporary among the upper-middle-class people who never discuss politics or indeed any subject outside their own relationships and their own emotions. Delicate and revealing as is this work, one cannot help but feel how removed it is from all the harsher realities of the year 1938 when it appeared and, indeed, this fiction, which was so competently represented in the first three decades of the twentieth century, was to come to an end. A more sustaining quality is to be found in the strange complexities of Iris Murdoch's (b. 1919) talent which has matured from *Under the Net* (1954) to *The Sea, The Sea* (1978). Other women writers who have claimed attention are Muriel Spark (b. 1918), particularly in her story of a schoolmistress in *The Prime of Miss Jean Brodie* (1962), and Edna O'Brien (b. 1936), the Irish writer, in a series of novels beginning with *The Country Girls* (1960).

Many practised the novel with intelligence and skill without adding substantially to its form. Without naming all the writers of this category, four may be taken as examples: Compton Mackenzie (1883–1972), Hugh Walpole (1884–1941), J. B. Priestley (b. 1894) and L. P. Hartley (1895–1972). Of these writers Mackenzie was by far the most prolific. His early novels broke new ground, particularly in *Carnival* (1912) and *Sinister Street* (1913–14): the latter, the most ambitious of his works, is a study of the growth of human temperament, and had the prudishness of his public been less pronounced, it could have been an important work rather than a bold period piece. Many of his later novels were entertainments such as *Whisky Galore* (1947). He was continuing with his vast autobiography, *Octave Nine*, well into his eighties. He was a grand old man of letters, the like of whom modern conditions cannot produce. Hugh Walpole, beginning with *The Wooden Horse* (1909), studied English types, sometimes, as in *The Cathedral* (1922), in a manner reminiscent of Trollope. His later long historical novel, *Rogue Herries* (1930), in an ample narrative vigorously explored a number of aspects of character. J. B. Priestley's meteoric rise with *The Good Companions* (1929) was followed by *Angel Pavement* (1930) and other novels. Those who dislike popularity have vehemently attempted to minimize his achievement. Beginning with his Yorkshire background, he has, in his expansive volumes, been able to elucidate much in the contemporary scene. He has appealed to a vast audience that was not aware of fiction before it encountered his work, a similar audience to that Dickens captured. Similarly L. P. Hartley exercised a consistent talent in the short story and the novel, with sensitive studies of English life as in *The Shrimp and the Anemone* (1944) and *Eustace and Hilda* (1947). He gained a much extended reputation in the last years of his life through the brilliant film version in 1971 of his attractive novel *The Go-Between* (1953). It increased the audience for his whole work, including *The Harness Room* (1971).

Of writers of a younger generation it is possible only to make a selection. Joyce Cary (1888–1957) added new strains to the novel. His early themes had an African background, *Aissa Saved* (1932) and *An African Witch* (1936), to which he added later the most notable of these studies, *Mister Johnson* (1939). They show much understanding of the problems of Europeans and Africans in a contemporary setting. Among his other novels there were three linked volumes *Herself Surprised* (1941), *To Be a Pilgrim* (1942) and *The Horse's Mouth* (1944), which appeared during the Second World War. They showed a great zest of life, an emphasis on the colour and the delight of living all held within a modern, picaresque theme, particularly in the person of Jimson, the rogue hero.

One of the difficult writers to assess is Charles Morgan (1894–1958). In his novels he analysed the finer shades of feeling on a background that was elegant and mystical. He found a wide public for *Portrait in a Mirror* (1929), *The Fountain* (1932) and *Sparkenbroke* (1936). Critics in England were a little sardonic in their approach, but in compensation he gained warm recognition in France.

Among writers born in the first decade of the twentieth century George Orwell (1903–50) had an impressive and individual talent. A social historian in assessing what happened to England in this period could not do better than study Orwell. He had the conventional education of the upper-class Englishman, but his family was comparatively poor: of this he grew conscious at his preparatory school, and though Eton treated him with kindliness, he left to go not to a university but

A still from Michael Anderson's 1955 film of George Orwell's *1984*; a cruel vision of the ultimate totalitarian world

to the Imperial Police in Burma. There he developed the guilt complex about imperialism so common in his generation. All this resulted in his first novel *Burmese Days* (1934). In his view there was not only imperialism to be expiated, for he had a vision of all the down-trodden and wished to associate himself with them. From 1927 to 1933 he buried himself in poverty, and there emerged the largely autobiographical *Down and Out in Paris and London* (1933). By a different route from his left-wing contemporaries he had come to see the desolation of poverty and unemployment in France and England, and there followed a series of novels in which these problems were implied or openly discussed: *A Clergyman's Daughter* (1935), *Keep the Aspidistra Flying* (1936) and *Coming Up for Air* (1939). They gained less attention than they deserved because Orwell was so separate from the left-wing literary groups and this isolation also affected the reception of his essays, *The Road to Wigan Pier* (1937). In an age of 'committed' writers it was harsh to hear Orwell say: 'No one who feels deeply about English literature, or even prefers good English to bad, can accept the discipline of a political party.' In the Spanish Civil War he was anti-fascist but highly individual and the literary result was *Homage to Catalonia* (1938), one of his most attractive books. His essays in *The Lion and the Unicorn* (1941) showed him regarding the English people with affection, though affirming that England was 'the most class-ridden country under the sun'. In *Animal Farm* (1945), possibly influenced by Swift, he portrayed the animals taking power and finding in it their own corruption. Finally there came *1984* (1949), with its cruel vision of the ultimate totalitarian world where all is controlled for power, a vision far more scarifying than that in Aldous Huxley's *Brave New World*.

Orwell's originality lay in his awareness of the shape of contemporary England: in this he anticipated younger writers such as Kingsley Amis (b. 1922). Amis's most brilliant novel was *Lucky Jim* (1955) but a comparison with Orwell soon defines the missing dimensions. A similar approach appears in John Braine's (b. 1922) *Room at the Top* (1957). A number of Orwell's contemporaries still moved among the upper-middle classes, though often with an ironic eye. Such was Evelyn Waugh (1903–66), one of the ablest novelists of his generation. He had passages and scenes of outstanding brilliance. His brother, Alec Waugh (b. 1898), gained an early popularity with what seemed at the time a bold documentary on public schools, *The Loom of Youth* (1917), but his later novels were mainly 'entertainments'. Evelyn Waugh's early novels shared something of Aldous Huxley's satiric criticisms of sophisticated society, but Huxley's figures were more intellectual, Waugh's more aristocratic, and Waugh abandoned himself more completely to high comedy. He had a farcical contemptuousness that was all his own, as in *Decline and Fall* (1928) and *Vile Bodies* (1930). His travels in Africa, and particularly in Abyssinia, led to *Black Mischief* (1932), *A Handful of Dust* (1934) and to the comic satire on journalism *Scoop* (1938). Waugh became a Catholic convert and, as a result, a depth of seriousness mingled with the comedy of *Brideshead Revisited* (1945). This portrayed a nostalgia for a vanished England: an England that was partly the day-dream of a man of middle-class origins about the grandeur and elegance of aristocratic society. He returned to satire among the American crematoria in *The Loved One* (1948), but his major work of this later period was the trilogy of the war period *Men At Arms* (1952), *Officers and Gentlemen* (1955) and *Unconditional Surrender* (1961), revised and reissued in one volume as *Sword of Honour* (1965), in which his hero, Guy Crouchback, becomes the symbol of the defeated romantic. In the middle of work on this trilogy the attacks on him as a reactionary led to a moving self-analytical novel, *The Ordeal of Gilbert Pinfold* (1957), which may yet remain one of the most revealing literary documents of the period. At the time of his death he was engaged on an autobiography, a part of which has been published but can add little to his reputation.

Many have given a high place to Malcolm Lowry's (1909–57) *Under the Volcano* (1947), a study in alcoholism, which was neglected for a time after Lowry's suicide, but gained a wider public when revived for radio.

Something similar to Waugh's cultivation of an elegant past appeared in the novels of Anthony Powell (b. 1905). As early as 1931 in *Afternoon Men* he exposed the foibles and extravagant behaviour of an aristocratic society no longer secure in its tradition. In the war years he prepared a volume on the antiquarian John Aubrey and returned to fiction determined to 'produce a really large work about all the things I was interested in – the whole of one's life in fact'. This became *A Dance to the Music of Time*, including volumes such as *A Question of Upbringing* (1951), *A Buyer's Market* (1952), *The Acceptance World* (1955), *At Lady Molly's* (1957) and *Casanova's Chinese Restaurant* (1960). Without any falling in standard it has been continued with *The Soldier's Art* (1966) which brings the narrative to 1941 and *The Military Philosophers* (1968) which continues this portrait of an age to the end of the Second World War. In these later novels the prose is often pleasingly elaborate. The characterization owes something to Aubrey, a little more to Dickens, and the method is indebted in a general way to Sterne and Proust. The credible is continuously in contest with the extravagant and both win. It has been estimated that there are already two hundred characters in this work: they all know each other, but in different contexts, and make up the intimate intricacy of upper-middle-class English life. The penultimate volume was published in 1973, as *Temporary Kings* and the whole series was completed with the twelfth and final volume, *Hearing Secret Harmonies* (1975). How it will endure cannot be said, but it is a major achievement in fiction, and its main character Widmerpool is not easily to be forgotten.

Evelyn Waugh's name has been linked with that of Graham Greene (b. 1904) because they were both Roman Catholic converts, but as novelists they have little in common. Greene is a realist, though he has given the name 'entertainments' to some of his thrillers, such as *A Gun for Sale* (1936), *The Confidential Agent* (1939), *The Ministry of Fear* (1943) and his brilliant script for the film *The Third Man* (1950). Even among these excitements an element of moral inquiry prevails. His more serious novels: *England Made Me* (1935), *The Heart of the Matter* (1948), *The End of the Affair* (1951) – with *Brighton Rock* (1938) poised somewhere between an 'entertainment' and a novel – show him as an outstanding novelist, presenting character and emotion with sureness and a cunning control of narrative. He has Maugham's delight in strange places and a ruthlessness in exploring human experience, but with Greene the Catholic element, as in *The Heart of the Matter*, does give an added depth. In these novels he presents 'good' and 'evil' in the theological sense, as distinct and sometimes even contradictory to kindness and to attempts at socially commendable behaviour. The hero of *The Heart of the Matter* is led to adultery and suicide and so, theologically, to damnation solely because of an earnest instinct towards kindliness. Some critics felt that with *A Burnt Out Case* (1961) there were signs that his best work had been achieved, but in *The Comedians* (1966) he showed himself still, effectively, occupied with the problems of good and evil on a brilliant and well-defined background in Haiti.

Another novelist whose main contribution has been to contemporary realism is Christopher Isherwood (b. 1904), who associated with W. H. Auden in his plays and wrote two vivid documentary novels of pre-

Nazi Germany in *Mr Norris Changes Trains* (1935) and *Goodbye to Berlin* (1939). He has an economy of style and a modest approach to themes illuminating the helplessness of ordinary individuals as a civilization begins to collapse. *Mr Norris Changes Trains* was a fantasy with a Berlin background of the immediate pre-Hitler period, illustrating the decadence of Berlin life, but also giving vivid pictures of the rising cruelty of the Hitler groups. The central theme is too fantastic but this contrasts with the passages where the gangsterdom of German politics during these years is illuminated. *Goodbye to Berlin* is nearer to reporting. Isherwood contrived to use a background which he knew well to define a unique moment in these decades. He went to the United States with W. H. Auden before the Second World War and his later novels, such as *Prater Violet* (1945) and *The World in the Evening* (1954), have less significance. Rex Warner (b. 1905) was again a writer whose best writing belonged to the impact of the revolutionary political movement of the thirties. A classical scholar, a critic and translator, he wrote two political allegories in the form of fiction: *The Professor* (1938) and *The Aerodrome* (1941). They illustrate the inadequacy of liberalism and tradition when faced with totalitarian power.

Contemporary with these, but seemingly untouched by current influences, was Henry Green (1905–73), a writer of much originality, who wrote a series of novels usually with one word titles. *Blindness* (1926), *Living* (1929), *Caught* (1943), *Loving* (1945), *Back* (1946), *Concluding* (1948), *Nothing* (1950) and *Doting* (1952). He looks at the human scene with an independent freshness, almost as if it had never been viewed before. In *Doting* he contrived to conduct the whole action in dialogue, but yet without any complexity. The seeming simplicity of his approach may at first sight conceal his skill. A most individual talent also appeared in William Golding's (b. 1911) *Lord of the Flies*, describing a group of English boys on a desert island.

In 1937 Lawrence Durrell (b. 1912) published in Paris a novel called *The Black Book*, a flamboyant and obscene extravaganza which could not appear in England for another thirty years. His reputation principally rests on *The Alexandrian Quartet*, a series of novels first published between 1957 and 1960: *Justine*, *Balthazar*, *Mountolive* and *Clea*. These explore love in all moods, and passages of great beauty mingle with studies of corruption and intricate sensual exploration. Durrell has a power of imaginative prose, but whether his brilliant and exotic work will develop remains questionable. In his uproarious *Tunc* (1968) and its successor *Nunquam* (1970) he uses all the licence of which the modern novelist has possessed himself, but where he will ultimately go as a novelist is uncertain. Among writers with an individual tone is David Jones (b. 1895) with *In Parenthesis* (1937), a first novel and war record with a mystical background (it is written partly in prose and partly in free verse). Many regretted that his writing drew him away from his brilliant work as a pictorial artist. Another novelist who began in the thirties but who is best known for a later work in several volumes with an exotic setting is Olivia Manning; her *Balkan Trilogy* comprises *The Great Fortune* (1960), *The Spoilt City* (1962) and *Friends and Heroes* (1965).

Out of the Second World War came a new tradition of realistic fiction attempting to place on the current scene the scientist, the psychologist and the new men of bureaucratic power. A popular attempt was made by Nigel Balchin (1908–70). *The Small Back Room* (1943) shows with all appearance of authenticity the rivalries of scientists in competing war-time groups, while *Mine Own Executioner* (1945) was the story of a psychiatrist. In a similar way a contemporary success was obtained by C. P. Snow (b. 1905) who, drawn from Cambridge into the war-time Governmental machinery, explored in fiction 'the corridors of power'. He planned a novel sequence of some eleven volumes under the general title of *Strangers and Brothers*. Of these *The Masters* (1951), which showed the rivalries of personalities within a college in Cambridge, obtained a wide recognition, as did *The Conscience of the Rich* (1958) and *The Affair* (1960). Some complained of a certain flatness in the style, but with Snow the novel did return to contemporary problems and a gift for narrative allowed them to be explored with vivacity. He gained a wider popularity when *The Masters* and *The Affair* were successfully adapted as plays. In 1968 in *The Sleep of Reason* he added to the *Strangers and Brothers* series with a novel most sensitive to the violence and psychotic crisis present in some elements of a rapidly changing society. The sequence was concluded with *Last Things* in 1970.

Another acute observer of the contemporary scene was Angus Wilson (b. 1913), particularly in his early novels such as *The Middle Age of Mrs Eliot* (1958).

In the fifties and most particularly in the sixties there was a decline of censorship and a licence to authors unprecedented in English literature. The abolition of stage censorship is recorded elsewhere but the same conditions were becoming available to the fiction writer. The turning-point was the failure of the charge of obscenity against the Penguin edition of *Lady Chatterley's Lover*. After that it was easy to publish an unexpurgated paperback edition of James Joyce's *Ulysses* It is ironic to contrast this with the continuous battle Joyce had with the censors and the police in his own lifetime. But these volumes were moderate compared with the text of some more recent English and American novels. In 1969 the Arts Council, the Government-sponsored body to support the arts, received the report of its own commission on censorship which recommended unanimously that the law on obscenity be abolished. The Government showed no eagerness to turn the findings of the report into law, but English fiction entered the seventies with a greater verbal permissiveness than at any period of history.

è Cœlo Salus

A true and full coppy of that which was most imperfectly and Surreptitiously printed before under the name of: Religio Medici.

Printed for Andrew Crooke 1656

The frontispiece to the 1656 edition of Sir Thomas Browne's spiritual autobiography, *Religio Medici*

Chapter 13

English Prose to the Eighteenth Century

WHEN LIFE is the criterion and not art, the prose of a nation is far more important than its poetry. Into prose go its laws and proclamations, its prayers and its politics, and, in modern times at least, its philosophy and history. Yet it is necessary to recall that in the earliest periods verse was used for many of the purposes where prose now is the natural medium.

The best that a nation can ask of its lawgivers, politicians and philosophers is a prose that is unpretentious, unambiguous, and unadorned. Apart from all this, the artist employs prose in a number of ways, in fiction, in the essay and in drama. Often he uses prose with elaborate patterns and richly decorative words. The artist may also use a simpler prose, but with him the simplicity will be accompanied by power and eloquence. Rhetoric and the quest for harmony will always be beckoning him away from simplicity to more elaborate effects. Any study of prose is complicated by the very varied purposes for which it is used. In this chapter the novel and drama are eliminated, for they have already been considered, and an attempt is made, not to record the work of all the other important writers who have employed prose, but only of such as have added to the possibilities of English prose as a medium of expression.

Behind English prose, from the Anglo-Saxon period to the eighteenth century, is the pattern of Latin. Boethius's *Consolation of Philosophy*, a Latin work of the sixth century, was translated by King Alfred (d. 899), by Chaucer (d. 1400) and by Queen Elizabeth (d. 1603). A single Latin work had retained such distinguished popularity for over seven hundred years. Throughout that period most educated people could speak and write Latin, and some of them regarded Latin as the language in which all literature should be written. Even as late as the seventeenth century, Francis Bacon was afraid that English would 'play bankrupt' with authors and determined that all he valued most in his work should exist in a Latin version. Even in the eighteenth century Latin still held a dominant place.

Early pre-Conquest literature had both a consciously mannered prose, such as Ælfric used, and the simple language of the compilers of King Alfred's *Chronicle*. The simple prose lives on much better than the mannered prose, in movement it is modern. Much of it is a bare and direct record of fact, but when the chronicler has to express an emotion he does so with a sincerity which is still intelligible. W. P. Ker translates a passage made by a Peterborough monk describing the misfortunes of the reign of Stephen, which is one of the most effective:

> Was never yet more wretchedness in the land, nor did the heathen men worse than these men did. For never anywhere did they spare either church, churchyard, but took all the wealth therein, and afterwards burned the church and all together.

Although the *Chronicle* began under Alfred's guidance, it continued for two and a half centuries after his death, and for almost a century after the Norman Conquest. It is sometimes suggested that English prose died out with the Conquest, but this is not true. What did die was the elaborate and mannered prose, such as that of Ælfric. What lived on was the simple, natural prose, such as the monks at Peterborough continued to write to 1154. There is thus a continuous tradition in English prose, though after the Conquest English is for a time debased, and has to struggle for its existence. So in these centuries, when French is the fashionable and official language, English is still used, though the works in which it was employed were unexciting.

The most important event in fifteenth-century prose was the establishment by William Caxton of his printing press in England in 1476. Caxton was not only a printer but a translator, and much concerned with the problem of extending the vocabulary of English. His own influence, and still more that of the printing press, helped to break down the anarchy of dialects and to give England a standard language.

Among the works which Caxton printed was Sir Thomas Malory's

A woodcut of an angler from *The Book of St Albans*, printed in 1496 by Wynkyn de Worde on his press at Westminster

Morte d'Arthur (written about 1470 and printed in 1485). Composed in a prose intelligible to any modern reader, the words in Malory's sentences have a beauty of movement which cannot escape unnoticed:

> And thus it passed on from Candlemass until after Easter, that the month of May was come, when every lusty heart beginneth to blossom, and to bring forth fruit; for like as herbs and trees bring forth fruit and flourish in May, in like wise every lusty heart that is in any manner a lover, springeth and flourish-eth in lusty deeds. For it giveth unto all lovers courage, that lusty month of May, in something to constrain him to some manner of thing more in that month than in any other month, for diverse causes. For then all herbs and trees renew a man and woman, and in like wise lovers call again to their mind old gentleness and old service, and many kind deeds that were forgotten by negligence.

Malory's work was a translation from the French, 'a most pleasant jumble and summary of the legends about Arthur', and through his work the chivalry and romance of the Middle Ages were recorded. As a complement, Lord Berners, in his translation of Froissart's *Chronicles* (1523–4), gave the realistic life of the same period. Froissart had narrated the life of the fourteenth century as he had seen it, and his vividness and honesty have made him a great descriptive historian. Berners allows Froissart's French to guide him into an English which is firm, intelligible, and simple.

Meanwhile, the Bible, which had been appearing in various forms in the vernacular, was approaching the translation in which it was to become for centuries the best-known book in English. The Bible as it is known today owes its form mainly to the labours of two men, William Tyndale (1490–1536) and Miles Coverdale (1488–1568). Already in the fourteenth century John Wycliffe (1324–84) had laboured to make an English version, but his renderings were based on the Vulgate, or Latin

An illustration from the 1634 edition of Malory's *Morte d'Arthur*. Arthur is shown surrounded by his knights at the Round Table

version, and his English was literal and stiff. His influence on the development of English prose has been exaggerated. Tyndale, who at Vilvorde in 1536 was strangled at the stake for heresy, his body afterwards being burnt, gave to his prose the simple vigour of phrase and the strong cadences, with which the Authorized Version of 1611 has made us familiar. Miles Coverdale completed the work which Tyndale had begun. No book has had an equal influence on the English people. Apart from all religious considerations, it afforded, to all classes alike, an idiom in which the deeper emotions of life could be recalled. It gave grace to the speech of the unlettered, and entered into the style of the most ambitious writers. Its phrasing coloured the work of poets, and its language is so embedded in our national tradition that if the Bible is forgotten a precious possession will be lost.

The sixteenth century had nothing in its prose to match the excellence of the drama, yet scholars had been preparing the way for the acceptance of English as the standard medium of expression. So Roger Ascham (1515–68), a tutor of royal ladies, including Queen Elizabeth, wished that England might be for learning and wisdom 'a spectacle to all the world beside', and he attempted to carry out his aim in *Toxophilus* (1545), a dialogue on the art of archery, and in *The Schoolmaster* (1570). The ordinary life of England does not come much into Elizabethan prose, though, as has been seen, Robert Greene, Thomas Dekker and the other novelists and pamphleteers with their picaresque narratives show something of the English Autolycuses in action. Translation, chronicle and history still continued as the main work of prose. In 1579 Sir Thomas North published his version of Plutarch's *Lives of the Noble Grecians and Romans*, the most famous of all the Tudor translations; Shakespeare was content to employ not only its themes but its very phrases in his Roman plays, particularly in *Antony and Cleopatra* and *Coriolanus*. The Elizabethan translators, like some of the sailors of the time, were freebooters, and North translated not from the original, but from the French of Jacques Amyot. He employed also his own gift for happy and ingenious phrasing. Apart from North, Shakespeare also used Philemon Holland's translation of Pliny's *Natural History*. This was an outline of the science of the ancient world, and included everything, from sober observation to winged beasts and monstrosities. It had a greater influence on Shakespeare than is commonly realized.

If the ancient world was rendered available by the translators, it was the chroniclers who laid bare the past of England and the deeds of Englishmen everywhere. Shakespeare again has given a special importance to the name of Raphael Holinshed, whose *Chronicles* (1577) were the basis for the English historical plays. Holinshed worked with collaborators, and he cannot compete with North in the dignity and beauty of his language. But he possessed a great lucidity, and whatever his prejudices, he had a clear conception of his great theme. If Holinshed gives

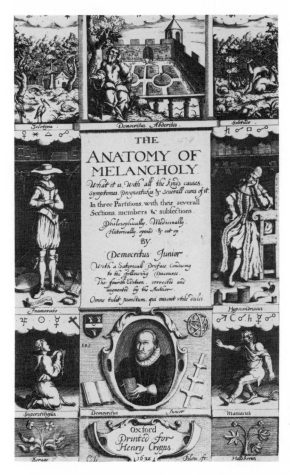

The title page of Robert Burton's *The Anatomy of Melancholy*. In this work, Burton describes and analyses the disease of melancholy, as suffered by scholars, recluses, clerics, lovers, maniacs and hypochondriacs

the background of England, Richard Hakluyt (1553–1616) gave the modern adventures and discoveries of his countrymen in *The Principal Navigations, Voyages and Discoveries of the English Nation* (published in 1589 and much enlarged in 1598–1600). Hakluyt's aim was a practical one: he wished to find 'ample vents' for our manufactured goods and to develop colonial possessions. His work is largely a compilation, made from the accounts of the explorers themselves. When he writes himself, he has a strength and even at times a haunting beauty. Hakluyt described the discovery of the geographical earth, but in the seventeenth century Robert Burton (1577–1640), in the strange but fascinating *Anatomy of Melancholy* (1621), explored the human mind with the aid of all the learning of the classical world. He was a marauding scholar, who found his prizes all equally worthwhile, and all equally relevant to the great purpose which he had in hand. He examined the disease of melancholy, Hamlet's disease, which was to that period what neuroses have been to the twentieth century.

The great prose writer of the early seventeenth century was Francis Bacon (1561–1626), and it is not without significance that the middle of his career should coincide with the publication of the Authorized Version of the Bible. If the Bible gave religion its great document, Bacon encouraged the methods of scientific investigation, which later were to challenge Christian thought. Bacon himself is orthodox enough in his religious professions, but the attitude he encourages came into conflict with faith, and indeed with any mystical view of human experience. Most of Bacon's work is in Latin, and it is ironical that the greatest prose writer of the time should have mistrusted the permanence of English as a language. Bacon is the most complete representative of the Renaissance in England, learned, worldly, ambitious, intriguing, enamoured of all the luxury that wealth in his times could supply and, while knowing so much, almost completely ignorant about himself. One can picture him in his study, in the half-light, with music playing softly in an adjoining room, running his fingers through a heap of precious stones, while his mind all the while is contemplating the nature of truth, unless, of course, it is engaged with political intrigue. His *History of Henry the Seventh* gave historical writing in England the first work which had design. His unfinished narrative of *The New Atlantis* told, in simple prose, an adventure story of a journey into an imaginary island in the Pacific while, in the manner of H. G. Wells, embedding in the middle a plea for historical research. *The Advancement of Learning* (1605), a portion of his great scientific work, described the condition of knowledge and the way in which it might be improved. None of these can equal in human interest the *Essays* (1597). The essays added in the editions of 1612 and 1625 are in each instance significant of different periods of Bacon's life. In 1597 with such essays as 'Of Studies', Bacon informs the ambitious young man how he can make his way in the world. In 1612 he has a wider range of theme and suggests the responsibilities of power. The third volume, with its essay 'Of Gardens', hints at the release of retirement. The essays are compact in style, almost gnomic, with a pretty

The exodus from London during the plague of 1625, from *A Looking-Glasse for City and Countrey,* published 1630

balance in the phrasing, and with images, such as, 'men fear death as children fear to go into the dark', which have become part of the common tradition of English speech. In arrangement they are precise and well-ordered, as one would expect from a scientist, and in this they contrast with the happy and informal intimacy of Montaigne.

The first half of the seventeenth century was a period of religious controversy, of Civil War and of the triumph of Puritanism. The great monuments of its prose have solemnity and seriousness and an impressive grandeur. The modern reader, who comes upon them for the first time, will feel a sense of remoteness, but he cannot easily fail to perceive a majesty, present in that age, which has never returned into the language. Prose was to discover itself in other ways, to become more pliable, more useful, even more human, but no one repeated the magnificent and sombre eloquence of Sir Thomas Browne, Jeremy Taylor or John Milton.

Sir Thomas Browne (1605–82) was a physician, resident in Norwich, who lived through the Civil Wars, but seemed entirely unaffected by them. He was learned in the science of his time and he knew Bacon's method of investigation. Not less was he attracted to religion, and he had read widely in classical and modern authors. He seems to stand, as does so much of the seventeenth century, midway between the modern and medieval ways of thought. Some of his science belongs to modern investigation, but he was seriously interested in popular superstitions, such as whether elephants have joints. He had a tolerance in religion and confesses that he could 'never hear the Ave-Mary bell without an elevation', but he believed in witches, and his evidence sent some of these unfortunate women to their death. He had a longing for the incredible and for the incidents in the Bible which are magical, though he knows how remote they are from the records of experience. This duality in his mind does not lead to fretfulness, though it may account for his gentle melancholy. He admires reason, but he sees that human life is part of greater experience. Whatever his theme, he is conscious of the great spectre of death at the end of the road. It is the theme of death which informs his *Hydriotaphia, or Urn Burial* (1658), where his solemn prose rises to its most imaginative and majestic effects.

More varied is his spiritual autobiography *Religio Medici* (1643), written before he was thirty. Seldom has English stretched itself to the harmonies which Browne controls in his long sentences, marshalled with words, many of them of Latin origin and all of them well-sounding. The age which produced Sir Thomas Browne also possessed in Jeremy Taylor (1613–67), the most eloquent preacher that the English Church had known. He is best remembered for his *Holy Living* (1650) and his *Holy Dying* (1651), but his sermons surpass these in the passion and splendour of their language.

The political controversies of the age drove John Milton to write in prose, that is to write, as he himself described it, with his left hand. Much of his most interesting prose was in Latin, his defence of the English people and his expression of his own very individual views on Christianity, the *De Doctrina Christiana*. Two pamphlets will always remain of importance: his defence of the encyclopedic method in education, published as *Tractate on Education*, and his plea for free speech and writing in the *Areopagitica* (1644). Milton appeared at his best in this second pamphlet, where he expressed his finely founded belief in the rightness of the human spirit if left to develop unrestricted. As elsewhere, he voices his love of England, or of what he hoped England might be, 'a noble and puissant nation rousing herself like a strong man after sleep, and shaking her invincible locks'. His prose does not read easily. He was so familiar with the·Latin sentence, which can be well-ordered even when it is elaborate, that he forgot that English cannot contain a multitude of clauses in a single sentence without confusion.

One writer stood apart from all these tendencies, and yet of all the prose authors of that age he has made the greatest appeal to posterity. Izaak Walton (1593–1683) published his *Compleat Angler* in 1653, and since then the volume has never lacked readers. Not less valuable are his lives of Donne, Hooker, George Herbert and Sir Henry Wotton. Walton had a long life, stretching from the Elizabethan Age to the Restoration, and his amiable optimism seems untouched by the troubles of his country in those years. His *Angler*, which coincides with the Civil War, is a gentle praise of the sport of angling, and of the English countryside through which it led him.

With the Restoration of 1660, English prose seems to make a new beginning. The Court had been to France and had learned there, as far as prose was concerned, the virtues of lucidity, for which the French have been justly praised. Lucidity had never been absent from English prose, as the language of the Bible shows, but the ambitious writers, especially of the early seventeenth century, had aimed, not at lucidity, but at grandeur. The change comes, not from any deliberate imitation of French prose, but because English prose-writers attempted the easy, sociable sense which French prose possessed. Jeremy Taylor's prose is processional prose; it will not do the tasks of a maid-of-all-work. Sir Thomas Browne's prose is prose in canonicals; it will not serve for conversation. The change can be exaggerated, for some Restoration writers are stiff and dull. Much of the interest of the age lay in science and philosophy, and these studies exacted from prose precision and bareness. While the Court was enjoying the comedies of Wycherley or Congreve, the Royal Society was being founded, with a Royal Charter in 1662, for the investigation of scientific problems. In prose it attempted to exact from its members a 'a close, naked, natural way of speaking'. Its scientific explorations were less precise than those of its successors in the twentieth century.

This spirit of inquiry extended beyond science into literature and philosophy. John Dryden, a figure symbolical of his age, applied himself in prose to examine the workshop of literature in essays modelled on those of Corneille, of which *The Essay of Dramatic Poesy* (1668) is the earliest, and the *Preface to the Fables* (1700), written in the year of his death, is the most engaging, especially in the comparison of Chaucer and Ovid. Dryden had some of the old mannerisms in his prose, but, at his best, he combined 'the other harmony of prose' with an easy manner of creating an informal atmosphere, and of allowing the reader to enter into the development of an argument.

The scientists, as has been suggested, deliberately encouraged simplicity, but the virtue had penalties, for the age produced few works of the imagination, apart from Bunyan's allegories, composed by a mind neither helped nor hindered by the tradition of his time. It was well that this economy and clarity in prose coincided with the beginning of the most important period of English philosophy. Of these philosophers the most alarming was a timid man, Thomas Hobbes, who, born in 1588, contrived to cling to the existence which he was always afraid to lose, until his death in 1679. Hobbes suggested that human life, including thought, was the result of physical changes. Our senses received impressions and we registered reactions to them, and that was the sum of experience and of morality. As we were all registering these reactions, the world would soon be reduced to a state of anarchy if there were not some control. Hobbes was a seventeenth-century totalitarian. But he was not a revolutionary who wished himself to be at the centre of power. That he discreetly reserved for his Stuart masters. In his *Leviathan* (1651), in which he relates his theories to politics, he makes it amply clear that the monarchy alone can preserve society from disruption.

The frontispiece illustration to the 1651 edition of Hobbes' *Leviathan,* an appeal for the restoration of the monarchy, which alone could preserve society from anarchy

Hobbes's extreme materialism was modified in the philosophy of John Locke (1632–1704), who developed a system in which knowledge was based on experience, but experience itself was not so closely related to physical reactions as in Hobbes. Locke's *An Essay Concerning Human Understanding* (1690) had a wide influence both on the Continent and in England. It is one of the greatest works of English philosophy, and one of the most typical of the English temperament. The abstract is held in a nice compromise with the concrete, and all is related to the test of experience. Both Hobbes and Locke write with clarity. Hobbes has a strange acrid beauty in his prose and Locke has lucidity without much charm.

The science of the time was interested in the human mind, and at the same time men became more interested in themselves, as can be seen in the diaries, the journals and the histories which survive from this age. Before the Restoration, the individual voice was seldom heard, or, if it were heard, it was on some important or public occasion. But now, for the first time, there walked through English prose a man discussing the intimate details of his own life. He was not an ordinary man, but he wrote of the things which the ordinary man has known. He wrote for himself, in secret, but his work has been transcribed, and so Samuel Pepys (1633–1703) has become the most famous prose writer of the late seventeenth century. Even if Pepys had not kept a diary he would have been a great figure in the history of England, the founder of the Royal Navy, an outstanding Civil Servant and a President of the Royal Society. In his diary, he revealed the other Pepys, privately for his own eye, and without shame, his pleasures and vanities, his philanderings, and the details of each passing day. The following is typical of his more innocent passages where he shows how he relaxed after a day at the office:

> Thence we went to the Green Dragon, on Lambeth Hill, both the Mr Pinkney's, Smith, Harrison, Morrice, that sang the bass, Sheply and I, and there we sang all sorts of things, and I ventured with good success upon things at first sight; and after that I played on my flageolet, and staid there till nine o'clock, very merry and drawn on with one song after another till it came to be so late. After that Sheply, Harrison and myself, we went towards Westminster on foot, and at the Golden Lion, near Charing Cross, we went in and drank a pint of wine, and so parted, and thence home, where I found my wife and maid a-washing. I staid up till the bellman came by with his bell just under my window as I was writing of this very line, and cried, 'Past one of the clock, and a cold, frosty, windy morning.' I then went to bed, and left my wife and the maid a-washing still.

Nothing in English literature can compare with this confession, not even Boswell, for Pepys's interests were wider than Boswell's. The human mind itself gained some liberation from the way in which Pepys records himself.

Pre-eminent though Pepys was, there were others in his age who shared his interest in recording their own lives. Pepys's friend, John Evelyn (1620–1706), a fellow-member of the Royal Society, a courtier and a country gentleman, kept an account of his more discreet existence. He was interested in gardens, in courts, in travel, in smoke-abatement and in himself. Wealthy, cultivated and widely travelled, he is a notable contrast to the conception of the licentious Restoration courtiers which the popular imagination gathers from the work of writers such as the Earl of Rochester.

Pepys and Evelyn described their own lives, but when Edward Hyde, Earl of Clarendon (1609–74), came to write of himself he found that he had to write the history of England in his own time. He was one of Charles I's advisers and he was in exile with Charles II until the Restoration, when he became Lord Chancellor. The later years of his life were spent in exile again. His *History of the Rebellion*, published in 1702, is the first work in England since Alfred's *Chronicle* in which great events are recorded by a man who was himself a central figure. Even if his style is not easy, it gives an impression of the great days through which he lived.

The intimacy, which appeared in Restoration prose, lives on in the days of Queen Anne, the most sociable period of English literature. Much of the prose of the age went into the novel, but some of the fiction writers were talented in other ways. Daniel Defoe, who is often rembered only for *Robinson Crusoe*, did much to establish English journalism, and in his paper, *The Review*, set the eighteenth century upon the genial task of composing the periodical paper. This employment developed with Sir Richard Steele (1672–1729) and Joseph Addison (1672–1719). Addison had varied success before he became a writer of periodical essays. In 1704 his poem *The Campaign* celebrated the victory of Blenheim. His tragedy, *Cato*, was very popular in 1713. Yet his real fame derived from his association with Steele in *The Tatler* between 1709 and 1711. Together they joined in the production of *The Spectator* (1711–12) which was later produced by Addison. Manners, fashions, literature, stories, moral reflections, all took a turn as themes in brief papers, which were addressed consciously to a middle-class audience. Both Steele and Addison came to understand precisely what was required, though Addison had to turn himself from a rather stiff and formal scholar into a man who could talk genially. The periodical essay was the eighteenth-century equivalent of the broadcast talk, and Addison found that a group of recognizable characters made his task easier. So he developed the character of Sir Roger de Coverley (originally introduced by Steele), and other members of the Spectator Club.

Steele and Addison wrote for their audiences, determined not to give offence. Jonathan Swift (1667–1745) wrote, without regard for any man, the vision of life as he saw it. The long list of his satires extends from *The Battle of the Books* and *A Tale of a Tub* (1704) to *Gulliver's Travels* (1726),

'Coffee-House Jests':
Coffee-houses were
first introduced into
London in the time of
the Commonwealth and
were much frequented
in the seventeenth and
eighteenth centuries for
the purpose of political
and literary discussion.
Dryden, Wycherley,
Addison, Pope and
Congreve used to meet
at Will's Coffee-house
in Russell Street

and beyond, into the more bitter works of his last period. Swift has often been presented as a diseased misanthropist, who saw his fellowmen as the Yahoos of the fourth book of *Gulliver*. Little of this is true. Swift had a mind overvexed by the inconvenience and inadequacies of the physical apparatus of the human body, of its uncleanliness and its odours and of the absurdity of the sexual act, when it is considered methodically by a non-participant. But his *Journal to Stella* shows that his fellowmen liked him, and that to Esther Johnson, whom in many, if not all, senses of the word he loved, he could show a genuine affection. The *Drapier's Letters* (1724) revealed his hatred of political chicanery and his genuine understanding of the Irish people. Proud he may have been, and even arrogant, but this arose from the dread possession of a vision

Gulliver in Lilliput

unlike that of ordinary men. His insight would not permit of any concealment, and *Gulliver*, apart from being a good story, is the indictment of the human race for refusing reason and benevolence as a way of life.

The Forum in Rome, by Canaletto. In the eighteenth century historians began to try to interpret the past, and the Grand Tours to take in the archaeological as well as the social centres of Europe

Chapter 14

Modern English Prose

IN THE eighteenth century the subjects of study to which man applied himself became more numerous and more systematic, and it was the good fortune of England that prose in that age had become a pliant and serviceable medium. It was a century full of speculation and fierce questioning, a century with powerful minds that applied themselves to the problems of the nature of life, and set out solutions which have been the basis of much later thought. It was a century, above all others, when England led Europe in philosophical speculation. The centre of interest was human experience, and what could be learned from it of the nature of life, and here the eighteenth century looked back to Locke, if not always for guidance, at least for its terms of reference. Richardson and Fielding explored human experience in fiction. Historians were attempting, more ambitiously than before, to interpret the past of life and philosophers to expound the nature of reality itself. It was natural that in such a century the orthodox teachings of the Church should be open to criticism, and it was fortunate for the Church that in Joseph Butler (1692–1752) it found its ideal exponent. In his lucid work, *The Analogy of Religion* (1736), he attempted to find the justification for religion out of such limited knowledge as experience itself supplies.

Among the sceptical minds produced by the century, none is more original than Bernard Mandeville (1670–1733). In *The Fable of the Bees* (1714) he exposed the difference between private morality and the morality of states, suggesting, in an ironical manner, that the more corrupt a state is the more successful it will be. Though Mandeville has superficial disguises to preserve his mental respectability, his underlying intentions are clear, and much in his work reads like a modern condemnation of commerce and governments.

George Berkeley (1685–1753), like Mandeville, saw life as corrupt, but he approached the problem, not with irony, but with a generous and idealistic desire for reform, which led him to attempt a campaign among the settlers and natives in North America. While thus concerned with the practical side of life, he brought to the problems of philosophy one of the most acute minds of the age. In a series of volumes beginning

P.E.L.—P

with *An Essay Towards a New Theory of Vision* (1709), he expounded in a clear prose the theory that the material world does not exist and that human knowledge is based on the ideas within the mind. While materialism was increasing man's attachment to the concrete world, Berkeley reasserted an idealism which, though closely argued, has in it strong elements of mysticism. David Hume (1711–76) also attached his mind to the problem of knowledge, but with conclusions which seem to remove the unity which Berkeley achieved. He pursued the psychological studies of Descartes and Locke into the nature of human thinking, only to discover that the human mind, as an instrument for elucidating truth, is inadequate. The scepticism of his *Enquiry Concerning Human Understanding* (1748) has left a mark on human thought which has been permanent. Each brand of human knowledge has had to speak less complacently of its assertions since Hume wrote.

Hume was himself a historian, and the spirit of inquiry of the age led others to investigate the human past in a systematic way. The art of history, in this important period of its development, was fortunate in attracting one who was a master of English prose. Edward Gibbon (1737–94) began the publication of *The Decline and Fall of the Roman Empire* in 1776. A moving passage in his *Autobiography* records the completion of the great work in 1788. His theme was no less than the break-up of the ancient world and the establishment of modern civilization: from Rome in the second century to its capture by the Barbarians, to the enthronement of Charlemagne and the establishment of the Holy Roman Empire in the west and then forward, through the Middle Ages, to the capture of Constantinople by the Turks in 1453. The impression it makes is one of unity and of design. Gibbon had a mind powerful enough to control the wide areas he had to describe, a thoroughness in preparation and a skill in prose that gives to almost any sentence a delight, even when it is detached from its context. It was style that ultimately gave the work its unity, for it carried him safely over the barren places. At the centre of his work lay the story of Christianity and towards religion Gibbon was sceptical. He had the added dilemma that, for the middle sections of his work, it was upon the Catholic historians that he had to rely. One feels that his own religious education had wounded him, and that he revenged himself with irony and innuendo; so in his account of monasticism he writes, 'Egypt, the fruitful parent of superstition, afforded the first example of the monastic life', and such examples are numerous. This hostility to Christianity gave to the centre of his history an emptiness which only the unvarying excellence of his style conceals. In compensation, he had aloofness and detachment, and an honesty in examining all the sources available. He had a very modest belief in human nature and very little faith in progress, and so, in the age when Rousseau was writing and England was losing the American colonies, he turned back to the decay of that classical world, which to him had come as near to an image of perfection as human life was likely to afford.

Among Gibbon's friends was Dr Samuel Johnson (1709–84). His powerful personality, and his long literary career, made him the dominating literary figure of the century. His reputation owes much to the art of James Boswell (1740–95), whose *Life of Johnson* was published in 1791. The publication in the middle of the twentieth century of Boswell's own journals and diaries has established him as a major writer, independently of the *Life*. It was the Johnson of the later years that he recorded, working from minute records of his sayings and his mannerisms with a realistic art that has no parallel. The capacity, the wit and the downrightness of Johnson, along with his often kindly and always devout approach to life, are the elements of the portrait which Boswell has created, and without his biographer Johnson would be a lesser man. He would still occupy a foremost place in the literature of his age. Part of his contribution belonged to those systematic studies which made such progress in the eighteenth century. His edition of Shakespeare (1765) helped in the eighteenth-century task of interpreting the text of the plays, and one can often find clarity in Johnson where other editors remain obscure, though the modern view is that Johnson and other eighteenth-century editors left deliberately unexplained passages where

'The Procession' by Rowlandson. Dr Johnson and Boswell are followed by Johnson's negro servant

Shakespeare indulged in bawdiness. The *Preface* to this edition, a brave piece of criticism, finally rescued the plays from the more pedantic judgement of neo-classic criticism. His central work – and nowhere is the clarity of his mind seen more firmly – was the *Dictionary* (1747–55). The *Plan*, issued in 1747, defined his purpose as to produce 'a dictionary by which the pronunciation of our language may be fixed and its attainment facilitated; by which its purity may be preserved, its use ascertained, and its duration lengthened'. The *Dictionary* itself followed in 1755 and upon it all later lexicographic studies in English have been based. No one has equalled him in describing clearly to the English people what the words in their language really mean. To these great tasks he added, in his later years, *The Lives of the Poets* (1779–81), in which, in a prose that often matches his conversation, he gives an account of English poetry from Cowley to Gray. Nothing in Johnson can compare with the three great achievements referred to above. His *Rasselas* has already been mentioned in the history of fiction. In *The Rambler* and *The Idler* he applied himself to the periodical essay, and introduced into his essays a deeper moral gravity than Addison practised. In these papers, he wrote hurriedly, with the printer often at the door, waiting for 'copy'. As a result the formality of his settled style becomes emphasized, greatly contrasting to the style of Dryden. His wisdom, his prejudices and the range of his interests are nowhere better seen than in *A Journey to the Western Islands of Scotland* (1775). He undertook the journey with Boswell who recorded his own version in *Journal of a Tour of the Hebrides* (1785).

Compared with Johnson's the mind of Oliver Goldsmith (1730–74) seems puny and inadequate, but in creative talent Goldsmith was more richly endowed. As Johnson said of him in an epitaph, he attempted every type of literature and each type he attempted he adorned. His dramas and his novel have already been mentioned, and his hack-work of history is best left without record. His essays, however, showed his individuality, and in *The Citizen of the World* (1762) he comments on life through the imaginary letters of a Chinese visitor.

The variety of Johnson's circle can be seen by the fact that it included not only Oliver Goldsmith, the impoverished writer, who economically never escaped from Grub Street, but Edmund Burke (1729–97), who stood high in the councils of the nation. Apart from an early treatise on aesthetics, *The Sublime and Beautiful* (1757), Burke's main work is to be found in a series of political pamphlets, mainly delivered in the form of speeches. On two major issues he expressed himself with emphasis. He opposed the Government in its attitude to the revolting American colonists in *On American Taxation* (1774) and *On Conciliation with the Colonies* (1775). With even more vehemence he attacked the French Revolution, notably in his *Reflections on the Revolution in France* (1790). In these, and in a number of speeches, including his attack on Warren

Hastings, the body of his prose and his political doctrine is to be found.

Burke's oratory becomes a part of English history. He had to undergo a change of thought which looked like inconsistency. In defending the American colonists he seemed to be defending freedom and in opposing the French Revolution he appeared to be on the side of tyranny. Actually, there is no change, but an inner consistency. Burke was opposed to abstract theory. The French Revolution was to him a dangerous experiment in bringing a theoretical philosophy into practice. The Government's attitude to the American colonists seemed also to be an attempt to impose 'metaphysical' claims upon them. Burke, like so many others in his century, based his thought on experience. The first law of society was man's relation to God, and the image of that law was to be found, not in paper-made theories, but in custom and tradition. Burke is the great exponent of conservatism, for while he relies on experience, he will not trust solely to the reason, because he finds that experience itself is not governed by the reason. Burke in his prose always has the spoken word in mind and, though he argues closely, he has the audience in view. This contact with the audience gave him the eloquence and the passion which entered into some of his best-known passages. He was freer in his effects than Johnson or Gibbon, and, at times, he introduced phrases which Johnson thought too familiar. These vary a style whose main effect is an ornate and rich movement, though never beyond the control of the informing mind. This sense of tradition, his belief that the greater problems of life are not submissive to reason, gave his conservatism a glowing and romantic quality.

Much that is most attractive in the prose of the eighteenth century goes into the private letters and journals of an age that had the leisure and cultivation to make correspondence a fine art. Thomas Gray, whose poetical production is slender and impersonal, reveals, in his letters, his 'white' melancholy and a mind as learned in literature as any in his age. William Cowper is more lively in his letters than in his poems. He captures all the details and oddities of everyday life into his amusing descriptions. John Wesley (1703–91), the founder of Methodism, in his diary gives a vivid and human account of the movement for which he struggled. Horace Walpole (1717–97) exercised all his wit and observation to make his vast collection of letters a memorial of eighteenth-century life. An accomplished art is also to be found in the letters of the Earl of Chesterfield (1694–1773) to his illegitimate son, Philip Stanhope. A nobleman of the older school, he set out, in deliberate and epigrammatic phrases, the philosophy that treasured good manners and the arts of pleasing, and distrusted enthusiasm and sentimentality or any form of boisterousness. To read Chesterfield and Wesley together is to see how varied were the ways of thought that the eighteenth century pursued.

In reading the letters of Horace Walpole one realizes that the eighteenth

John Wesley, the founder of Methodism, preaching on his father's tomb
Right: Samuel Taylor Coleridge, 'table-talking'. From a drawing by Max Beerbohm.
Thomas Carlyle described Coleridge's voice as 'a plaintive snuffle and singsong',
in which he preached 'earnestly and also hopelessly the weightiest things'

century had longings for some world of mystery beyond the elegant drawing-rooms in which so many of Chesterfield's days were spent. Some of that desire was satisfied by James Macpherson (1736–96) in a series of narratives, known collectively as *The Works of Ossian*. Macpherson is one of the most pathetic figures in our literature. With some knowledge of Gaelic traditions, he invented in a rhythmical prose a number of narratives which he alleged to be translations of early poems. As such they were accepted by many strong minds, but when their authenticity was questioned, Macpherson had to sit down and try to invent the originals of his own invention. He answered strongly to some needs in his age, and not in England alone, for the sombre and vague grandeur of his narratives attracted Goethe and Napoleon. Had he been content to come forward as an original and creative writer, his own career would have been less troublesome and he would still remain a formative influence in his age. He was answering the same need which in verse was satisfied by Thomas Percy's (1729–1811) collection of early ballads and poems, known as the *Reliques of English Poetry* (1765).

The main energies of romanticism in the early nineteenth century went into verse and the novel, but a new prose develops at the same time. S. T. Coleridge gave to literary criticism a deeper and more philosophical interpretation, both in his lectures and in the *Biographia Literaria* (1817). His original mind also conceived a more subtle and revealing vocabulary for criticism. If his philosophy is, in expression, fragmentary, his conception that faith depends on an active will to believe obviously influenced nineteenth-century thought.

Charles Lamb (1775–1834) has endeared himself to generations of Englishmen for his *Essays of Elia* (1823) and *Last Essays* (1833). Lamb

belongs to the intimate and self-revealing essayists, of whom Montaigne is the original, and Cowley the first exponent in England. To the informality of Cowley he adds the solemn confessional manner of Sir Thomas Browne. In style, he makes an intricate mosaic of earlier writers, particularly those who affected the grand manner. This elaboration he uses in a gently humorous way, amid the sentiments and trifles of every day. To understand his personality and his intention is not so simple as may at first appear. Is 'Elia', the sentimental, smiling figure of the essays, really Lamb or only a cloak with which Lamb hides himself from the world? He understood the great things in the literature of his time, the poems of Wordsworth and Coleridge, and in criticism he has a sympathy for the harrowing moments in literature. He can criticize *King Lear* with understanding, but when he comes to write himself, he composes a dissertation on roast pork. It may be that a solution can be found on that September evening in 1796, when his sister Mary, in a fit of insanity, stabbed her mother to death and wounded her father. Lamb devoted his life to the care of his sister, and the part of his mind which was creative could not face tragedy, though he could understand tragedy when he found it in the works of others. So in the essays he plays with trivialities, though as Walter Pater has said, 'we know that beneath this blithe surface there is something of the domestic horror, of the beautiful heroism, and devotedness too, of old Greek tragedy'. Brilliant though his essays are, Lamb's popularity in the twentieth century has diminished.

One of the best-known figures in Lamb's circle of friends was William

Charles Lamb: 'We know that beneath this blithe surface there is something of the domestic horror, of the beautiful heroism, and devotedness too, of old Greek tragedy.' – Walter Pater. In 1796 his mother was killed by his sister Mary in a fit of insanity. Lamb, who was subject to fits of derangement himself, looked after her for the rest of his life

Hazlitt (1778–1830), whose essays still read with some of their original freshness. Part of Hazlitt's training had been as a painter, and he used words as if he enjoyed their colour. In his numerous essays he was always downright in his opinions, and he used pungent and illuminating phrases to reveal his judgements. As a personality he was as difficult as Lamb was kindly. There was a violence in his judgements, not only in his hates, but in his attachments. Though he was a Radical, he believed in Napoleon and he spent his last years struggling to write his life. The effect of his personality on his own life can be seen in *Liber Amoris* (1823), where he appears as a Rousseau with a sense of irony. Of his many volumes of essays the most effective is *The Spirit of the Age* (1825), in which he gave critical portraits of most of his contemporaries.

As a critic Thomas de Quincey (1785–1859) is less reliable than Hazlitt, but in the *Confessions of an English Opium Eater* (1821) he brought into prose a new accent. He described his experiences and his dreams as an opium addict, and for the dream descriptions he employed a 'poetic prose', elaborate and sonorous in its effects. In refreshing contrast is the prose of William Cobbett (1763–1835). He wrote voluminously, breezily, often pugnaciously, and he had a natural gift for exciting the reader in his experiences and his views. Of all his works, *Rural Rides* (1830), which describes his journeys on horseback through England, is the most effective. He shows the counties as they were, with a quick eye for detail, especially for a 'field full of turnips', and there is often an unaffected beauty in his descriptions. While Cobbett will always find readers wherever his works circulate, opinion is more likely to differ on the merits of Walter Savage Landor (1775–1864). His tempestuous and eccentric personality separated him from his contemporaries, and it has kept both his verse and his prose apart from the tradition of literature in his age. His prose is certainly far more readable than his poetry, and the *Imaginary Conversations* (1824–9) show the range of his knowledge, and the beauty which he could command from words.

Throughout the nineteenth century there was an audience for solid periodicals and reviews. Though these were organized mainly on a political basis, they devoted ample space to the criticism of literature. The longest-lived of these journals was *The Gentleman's Magazine* (1731–1868), which continued in existence from the age of Pope to the age of Browning. In the first decade of the nineteenth century the great political journals began circulation with *The Edinburgh Review*. The most powerful of all such periodicals, it had as editor Francis Jeffrey (1773–1850), who as a literary critic exercised his talents in demolishing the romantic poets. One of its most brilliant contributors was Sydney Smith (1771–1845), whose mind is satiric but witty. He is frequently prejudiced, but like Dr Johnson he can give the impression of a monopoly in common sense. Sometimes he is reminiscent of Swift, and sometimes of Macaulay, but he is more genial than either in the careless exuberance of his wit. *The Quarterly Review* (1809) began publication as a Tory answer to the *Edinburgh*, and Scott was for a time one of its contributors. It was followed by *Blackwood's Edinburgh Magazine*, in which J. G. Lockhart, Scott's son-in-law and biographer, was a leading spirit and one of the most virulent of contributors. *Blackwood's* is often remembered only for its scurrilous attacks on Keats, but this is unjust, for it contained much lively writing, including John Wilson's *Noctes Ambrosianae*, written under the name of 'Christopher North'. All these reviews showed the presence of an alert and educated public which continued to exist throughout the nineteenth century.

Literary production in the nineteenth century is so voluminous and varied that only the works which have a fresh approach to prose can be considered. This is less unjust than it may seem, for only in Charles Darwin did the century possess a mind capable of making a contribution as powerful as that of Hume or Burke. Darwin (1809–92) would have disclaimed any right to be considered as a literary artist, yet the clarity of his style and his very quietness in presenting his profound conclusions, give to much of his work the qualities of a work of art. In *The Origin of Species* (1859), and in *The Descent of Man* (1871), he brought to light conceptions of the origins of man which challenged orthodox religion and accepted opinion everywhere. His own investigations and conclusions he had stated with great caution and in this lies much of his artistry.

The consequences of his thought could not be avoided, and they were emphasized in the clear, insistent prose of T. H. Huxley (1825–95) in works such as *Man's Place in Nature* (1863).

Both Darwin and Huxley were more effective as writers of prose than the political philosophers of the early part of the century. As thinkers, the radical philosophers have their own importance, for they developed the twin conceptions of individuality and *laissez-faire*, which are behind so much English thought in the nineteenth century. As literature, their work is less attractive. Jeremy Bentham (1748–1832) wrote clearly, and one can appreciate the mind controlling the complexity of the material, but Bentham must be judged as a thinker, not for his prose style. He was one of the great 'seminal' minds of the century. He covered morals, ethics, legislation, politics, penal reform and philosophy, at the basis of which was formulated the principle of 'utility'. 'It is the greatest happiness of the greatest number that is the measure of right and wrong.' There were other writers who also belong more to the history of thought than to literature, narrowly interpreted. T. R. Malthus (1766–1834) published in 1798 his *Essay on the Principle of Population* which proved a corrective to Rousseau and Godwin and others who took an optimistic view of the world's future. He saw the problem which in the twentieth century is the major problem for the survival of civilized man. Outstanding among the philosophers associated with Bentham were James

Darwin's ship, *The Beagle* being careened at Santa Cruz in 1838. *The Origin of Species* and *The Descent of Man,* the books which resulted from Darwin's voyage, brought to light conceptions of the origins of man which challenged orthodox religion and accepted opinion

Mill (1773–1836) and his son John Stuart Mill (1806–73) whose essay *On Liberty* appeared in 1859 and whose revealing *Autobiography* was published in 1873.

The glamour which the philosophers of politics lacked was found in full measure in the prose of Thomas Babington Macaulay (1800–59). He brought to the composition of his essays a mind that was richly stored with detail and brutally clear in its convictions. This allowed him to set forth his theme with a simplicity that avoided every compromise, and this firm outline, once defined, he decorated with every embellishment of allusion and picturesque detail. Such a method he followed in his studies of Bacon, Johnson and Warren Hastings, and it serves admirably as long as the first simple formula is sound. Brilliant though the essays may be, they do not compare in solid worth with his *History of England* (1849–61). Though sometimes dismissed as a mere justification of Whig policy, this work has security and design combined with Macaulay's unsurpassed use of detail. In no earlier work had the life of England been made to live so clearly, and though Macaulay had no predecessors, he may have gained something from Scott's imaginative treatment of the past and from Gibbon's mastery of form.

The nineteenth century was to produce many historians, Froude, Lecky, Hallam and others, but the most original was Thomas Carlyle (1795–1881), who used history only as one of the methods of his teaching, but attempted on the whole to use it honestly. He addressed himself to his age in a long series of volumes, of which the most impressive were

Sartor Resartus (1833–4), *On Heroes and Hero-Worship* (1841) and *Past and Present* (1843). He also composed a series of historical studies of which the earliest, *The French Revolution*, gained him his reputation in 1837. The reader is affected by the style even before the thought can make its impression. The sentences come cascading forth, tumbling and spluttering, as if the very words were in a fury with the world. The effect varies from a comic irony to genuine eloquence, and Carlyle has added to his native gifts by a study of prose writers such as Sterne and Fichte, the German philosopher, both of whom attempt ever to startle the reader with their language.

Carlyle, in his prose, is attempting to stir his age from its complacency. He possesses a strange unformulated mysticism which distrusts the reason and above all opposes the materialism of the Utilitarians. For him, the individual is the centre of life, and, as he shows in *Sartor Resartus*, the individual must overcome his hesitations and doubts, and affirm himself in faith and activity. Only thus can the corruption of society be checked, and he discovers in the individual at his highest the mystical figure of the 'hero'.

Carlyle tried to lead England back to a more spiritual life by a self-conceived doctrine. It was the same urge, working through a very different channel, that led others, through the Oxford Movement, to a new movement in the English Church and in some instances to Roman Catholicism. At once the most attractive personality in the group, and the most distinguished prose writer, was John Henry Newman (1801–90). He recounts his own spiritual history, in a most moving manner, in his *Apologia pro Vita Sua* (1864). He was the master of a supple prose, dignified but resilient, and his mind, though moved by emotion, was disciplined by a fine intellect. These qualities allowed him to convey to his conversion to Roman Catholicism a human quality which gives a permanent attraction to his record. Newman also published in 1870 *The Grammar of Assent* which examined the nature of belief much in the manner of Coleridge's *Aids to Reflection*. As a poet his dramatic monologue of the soul leaving the body at death, *The Dream of Gerontius* (1865), had wide popularity especially after it was set to music by Elgar, and there is always 'Lead Kindly Light' which he composed in 1833 on a voyage from Palermo to Marseilles.

Of all the writers who felt that the nineteenth century was inadequate, John Ruskin (1819–1900) expressed himself most voluminously. In *Modern Painters* (1843–60) he championed the art of Turner and constructed a philosophy of the aesthetic which, in his mind, is almost a substitute for religion. In *The Seven Lamps of Architecture* (1849) and in *The Stones of Venice* (1851–3) he expounded the principles of architecture and eulogized the Gothic, to a generation that sadly misinterpreted his lessons. The arts led him to the craftsmen who are responsible for them and this, in turn, directed his attention to the shabby commercialism of his age, which he attacked in *Unto this Last* (1862). Among his later and more informal works were his letters to working men entitled *Fors Clavigera* (1871–84) and his autobiography, *Praeterita* (1885–9). Early in his life he was deeply impressed by the paintings of Turner, and the effects of light which Turner created led him to his basic aesthetic creed of the truth of vision. From this passionate attachment grew the faith that beauty was valuable not for itself but as a symbol of the divine in human life. He was thus led to his admiration for the Gothic and to a belief that the craftsmen who built the cathedrals were virtuous men exercising their skill for the glory of God. He set this work against the shabby mass productions of a mechanical age.

He challenged, at least by implication, the whole basis on which a commercial society rests, and his influence lived on in William Morris, and in numerous other less well-known followers. With all his strength and vision, Ruskin had in him some element of weakness. To read his work is to listen to someone shouting continuously, and so loudly that one is distracted from the argument. It is true that his prose could at times assume the garments of magnificence, but even at their grandest the reader feels that the effects have been produced to overawe him. The quieter manner of his autobiography is a relief from the rhetoric of some of the earlier volumes. Yet it must be remembered that there was no more powerful voice for reform throughout the whole nineteenth century.

To the criticism of England in the nineteenth century Matthew Arnold (1822–88) brought all the resources of his powerful intellect. He sees the English as a nation of 'philistines', dominated by a narrow dogma in religion, a petrified code of morality in conduct and with a complete shallowness of literary taste. His attack is not carried to its logical conclusions and varies in value. On religion his own views have a gloomy morbidity, but when he speaks of literature he attempts, for the first time in the century, to evolve standards by which works of art can be judged. Against the insularity of his age, he brings a European outlook, and his style, with its happy gift of definition and for the invention of just but memorable phrases, gives an added attraction to his thought. Outstanding were his lectures *On Translating Homer* (1861), his *Essays in Criticism* (1865–88) and his more general criticism of the social and religious problems of his age in *Culture and Anarchy* (1867) and *Literature and Dogma* (1873).

Among those who had studied Ruskin was Walter Pater (1839–94), though he studied him only to draw his own conclusions. While Ruskin had made art a religion, Pater made it an end in itself. In the *Conclusion* to *Studies in the History of the Renaissance* (1873) he set out his faith that the pursuit of beauty, whether in experience or in works of art was the most satisfactory activity that life offered. The concluding passage was omitted from the second edition as Pater feared that it might have misled

Wilde and some of his contemporaries, but it does define, with a poignant precision, what Pater believed:

> To burn always with this hard, gemlike flame, to maintain this ecstasy, is
> success in life. In a sense it might even be said that our failure is to form habits:
> for, after all, habit is relative to a stereotyped world, and meantime it is only
> the roughness of the eye that makes any two persons, things, situations, seem
> alike. While all melts under our feet, we may well grasp at any exquisite
> passion, or any contribution to knowledge that seems by a lifted horizon to
> set the spirit free for a moment, or any stirring of the senses, strange dyes,
> strange colours, and curious odours, or the work of the artist's hands, or the
> face of one's friend. Not to discriminate every moment some passionate
> attitude in those about us: and in the very brilliancy of their gifts, some tragic
> dividing of forces on their ways is, on this short day of frost and sun, to sleep
> before evening.

This quest he explored in the form of a novel in *Marius the Epicurean*
(1885). His own sensitive appreciation of literature and the other arts
he showed in a series of essays which seemed to recreate the originals of
which he spoke. The limitations of his philosophy are only too obvious,
for he rejects all social and moral obligations, but the prose in which he
describes his outlook combines precision of statement with a strange and
compelling charm. The great prose writers of the nineteenth century
from Carlyle to Arnold and Ruskin had been concerned with the problems of their age. These problems Pater rejects, just as in poetry they
had been rejected by the Pre-Raphaelites, and so with Pater the prose of
the nineteenth century may be said to have come to an end.

To write briefly of twentieth-century prose is difficult. In style the
most interesting developments were in drama and fiction, in Shaw and
Joyce. While commanding an ample rhetoric, Shaw matched Swift in
clear and idiomatic prose. *Pygmalion* and his admiration for C. K.
Ogden's Basic English show how deeply he thought about words.
Joyce stretched language beyond rational containment until ceasing to
be English it became a fantasy of his own creation. In between lies the
prose of a prolific half century, with style playing a varying part; sometimes the imagination finds an alliance with scholarship and criticism,
but often the frontiers of literature are left behind as one enters a solely
utilitarian world.

Imaginative forms suffered a decline. The essay, for instance, had been
revitalized late in the nineteenth century by R. L. Stevenson (1850–94)
in volumes such as *Virginibus Puerisque* (1881) and *Memories and Portraits*
(1887), and in travel books of similar material, *An Inland Voyage* (1878)
and *Travels with a Donkey in the Cevennes* (1879). In the essay and in his
verse he was a romantic, and in style a self-conscious artist. After Stevenson the essay flourished until the thirties when it was affected by the

**Right: The frontispiece illustration, by Walter Crane, to the first edition of
Robert Louis Stevenson's *Travels with a Donkey in the Cevennes***

declining number of periodicals, the pressure on newspaper space and the attractions of radio. Further, the temper of the age led away from rhetoric and the essay's self-sustaining elegance. Radio invited the conversational manner and this television accentuated. To read Lloyd George's early speeches is to step into another world. Sir Winston Churchill alone retained the grand manner and some of his eloquence will remain permanently in English literature. Like Macaulay he knew how effective the short and simple sentence could be amid elaborate periods. In compensation for rhetoric's decline there appears an increase in exposition and argument to which scientists such as A. N. Whitehead and philosophers such as Bertrand Russell have contributed.

Outstanding in the essay's final phase was G. K. Chesterton (1874–1936). He was also a prolific writer of short stories, one hundred of which were collected as *The Innocence of Father Brown* (1914). A poet of distinction in the ballad manner with 'Lepanto' and 'The Ballad of the White Horse', his prose had spectacular liveliness as if he felt that in a clamorous age style must advertise his thought. He has suffered neglect, as has his versatile contemporary, Hilaire Belloc (1870–1953), some of whose ballads have entered into the tradition of the language. In prose his history is too prejudiced to wear well, but certain essays and a volume such as *The Path to Rome* should have permanence. Sir Max Beerbohm (1872–1956), caricaturist and prose-writer, working within a narrower range, has greater security. His light-hearted, satiric novel, *Zuleika Dobson* (1911), has survived many changes of taste; the essays reveal an eighteenth-century wit, still untarnished; and his dramatic criticisms *Around Theatres* (1953) contribute, with Shaw's, to the small effective comment on the living drama in England.

In the twentieth century biography and autobiography established new traditions. Lytton Strachey (1880–1932) in his *Eminent Victorians* (1918), *Queen Victoria* (1921) and *Elizabeth and Essex* (1928) broke with the Victorian tradition of 'pious' biography, seeking not so much for truth, as the weaknesses and absurdities of great figures, so that, at first at least, the portraits were satirical. He belonged to the disillusioned age of the First World War, when events were greater than men, and he turned upon the past revengefully to undermine its legend of the heroic. In an early study of French literature he defined his admiration for Voltaire, and a mood of eighteenth-century wit and rationalism informs him. Finding in Queen Victoria a great theme, he handled it with artistic discretion. All that was incongruous in the Victorian age he exposed, while its insincerity he condemned with quiet but piercing innuendos. The work had a design as finished as a portrait, and while sceptical of the false and pretentious, he came almost to admire the ageing Queen in passages not without pathos. In economy of effect he is with Swift. In autobiography Sir Osbert Sitwell provided the major period piece in a number of volumes beginning with *Left Hand, Right*

Hand (1945), portraying in a prose of baroque profusion the sophisticated and aristocratic life of his time. Richard Church, using a background of a simpler social order, brought his poet's and novelist's skill to *Over the Bridge* (1955) and *The Golden Sovereign* (1957).

Apart from Strachey other historians tried to break down the older traditions in history and biography. Philip Guedalla (1889–1945) attempted to return to Macaulay and illuminated his narrative with striking visual detail. He had not Strachey's satiric intention nor his qualities of style, but *Palmerston* (1926) and *The Duke* (1931), a study of Wellington, contrived to reach a large audience without making many concessions. The same was true of Sir Arthur Bryant (b. 1899) with *Charles II* (1931) and his study of Pepys, beginning with *The Years of Peril* (1935). Sir John Neale, despite unrelenting scholarship, was successful with his *Queen Elizabeth* (1934) as was G. M. Trevelyan in a *History of England* (1926) and his *Social History of England* (1944), which was so popular that a quarter of a million copies were soon sold. John Buchan (Lord Tweedsmuir), whose adventure stories had great popularity, composed historical biographies, including *Montrose* (1928), and Sir Harold Nicolson, essayist and critic, wrote finely fashioned volumes such as *Curzon: The Last Phase* (1934). To this distinguished work in history can be added that of economic historians such as Mr and Mrs J. L. Hammond's *The Town Labourer* (1917) and *The Skilled Labourer* (1919), and a volume which will be remembered for originality of thought and quality of style, R. H. Tawney's *Religion and the Rise of Capitalism* (1926). The most ambitious of all these ventures was A. J. Toynbee's *A Study of History* (1934–61); some have found Toynbee too subjective but few can fail to admire the sweep of learning and comprehension in this study of the rise and fall of civilizations.

Foremost among writers belonging to the history of thought rather than to imaginative literature was J. M. Keynes, later Lord Keynes (1883–1946). Internationally famous as an economist, he was also a friend of artists, and the first Chairman of the Arts Council. His *Economic Consequences of the Peace* (1919) affected history in a way that made it one of the most important books on the inter-war period. It had independent literary qualities in descriptions of President Wilson, Clemenceau and Lloyd George. Keynes's imaginative qualities showed more amply in *Essays in Persuasion* (1931) and *Essays in Biography* (1933). The social and economic studies of Sidney and Beatrice Webb belong solidly to thought without any adornments of style, but Beatrice Webb's autobiography is a moving book admirably expressed.

In criticism I. A. Richards attempted to examine problems in depth in *Science and Poetry* (1926), which followed, though indirectly, Matthew Arnold's separation of poetry from history, science and religion. Already in 1924 he expressed similar views in *Principles of Literary Criticism*. His thought had come from his association with C. K. Ogden, an original mind and a student of Jeremy Bentham, and together they wrote *The Meaning of Meaning* (1923) which, among other things, defined the difference between words in poetry and in other forms of writing. The University of Cambridge, the centre for Ogden and Richards, also harboured, if at times a little grudgingly, F. R. Leavis (1895–1979), who treated literature seriously and with a puritanical fervour. If literature was to be the centre of culture, he was determined that only the best would suffice. He proceeded to select the best, if perhaps in too arbitrary a way. In compensation there was distinction of mind and critical acumen, and no assessment of what happened in criticism is intelligible without acknowledging his contribution. He was early to champion D. H. Lawrence and T. S. Eliot. He elevated George Eliot's reputation as a great and adult writer. His journal *Scrutiny* was a courageous and important venture, as were his own volumes, including *New Bearings in English Poetry* (1932), *The Great Tradition* (1948), *D. H. Lawrence* (1955). In 1963 the whole run of *Scrutiny* from 1932–53 was republished.

Among imaginative writers T. S. Eliot gave major attention to criticism, and from 1922 to 1939 edited a journal of considerable influence, *The Criterion*. He succeeded in changing much in the taste of his generation; in introducing Donne, the metaphysicals, later Elizabethan and Jacobean drama, and in describing with a poet's insight the ways of imaginative thought. *The Sacred Wood* (1920), the earliest and most original of these volumes, was followed by *Homage to John Dryden* (1924), *For Lancelot Andrewes* (1928) and other volumes. Often destructive, as in his comments on Milton, Hardy and Meredith, his mind could stretch itself in response to his poetical intuitions, and open new regions of understanding. The later volumes are more rigid and arbitrary with *Dante* (1929) standing between these and the original early volumes.

Cyril Connolly (1903–74) in his journal *Horizon* (1939–50) sustained, in war-time, the graceful image of an earlier Western civilization. Many of his contributors shared his wit and irony, and a nostalgia for days past. In his *Enemies of Promise* (1938), a mixture of autobiography and criticism exists with an imaginative talent that lacks the creative energy to exert itself, and in *The Unquiet Grave* (1944) and *The Condemned Playground* (1944) the mood recurs; playfulness, perception and a sense of the author wishing he had been born in another age. Against the ironic mood of Connolly and his contemporaries stands T. E. Lawrence (1888–1935), still one of the most puzzling figures. On the western front the First World War obliterated personalities, but Lawrence in Arabia could gather 'all the legendary atmosphere of a hero'. In 1926 *The Seven Pillars of Wisdom* gave to a limited audience an account of his Arab campaigns and to pay for the splendour of this production he issued an abbreviated form, *The Revolt in the Desert* (1927), which became known to a large public. After his death a remarkable collection of his letters was published. A complex personality, sometimes seeking obscurity, but unable

T. E. Lawrence in Arabia,
where he gathered 'all the
legendary atmosphere of a
hero'

to avoid the temptations of power and publicity, he was divided in himself by his illegitimate birth and a strange mixture of austerity and romanticism, which appeared in the style and rendering of his remarkable tale. His later self-tormented life led him to become a private in the Air Force; after his death there was published *The Mint* (1955) where he recorded his life as a serviceman. Romanticism had been exorcised and realism dominated with all its crudity, enough for Ralph Fox, a communist writer, to describe him 'as certainly, among the most remarkable figures of Modern England'. As a prose writer he could vary from the tawdry to the profoundly moving, but he had a uniqueness of experience, and Lawrence riding into Damascus may be the last man with an individual story to tell of modern warfare.

Arabia also claimed one combining courage in travel with a more disciplined and classical style. With Freya Stark one has not the glamour of a war hero, but the single, private traveller, a woman in a Muslim world. Beginning with *Baghdad Sketches* (1933) she continued with *The Southern Gates of Arabia* (1936), *Beyond the Euphrates* (1951) and *The Coast of Incense* (1953). She became one of the great travel writers in English and her imaginative power was confirmed by her autobiography. As the world grows smaller and the universe crowds in upon the earth, these records of the individual and lonely traveller will grow rarer and become more precious.

Even in its noblest forms, printing is ugly compared with the exquisite beauty of a manuscript such as the early medieval *Book of Kells*

Epilogue

THE STORY of English literature, told with an almost brutal brevity in the preceding pages, is based on a tradition that has extended for nearly fifteen hundred years. The list of writers whose names have been omitted is formidable: I have tried to concentrate on those who with the originality of their genius have modified the shape of the tradition, and above all on writers whose work has continued to be read by the generations after their death. Thus the literature here surveyed has stood the test of time, has secured the permanent values of tradition. As Dr Johnson said of Gray's *Elegy*: 'Had Gray written often thus it had been vain to blame and useless to praise him.' The judgements in this volume have not been merely personal but the basically considered conclusions of generations to which a mere patina of personal predilection is added.

For over a thousand of the years recorded in this story the majority of the population was illiterate and it was only in 1870 that education, including reading, became compulsory, and even then not without 'severe opposition'. As has already been emphasized those very early centuries of English literature were of major importance. The main strength lay with the Church, for the Church contained men of learning, and monasteries were safer than most places for the preservation of manuscripts. I have always found it moving that while Augustine came with Christianity from Rome to what is now southern England, it was Irish monks who at that period brought Christianity to Northumbria and to Scotland. While for centuries Ireland has been the ineradicable stain on English history, the first contact between the two countries was to be found in the Irish monks, fleeing from the Vikings and bringing with them the peaceful message of the Faith. How advanced was their culture can be seen from *The Book of Kells*, the most splendid Western manuscript of the early Middle Ages, which since the seventeenth century has been preserved in the library of Trinity College, Dublin. For centuries manuscripts were few, the audience very small, the clergy, courtiers and a narrow circle of noblemen and scholars, but the survival of what was available is little short of miraculous. I have quoted in the text Boethius's *Consolation of Philosophy*, translated by King Alfred

Chaucer and Queen Elizabeth I, a survival of seven hundred years. How many modern authors can hope to compete with that? Dante quoted his words, and so did Shakespeare, for Hamlet's 'There is nothing either good or bad but thinking makes it so' is a direct quotation from Boethius, as is 'That last infirmity of noble mind' from Milton's *Lycidas*.

The tragedy of human life lies in the continual destruction by men and women of their own achievements, the multitudinous lost manuscripts, the buried talents, the forgotten books, the destruction by war from the burning of the library at Alexandria in Caesar's time to Hitler's burning of books. But the perpetual compensation is that man, despite every despoliation, never ultimately despairs; there is a continual renewal, the awakening to new imaginative possibilities and the invention of new techniques. Who could have imagined before Chaucer's birth in 1340 that he would create characters such as the Wife of Bath, acceptable, with dramatic modifications, on the twentieth-century stage? Who could have foreseen the arrogant but sublimely courageous expansion of the human spirit that came with the Renaissance? Ten years before Marlowe's birth in 1564, who could have conceived the possibility of the creation of lines such as:

> ... the ripest fruit of all,
> That perfect bliss and sole felicity,
> The sweet fruition of an earthly crown.

And immediately after Marlowe, the unmatchable genius of Shakespeare brings a gift to English literature without parallel, and in its origins and achievement, whatever the critics may say, without explanation.

On the technical side the great change came with the invention of printing. Even in its noblest forms printing is ugly compared with the exquisite beauty of a manuscript such as *The Book of Kells*, but it introduced a new factor into the distribution of texts. In England the innovation came with the establishment of William Caxton's printing press in 1476. Our debt to him is formidable, as has already been recorded, but I doubt whether intellectually his was a mind of the first order. When he looked for books to translate and print he turned to the past rather than to the new movements that were developing around him. Yet printing was the invention that made possible the wider dispersal of literature and of books of all kinds. The restriction was illiteracy, and that in decreasing but formidable degrees was a factor, as has been noted, until the end of the nineteenth century: it is not extinct today.

It is a common weakness in humanity to exaggerate the importance of events that have happened in one's own lifetime, yet aware of this risk I would affirm that changes have occurred in the last half century more crucial to literature, and even to reading in general, than anything since the invention of printing. For the age of Caxton is being replaced

In December 1978, BBC Television started transmission of their series of Shakespeare's plays. All thirty-seven plays will have been recorded and transmitted by 1984. This picture shows Helen Mirren (left) as Rosalind, and Angharad Rees as Celia in a production of *As You Like It* that was seen by about one and a half million people on its first screening in Great Britain

by the age of Marconi, or if Marconi is too outdated a name, then by the age of electronics. I refer, of course, as has been suggested in the text, to the coming of film, radio and television, and in my own view to further ingenious inventions that may make newspapers as ineffective and outdated as the town crier.

Avoiding speculation and keeping to a conservative estimate, a play of Shakespeare's with international television coverage will have been seen by more people in one performance than by all the audiences viewing the play from its first Elizabethan première until the day of the television viewing. So powerful is this appeal that in 1979 a young man with only a limited previous reputation is offered £250,000 for a novel, text still unwritten, because the film and television moguls have calculated that they have found a winner. The spoken word has been restored to a new authority and can intrude into every home. The success it has given to some novelists has been as gratifying as it is surprising. Those who have read Leon Edel's biography of Henry James will recall the major tragedy in his life was his failure as a dramatist. What pleasure he would have experienced could he have seen the brilliant transference to the small screen of *The Spoils of Poynton*. Recently a novelist of average competence, L. P. Hartley, with a secure, respectable but modest audience, found himself just before his death internationally famous by the successful creation of a film, under the direction of Joseph Losey, of his novel *The Go-Between*. Yet with all these glamorous successes, the results of the transfer from novel to screen are sometimes unfortunate to the point of the disastrous. An outstanding example is Anthony Burgess's (b. 1917) *A Clockwork Orange*. Burgess is a serious writer with many publications to establish his quality. His novel analysed the corrupting influences of some phases of modern civilization, but the film was sensational, vulgar, bordering at times on the pornographic.

The effect of all these changes on publishing, on authors and the theatre is difficult to assess. The number of books published in England increases yearly though the majority of these have little to do with literature. But despite the temptations of television reading has increased. Popular education has not been totally without effect and the Open University demonstrates that many who lost opportunities early in life are anxious to recover them later. The paperback editions have also made a revolution in book purchases, for as has been suggested earlier the English have been a nation of book borrowers, through their excellent libraries, rather than a nation of book buyers. For many years authors have complained that the local libraries, maintained by taxation, bought one copy, or at best a few copies, of a book and circulated it to many readers, thus giving them a minuscule return for their labours. In 1979, after long debate, Parliament finally passed a Public Lending Library Act which would assign to authors some reward proportionate to the number of times their books were borrowed. Unfortunately only £4 millions a year is available for authors while it is estimated that the scheme will absorb £600,000 annually in administration. But as a gesture it is the first recognition of the writer by the State.

One of the major features of these last few decades has been the increased subsidy of the arts by the State. In 1976 the National Theatre was opened on the South Bank of the Thames, the consummation of a project cherished by artists for many decades and supported by Bernard Shaw among many others, yet impossible of execution without State aid. The resulting edifice is expensive and elaborate with three theatres within one complex, and its ultimate place in the theatrical life of the nation has yet to be proven. The major assistance of the State to the arts came through the agency of the Arts Council. It all began in a very simple way. Tom Jones, once Assistant Secretary of the Cabinet, realized that with the Second War many artists and singers would be displaced. With encouragement from the Pilgrim Trust and the Board of Education (now the Ministry of Education and Science) he found funds to establish the Council for the Encouragement of Music and the Arts (C.E.M.A.), so that artists might go to the remote places where many families had been evacuated. The response was encouraging and emphasized by Sybil Thorndike's early participation. When the Blitz came to London the singers and players went into the underground shelters and the Tube, and their popularity gave a *réclame* to the movement. Thus the beginnings were modest and practical, but through Tom Jones's combination of wisdom and guile the State was involved. So it became possible after the War to transmogrify C.E.M.A. into the Arts Council with Lord Keynes as its first Chairman, and if a personal note is permissible I served under him as his Vice-Chairman. Neither of us in those days would have thought that in 1977–8 the budget of the Arts Council would be £41,725,000. Some of the results have been admirable. Covent Garden and the New English Opera Companies have been able to produce, on a permanent basis, opera and ballet of an international standard. Outside London the provinces have been able to establish theatres and opera companies, outstanding among which is the Welsh National Opera. It may as a corrective be well to recall that the seasons of the Glyndebourne Opera in Sussex, founded by the late John Christie, have attained an unique and international reputation without any State aid. Nor should the pioneer adventures of Lilian Baylis in the Old Vic and Sadlers Wells be forgotten, for without State aid she discovered the major actors, the ballerinas and ballet directors without whom the most ambitious State-aided productions would have been impossible.

George Bernard Shaw receiving the deeds for the Cromwell Gardens (London) site of the projected National Theatre, together with a symbolic twig and piece of earth, on Shakespeare's birthday, 1938. Thirty-eight years later the theatre (inset) opened on a new site on the South bank of the Thames. Designed by Denys Lasdun, it has three auditoriums and can hold a maximum of 2,400 people

The Royal Shakespeare Company was another beneficiary of State aid. Its main contribution lay in the new settings and interpretations which its directors at Stratford imposed upon Shakespeare's plays. Some of these were of great beauty and ingenuity, but others were a combination of arrogance and a seeming indifference to the text and its author. It would be invigorating if the Company had to play before an instructed and critical audience such as that at Glyndebourne instead of at Stratford, mainly a tourist centre which will crowd the theatre whatever the presentation may be. Further, it is sad that we cannot see Shakespeare fresh without the dreary contamination of the classroom, and invariably knowing beforehand how the play will end.

Further Festivals of the Arts have been created, outstandingly in Edinburgh, and in a wet summer of economic depression Prince Albert's great Exhibition of 1851 was given a centennial commemoration with the 1951 Exhibition.

All this State aid has given a new status to the executive artist, the dancer, the actor and the producer, but there are few signs that it can assist the creative artist. With radio, television and new concert halls and opera houses it can be confidently affirmed that more people have heard the classics of music than at any time in our history. But the State cannot, at least in my view, assist the creative artist. He must have freedom, and often he will be a rebel, discontent not only with society as now organized but even with the act of living. It would require an ironist of the supreme order to portray Jonathan Swift applying for an Arts Council grant.

The two greatest artists of this the latest phase in our cultural history have not been writers. It is well to judge by international standards, and there stand out towering without comparison Henry Moore as a sculptor and Benjamin Britten as a musician. It is fortunate that before his death there was created at Aldeburgh a centre where in annual festivals Britten's work can be permanently remembered. His symphonies and his operas represent an achievement with which nothing in the literary art of these last decades can compete. Similarly Henry Moore stands commemorated in stone and bronze not only in England but in other countries.

The writer it can be admitted has had to face changes in the whole structure of society which have increased his problems. One can date the change in the theatre with John Osborne's *Look Back in Anger* (1956), or more generally with the coming of Harold Wilson's government of 1964, a period uniquely explored in its political aspects from 1964 to 1970 by Richard Crossman in *The Crossman Diaries*. The writer was working in an atmosphere where for all practical purposes censorship did not exist. In the theatre the office of the censor, as represented by the Lord Chamberlain, had been formally abolished by law, but as far as fiction was concerned the failure of the prosecution of D. H. Lawrence's *Lady*

A performance of Benjamin Britten's opera *A Midsummer Night's Dream,* at the Aldeburgh festival, 1964, with Peter Piers as Thisbe and Owen Brannigan as Pyramus

Chatterley's Lover in 1960 marked the end of censorship in general. Society and the police had an ill-defined battle with the pornography which reached excesses unacceptable to anyone who believed in a cultured society, but as far as the creative artist was concerned the barriers were down and this was emphasized by the passing of the Sexual Offences Act of 1967, by the initiative of Lord Arran, whereby homosexual acts between two consenting adults in private – with certain exceptions and treating twenty-one, not eighteen, as the critical age for adulthood – were no longer illegal. The text has already revealed how E. M. Forster was tormented by the criminal label attached to homosexuality, and he would be surprised how timid his secret homosexual novel *Maurice* would seem in the seventies. Dramatists and novelists seized on these newfound freedoms with avidity. The change was not alone in the portrayal of sex, but in violence and the inversion of the normal values of compassion and tragedy. An example occurs in the work of the ill-fated Joe Orton (1933–67) with *Loot* (1967) and *What the Butler Saw* (1969). In fiction a strange example occurs in the work of John Fowles, whose *The French Lieutenant's Woman* (1969) was rightly much admired. It had a nineteenth-century Dorset setting and a strong theme with much contemporary relevance, magnificently narrated. Yet he combines this with *The Magus* (1966) which seems, particularly in the revised edition of 1977, to reveal a world of sheer sexual fantasy.

The uncertainty of values in literature may be in part because England itself is uncertain of its own development. As one of our most discerning American critics said: 'You have lost an Empire but not discovered a role.' Some writers have solved the matter by ignoring the contemporary world and discovering a universe of their own. This may account for the extraordinary success of Professor John Tolkien (1892–1977), who beginning with *The Hobbit* (1937) continued with *The Lord of the Rings* (1954) and other volumes to imagine a world which is freshly conceived to the minutest detail. It even creates its own language, which was not difficult for Tolkien who was an erudite Professor of Anglo-Saxon. The popularity of his work has been immense and has developed into a cult. Allied somewhere in this retreat to a remote world has been the effect that increased knowledge of the universe has had on the human imagination. Man has reached the moon, but his imagination has explored far further afield into imaginary universes. There has developed a whole school of Science Fiction, with its own vast audiences, and with many writers of great skill and ingenuity. To assess their place in literature would be here too precarious an endeavour; one can only note their existence and the phenomenon to which they belong.

With the disappearance of the Empire and the narrowing of English life in power and responsibility there has been a certain nostalgia for the past. It can be seen nowhere more clearly than in the reassessment of

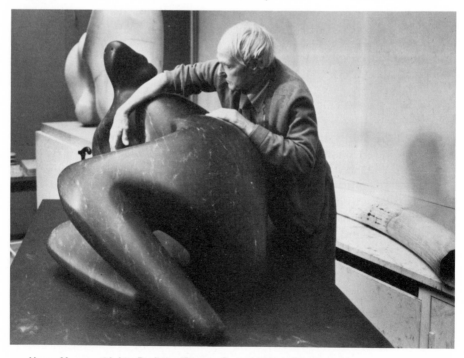

Henry Moore, with his *Reclining Figure: Curved* 1977, in black marble

Kipling's art, reinforced by excellent biographies by Angus Wilson and the late Earl of Birkenhead. E. M. Forster when he wrote *A Passage to India* was battening on the imperial privilege which it was his purpose to condemn. A kindlier view appeared in the novels of Paul Scott which have been mentioned in the main text, and there is an awareness that whatever its error England's more mature relation with India was the greatest event in its history. There is a further compensation in the work of writers such as V. S. Naipaul (b. 1932), an Indian who grew up in Trinidad but found his way to University College, Oxford. His *A House for Mr Biswas* (1961), portraying the grim life of Trinidad, has been followed by a number of novels, so much esteemed that he counts as a major figure among contemporary novelists.

The text has already suggested that the place of poetry in the community has diminished. Some hoped much, as has been already recorded, from the 'Movement' poets of the fifties, and from the influence of Sir William Empson (b. 1906) who had early composed a searching volume of critical examination into poetic language with *Seven Types of Ambiguity* (1930). It is difficult to discover any major traces of the 'Movement' in the seventies. What is remarkable is that poets have apparently not been affected by the profound development in the study of linguistics and the nature of language which extends from the propositions of Professor Chomsky in America, which if they prove to be true are as profound and revolutionary as those of Charles Darwin in the nineteenth century, to the studies of Professor Randolph Quirk in London, revealing for the first time the grammar of contemporary English.

Thus, one ends this epilogue with a note of uncertainty, as indeed is inevitable in viewing the shifting contemporary scene in literature. One can affirm with some certainty that the most ambitious achievement has been Anthony Powell's series of novels, given the general title *A Dance to the Music of Time*. They have given pleasure to thousands, but will they survive? And survival has been the criterion of merit throughout this survey. The suspicion sometimes arises that the vast tapestry of character and incident is too idiosyncratic, too attached to the oddities of the narrow personal scene, and if one may dare add the suggestion, too parochial to be read in fifty years' time by new generations. International comparisons are always helpful, and one may enquire where Powell will stand as compared with Proust, for they are writing on the same ambitious scale. Proust has never had a large audience, but it has been a permanent one and will continue, for he explores life in its continuing profundities. Does Powell succeed in a similar way? The future will show. This at least is true, that the novel has fallen from that central position it held in English life when Dickens died in 1870. Brilliant authors have succeeded him, but the conditions of life have changed with a revolutionary impetuosity.

I would not have the mood of this epilogue to be interpreted as pessimistic. England is more literate today than at any point of its history and there are more readers of books, and of books that deserve the name of literature, than at any time in English history. I have outlined the influences which combat for attention against the book, but it is clear that they have not in any dominating way been successful, though the competing media have been formidable. That the novel should no longer have a central place in literature is, in my view, inevitable for the novel depended on that close analysis of the private life which less leisurely modern conditions no longer permit. Further, there is this strange consequence of improved conditions of travel and communications that the variety of human experience diminishes. It is indeed the most frightening consequence of the technological, and in future of the electronic, revolution. A single example will suffice. The sea, which supplied such material for novelists from Smollett to Conrad, is no longer available as a theme. For the sea with its once varied cargoes and slow journeyings is now confined to oil tankers, pleasure cruisers and the dreaded and hidden weapons of war of which we are all supposed to be in complete ignorance. The aeroplane passes swiftly from one continent to another, and the passenger moves from one capital to the next finding only a replica of the centre which he last left.

The future is undisclosed, but in concluding this portrait I would affirm certain convictions. A tradition which has been maintained for over fifteen hundred years will not diminish. Alfred who died in 900 faced far more difficult conditions than we encounter today. For he developed our literature during the years of the most cruel invasion which this country has known. Further, this book has shown that without any explanation literature suddenly renews itself. It happened in the times of Chaucer and Shakespeare and it may happen again tomorrow, or within the next few years. Throughout the centuries critics have been prophesying literary bankruptcy, usually when the dawn of a new era is about to begin.

Ultimately I would assert that for the written word there is no adequate alternative whatever the media and the wonders of electronics may invent. For the enjoyment of a book is a personal experience. In a poem or a novel one may wish to turn back and contemplate, or have several volumes at hand for comparison. Further, if one is to consider the great philosophers as part of literature, Hobbes, Locke, Hume or Bertrand Russell, the text must be read several times before the full meaning exposes itself to the mind. Only with the book can we readers explore the individual word, and we as readers have been notoriously ungrateful to lexicographers. Dr Samuel Johnson, whose *Dictionary of the English Language* is one of the great books of English literature and a pivotal book in the development of English culture, defines 'the lexicographer' as: 'A writer of dictionaries; a harmless drudge, that busies himself in tracing the original and detailing the signification of words.'

The phrase 'harmless drudge' is obviously ironic for Johnson knew that 'the definition of words' is one of the most difficult tasks to which the human mind can apply itself. Johnson's original venture has so developed that anyone reading English today has available *The Concise Oxford Dictionary*, the most effective one-volume dictionary in any language, in the world.

I have quoted earlier the comment of the American statesman who said that England had lost an Empire but not found a role. That may be true of England but it is not true of the English language. The only means of world communication is English, with admittedly some concessions to American variations. Until the sixteenth century, and in many places even later, Latin was the international means of communication. For some centuries, and mainly through the influence of Napoleon, French in diplomatic and cultural circles became supreme not only in Western Europe but in Egypt, and generally in the Middle East. Today English is the supreme language and the consequent responsibilities are enormous. If there ever were a world society it would need English as a world language. Writers are not naturally aware of considerations of this kind. But their royalty statements will show them that they are writing not only for an English audience but for Americans, Russians and readers in many other countries. Thus I would end this portrait of English literature with a conviction that the possibilities for the future are incalculably great. Yet a more cautionary note must be added. Artists do what they want to do, not what might be most beneficial for humanity. One can hope, however, that the world distribution of English will lead Commonwealth writers to discover their medium in English. There are opportunities here unparalleled since the days of the Roman Empire, and such opportunities do not occur frequently in the mangled and tortuous history of humanity.

Index